medieval nuns at war

Medieval Nuns at War

Rebellious, Resilient and Rowdy Women

ELIZABETH A. QUILLEN

First published in Great Britain in 2025 by
PEN AND SWORD HISTORY
An imprint of
Pen & Sword Books Ltd
Yorkshire – Philadelphia

ISBN 978 1 39905 751 6

A CIP catalogue record for this book is available from the British Library.

Typeset in Times New Roman 11.5/15 by
SJmagic DESIGN SERVICES, India.
Printed and bound in the UK by CPI Group (UK) Ltd, Croydon, CR0 4YY.

The Publisher's authorised representative in the EU for product safety is Authorised Rep Compliance Ltd., Ground Floor, 71 Lower Baggot Street, Dublin D02 P593, Ireland.
www.arccompliance.com

For a complete list of Pen & Sword titles please contact:
PEN & SWORD BOOKS LIMITED
George House, Units 12 & 13, Beevor Street, Off Pontefract Road,
Barnsley, South Yorkshire, S71 1HN, England
E-mail: enquiries@pen-and-sword.co.uk
Website: www.pen-and-sword.co.uk

or

PEN AND SWORD BOOKS
1950 Lawrence Rd, Havertown, PA 19083, USA
E-mail: uspen-and-sword@casematepublishers.com
Website: www.penandswordbooks.com

Contents

Introduction

The idea for this book came from a place from which many book ideas are born – a graduate school seminar. I was tasked with finding a manageable piece of Latin text to translate. Naturally, I turned to Gregory of Tours' *History of the Franks*. It is an easy read with plenty of short, exciting moments in history. Conveniently, most of it has been translated into English, so corrections would be easy. Yet, what grabbed my interest was a series of lines in the table of contents referring to a rebellion in a convent. When I turned to the relevant pages in the edition in my library, the entries for the rebellion had not been translated, merely summarized. For a translation exercise, this was for the better. I had to do all the work myself. Yet, as I worked my way through Gregory's Latin, it became increasingly frustrating to think that this story of two illegitimate princesses leading a revolt over an election had been consigned to summary.[1] I felt compelled to translate the event in its entirety and make the convent the focus of a longer research paper. From there, it felt imperative to tell the story as often as I could. I recounted it at dinners, added it to my lectures, and submitted a short narrative of the event to a magazine. This story makes up the first chapter of this book.

In the chapters that follow, we will encounter several more stories and texts that have been sorely neglected. Not all of them, of course, but many. This is the unfortunate reality of writing a history of women, particularly religious women. In Chapter Two, I relied heavily on a singular translation of the works of a tenth-century German nun. Though Hrotsvit is not an obscure figure in medieval history and is often lauded for her accomplishments as a playwright, her works have only been fully translated by one woman, Mary Bernadine Bergman, herself a nun. All other translations are partial, and most historians ignore Hrotsvit's historical poems. Throughout the book, we will meet several anonymous or unnamed women who made their mark briefly, but brightly, in the pages of chronicles, poems, and letters. For this reason, I have included the names of several women who are known only through a singular mention, often their deaths. For some of them, there is nothing to say, but including their names seems vital to me as a small but intentional counter to frequent erasure. The women featured in this book come from a variety of walks of life. Some were royalty, legitimate or otherwise; others have origins so obscure that it is a miracle we know their names at all. Some put their minds to writing imperial histories or operating successful businesses; others preferred to organize soldiers or pick up the sword themselves. What unites the nuns here is their devotion to their convents. Even the subject of the final chapter, a runaway nun who became famous as a lieutenant in the Spanish army, never shied away from saving a nun from danger or spending an afternoon in a convent, discussing niceties and receiving little gifts.

There are a few themes that run through the book. The most prominent of these is the concept of enclosure. On the individual scale, enclosure is the act of sealing oneself in a cell or room for an extended period of time, perhaps for life, in order to be wholly devoted to contemplation and prayer. On a larger scale, the enclosure of nuns involves the construction of walls around a singular convent building or a complex of several smaller buildings or houses. Access to the interior of the convent would then flow through a single door which was itself separated by a room or series of rooms from where the majority of the nuns lived and worked. This requirement was included in the first Rule written for nuns and over the centuries the requirement was reiterated ad nauseum by the ecclesiastical authorities. As will become clear through the course of reading this book, however, enclosure was not a realistic expectation. It proved difficult to enforce, particularly in times of crisis or expansion. When it was strictly enforced, it was almost always to the detriment of the women living inside the convent walls. While male clerics insisted upon enclosure and encouraged nuns to aspire to as complete a version of it as possible, the female religious acknowledged not only the necessity, but the benefit of sending sisters out in pairs or groups to build important social networks for the convent and to experience the personal benefits of activities like missionary work and pilgrimage.

In a similar vein, the male authorities in the church discouraged the female religious from working, whether to provide for themselves or to produce goods, both tangible and spiritual, for others in the larger communities around them. Fortunately, this was not true of all male clergy and many female religious ignored their critics. The early days of female monasteries were dominated by women of noble or near-noble birth who remained closely involved with the politics of their time. In most instances, this was their means of maintaining the funds necessary to support their enclosed communities. In some instances, however, religious women involved themselves as intercessors and mediators for peace. As we will see in Chapter One, the former queen Radegund remained vigilant in her letter-writing campaigns to the Merovingian kings. While she could not secure peace among them, she was able to secure her own convent as a place where the daughters of any nobleman could live safely. Female religious, because they received a similar education as their male counterparts, also worked ceaselessly to produce texts and textiles that immortalized ideal images of the imperium of their day. The role of women in medieval book production has been well-documented and is highlighted in several chapters of this book.

As recruiting patterns for convents evolved, particularly in the later centuries of the medieval era, the daughters, sisters, and widows of craftsmen and merchants also took vows. Like their lay peers, these women involved themselves in making and using wool and silk. They also maintained gardens and orchards from which they harvested their own food and ingredients for medicines. In some places, where convents benefitted from generous patrons or savvy abbesses, there was money to be made from investing in property and renting to tenants working farmland or vineyards. Inside some larger convents, there were also rooms to be rented out to lay women, usually widows who were not ready to take their own vows. Nuns also oversaw small schools, educating young girls and sometimes boys. Certain convents became known for their embroidery work, their luxurious books, or their musical ability.

Oftentimes, despite the calls for stricter enclosure, the convents were centrally located in bustling cities. Naturally, they were centrepieces of the community, for better or worse.

The women who entered these institutions, particularly those who made the conscious choice as grown women to take their vows, understood the opportunities provided inside the walls. A convent was a place where an unmarried woman, by wedding herself to Christ, could focus on her studies and her crafts. For many this was a welcome alternative to secular marriage. For many families, putting a daughter, or several daughters, in a convent was the more affordable option. Convents also provided a comfortable and secure place to retire as a widow whether one took vows or not. Besides these material incentives, the placement of a family member in a convent, particularly a prestigious or beloved one, yielded great social and spiritual value. A Florentine convent, which provides the setting for Chapter Five, became a major node in the de' Medici political network and, consequently, became a premiere location for some of the richest Italian families to place their female relatives.

The intention of this book is to illuminate the variety of religious lives that women carved out for themselves over the course of the medieval period. It begins at the end of the sixth century with one of the earliest European convents and ends in the middle of the seventeenth century in a rural town in Mexico. Major monuments of the medieval will appear throughout: Charlemagne, the crusades, the inquisition, the Florentine Renaissance, and the 'discovery' of the 'New World'. Nuns and other female religious, like canonesses and beguines, were witness to and active participants in these moments. Yet, because the book spans such a long period of time – more than one thousand years – and travels across the whole of western Europe and into the Americas, it necessarily skims over several other events and people. For example, there is only passing mention of the Investiture Controversy which dominated papal politics and featured in the histories of nearly every European kingdom during the tenth and eleventh centuries.

The first chapter traces the early years of a royally founded convent, Sainte-Croix in Poitiers, France. The nuns of Sainte-Croix were working nearly from scratch to create a conventual lifestyle. They adopted a version of the earliest rule for virgins which had been written only a few decades earlier in the city of Arles in southern France. Their convent was built on the outskirts of a major town in the Merovingian domain. The threat of civil war and other violence was constant. The kingdom had not been completely or consistently Christianized. Royal and ecclesiastical authorities were in flux. It was an era ripe for contest and experimentation.

Saint Leoba, one of the main figures of the second chapter, worked in a similar atmosphere. She, accompanied by a handful of other nuns, aided Saint Boniface as missionaries along the frontier of Saxony in modern-day Germany. The exceptional circumstances of the eighth-century Germanic lands, paired with the ninth-century imperial project of Charlemagne, resulted in a network of imperially backed convents headed by the daughters of the imperial family. The convents of early medieval Germany produced playwrights, historians, and regents for the empire. These roots would later flourish into a conventual culture of visionary and politically minded women that bore fruit like Hildegard of Bingen, one of the most famous medieval nuns.

The third chapter spans the first century of the crusading movement. While there are specific individuals to discuss – Margaret of Beverely and Hildegund von Schonau – the chapter is more of a literary history. It is necessary to grapple with the complicated nature of chronicles and poems. There has been extensive and intense debate about the reality of women on the crusade. Contemporary sources constantly obscure the picture. Many women are described only as groups – a legendary battalion of wives, abducted prisoners, banished sinners – or they are unnamed individuals who may or may not have been real. The two nuns who receive most of the focus of the chapter were likely real, but the details of their life stories are complicated by the fact that they are recorded in poetry or hagiography. They also survived in pieces or were adorned with embellishments. The chapter concludes with a discussion of women who most certainly were real, but whose personal careers as commanders of small houses in military orders must rely on generalization or conjecture.

The fourth chapter scales back down to talk about a single woman who was not technically a nun. Marguerite Porete was a lone beguine, evicted from a house of other lay religious women, and forced to defend herself against inquisitors in Lorraine, a region of northeast France, and in Paris. Her work on the soul and its spiritual progress was an exemplary piece of theology, albeit a bit bolder than the typical beguine book. Her trial, held in Paris in late spring 1310, coincided with the much more famous trial of the Templars. United by a context of centralizing royal authority and growing ecclesiastical anxiety, Marguerite and the Templars burned because they could not be controlled. Marguerite refused to stop copying her book and refused to cooperate with her second and final inquisitor, William of Paris. Her execution was a pivotal moment in the history of female religious after which both ecclesiastical and secular authorities were increasingly anxious to control convents and the women inside them.

The women of Le Murate, discussed in the fifth chapter, grappled with this new reality. Their convent began as a group of unaffiliated devout women living in a house on a bridge in Florence. At the end of the fourteenth century, to save one of their sisters from an unwanted marriage, they were forced to associate themselves with a recognized monastic order. The growth of their convent was then dictated by their ability to navigate the complexities of de' Medici politics, panicked religious revivals in the face of a seemingly endless war for the Italian peninsula, and the growing costs of operating a convent in Renaissance Florence. The convent's success was primarily the result of one woman, Scholastica Rondinelli, who was clearly recruited by the convent after her husband died. Almost immediately after she took vows, she was made the abbess. Using her political connections to the leading families of the city she oversaw major building projects, established a successful apothecary, and secured the necessary funds to see her convent through several harrowing years after her death. The chapter relies heavily on one of the convent's own chronicles – not by taking it at face value as history, but by exploring the ways in which Sister Giustina Niccolini crafted a cohesive identity for the convent in the face of famine and war.

In the sixth and final chapter of the book, we spend very little time in a convent as the subject of the chapter, Catalina/Antonio de Erauso, spent very little time in a nun's habit. Instead, Catalina escaped the convent in which she and all but one of her sisters had been deposited as small children. From there, the young runaway began a life of adventure, both daring and violent. Erauso would only re-enter the convent to avoid being arrested for murder. The sensational case of the Lieutenant Nun became headline news in seventeenth-century Spain. The bulk of the historical work on Erauso has focused on gender and sexuality. This chapter does not ignore these topics but sets them off to the side in favour of exploring how Erauso manipulated the gaps between secular and ecclesiastical authorities and spaces in order to maintain to maintain a life of aimless, rambling freedom. Through this runaway nun's dramatic autobiography, we get a revealing glimpse of the day-to-day ambitions, schemes, and violence of a Spaniard in the colonies.

There is a popular saying which appears on bumper stickers, pins, tattoos, and elsewhere: Well-behaved women rarely make history. While pithy, and true enough about women's history generally, it is actually quite the opposite in the history of religious women. The well-behaved nuns of history have been canonized, chronicled, and used as exemplars down through the centuries. One has to think only of Caesaria of Arles, for whom the first rule for virgins was written; Hildegard of Bingen, whose visions and musical compositions are perhaps some of the most famous of the medieval era; Catherine of Siena or Teresa of Avila who were both lauded for their piety, but also their sharp insight and leadership. Nuns who led rebellions, forsook enclosure in the name of pilgrimage or preaching, or rejected the veil entirely because it was put upon them without their consent are more often erased or treated as fascinating, if cautionary, tales.

Concepts of 'well-behaved' have also changed dramatically since the medieval period and were not entirely static during those centuries. Some of the women discussed in this book would have been considered perfectly well-behaved in a different time than their own and others, who were lauded as saintly in their own time, would have been treated as impudent sinners, even heretics, in others. To be a good or well-behaved woman is to be constantly chasing a moving goal post. This book hopes to settle the goal posts in a different field entirely – not one based on orthodoxy or morality, but on audacity and determination.

Chapter One

War in the Convent

Founded among the Roman ruins and forged in the foggy darkness of the sixth century, the line of Merovech was cruel and sharp. The ever-shifting boundaries of the Frankish kingdoms carved out a battleground that stretched across Europe from Thuringia in the east to the Pyrenees in the west. Still the kings and their heirs seemed to be forever unsatisfied with their portions. No individual or institution was immune to the insidious influence of familial war. Sons and nephews were slaughtered, daughters and widows were exiled or held captive, and the hierarchies of the Christian churches were filled with loyal retired warriors and noble girls. The intermingling of nobility and clergy had been mutually beneficial. The nobility granted land, money, and protection to the clergy. In exchange, the clergy blessed kings with divine legitimacy and provided a mostly secure sanctuary for family members who were not needed for, or were no longer involved in, the politics of the time. Simultaneously, the closeness of the two institutions, the royal courts and the church, blurred ideas of authority. What happens when a queen founds and enters her own abbey? Can princesses be bound under the authority of a common woman within the walls of a convent? When nuns lead a violent rebellion, to which judicial authority should they answer?

This mélange of royal intrigue and righteous will is exemplified in the Sainte-Croix abbey founded in Poitiers by Radegund of Thuringia (d. 587), a captive princess and ascetic queen turned saint. From its foundation, this royal abbey toyed with the line between ecclesiastical and royal authorities. Queen-Saint Radegund invoked her powers both as a queen and as a deaconess. At different times, she sought the authority or protection of both the king and several bishops, wielding one against the other. All her machinations were in the pursuit of independence and prosperity for her community of pious noble ladies. Following her death, the blending of authorities was more difficult and the different women who wished to succeed the queen each chose one authority over the other. This division, provoked by the queen's death and a disputed election, would plunge Radegund's abbey, and the city of Poitiers, into a months-long conflict – a battle of wills and weapons between two princesses, Clothild and Basina, and their abbess, Leubovera.

This conflict came to a head in March 590 – a full year after it had begun – when mercenaries hired by Clothild and Basina stormed Sainte-Croix in the middle of the night. After a long winter of dwindling fuel and supporters, the time had come for the final attack. As the mercenaries breached the walls, the abbess, Leubovera, was carried from her rooms to an inner sanctum which housed a piece of the Holy Cross. There, suffering from gout, laid out on a blanket, the abbess led the nuns in prayer as the sounds of armed men pillaging and searching grew closer. When the men burst into the room, swords drawn, illuminated by candlelight, the women did not cower or panic. Instead, the prioress, Justina, extinguished the candles upon the shrine and threw a blanket over the abbess to hide her. In the shadowy chaos that followed, one of the mercenaries was stabbed to death by his own men, but the nuns were mostly spared, only their dresses falling under the mercenary blades.

They had come to take the abbess, but in the dark and with one of their own dead, the men were hurried and grabbed the prioress instead. It was only in the dawn light, after they had dragged her from the abbey – her veil torn and her hair loose – that they realized their mistake. Frustrated, the armed men dragged her back to the nunnery, likely right back to the darkened shrine. Perhaps by then the candles had been relit, the women coming to the aid of their abbess, assessing the damage, and beginning to offer up thanks only to hear the sounds of rushed footsteps, angry shouting, and a plaintive warning from their sister, Justina. After exchanging the women, likely tossing the gout-suffering abbess over a shoulder, the men returned to a nearby house where the princesses had been waiting. As Leubovera sat before Clothild and Basina, women whom she had known for several years now holding her captive, it must have been surreal to recall the meals and prayers before the previous spring. Sainte-Croix was not a small abbey, but at the time of Queen Radegund's death in 587, there were only 200-250 women residing there. The three women now embroiled in this conflict must have known each other, even done chores, and attended mass together. Much had changed in the year since Leubovera's election.

The election of Leubovera as abbess late in 588 was only the second election held in Sainte-Croix though the abbey had been founded at least thirty years earlier. Queen Radegund established her abbey sometime in the 550s but did not become abbess herself. Instead, she had taken on the title of deaconess. In Radegund's time this was an archaic term, a title which harkened back to the era of the Apostles.[1] There were two major benefits of being a deaconess, rather than an abbess or nun. First, and this was the most legally vital in Radegund's circumstances, was that the deaconess was not required to be either a virgin or a widow. At the time of her vows, Radegund was a runaway queen, still married to King Clothar (d. 561). We are told by one of her biographers, Fortunatus (d. 610), a bishop of Poitiers, a famous poet, and one of Radegund's close friends, that when Radegund decided to 'divest herself of the noble costume', she fled to Médard, bishop of Noyons, and demanded that he consecrate her as a *monacha*. The bishop hesitated to follow the queen's orders. Fortunatus describes a hectic scene in the church at Noyons. The queen and bishop, discussing the matter at the altar, were interrupted by a crowd of noblemen who had been sent to retrieve the runaway queen. Fortunatus writes that the men were not only harassing the bishop, shouting and cursing at him, but even broke down the door to the church and attempted 'to drag him brutally through the basilica from the altar to keep him from veiling the king's spouse'. Yet, these brutal nobles were no match for Radegund who, seizing the moment, clothed herself in monastic garb and accused the bishop of 'fear[ing] man more than God', leaving him 'thunderstruck'.[2]

Despite the melodrama of Fortunatus' consecration scene, Médard and Radegund had come to a pragmatic compromise which may have eased the political burden on Médard by technically allowing Radegund's marriage to stand. In the end, it did not matter as Clothar appears not to have forced the issue of his and Radegund's marriage any further. By Radegund's account, told to us by her two other biographers, the king rescinded his claim on her and provided the means for her to establish her abbey, even allowing Radegund to retain her royal allowance, and died only a few years later.[3]

A second benefit of Radegund's deaconess status was the substantial flexibility under her chosen Rule and within the church hierarchy. The status was an older one with far less rigidly defined responsibilities and requirements. This flexibility was intensified by Radegund's royal status and her determined personality. Though Radegund had set aside her crown and 'noble costume' in pursuit of an ascetic and holy life, she did not forsake the authority and power she had gained in her husband's kingdom. In fact, as a deaconess, freed from her marriage, she may have become more involved in the power struggles of her day. One of the nuns who grew up at the abbey in the later years of Radegund's life often highlighted Radegund's worldly authority and lifelong involvement in the politics of the kingdom:

> 'She was always solicitous for peace and worked diligently for the welfare of the fatherland. Whenever the different kingdoms made war on one another, she prayed for the lives of all the kings, for she loved them all… Whenever she heard of bitterness arising among them, trembling, she sent such letters to one and then to the other… And, likewise, she sent to their noble followers to give the high kings salutary counsel so that their power might work to the welfare of the people and the land… And who can tell what agonies she inflicted on herself? So, through her intercession, there was peace among the kings'.[4]

Radegund's flexibility under the Rule of her abbey extended to her participation in enclosure,[5] and her administration of the abbey's hierarchy. This latter point is relevant to the election of an abbess. The first abbess of Sainte-Croix, a woman named Agnes, was elected by the nuns there in 561. The first mention of Agnes comes in a letter of Radegund's, copied by the historian, Gregory of Tours (d. 593 or 594). There, Radegund describes her as 'my lady and sister Agnes, whom I had raised and educated from an early age in the place of a daughter'.[6]

Indeed, Agnes had been raised at court and seems to have been a constant companion to Radegund even before she fled her husband. So, it is likely that this election ran smoothly.

It is possible that Agnes had prepared Leubovera to be her successor much in the same way she had been 'raised and educated' by Radegund, but this is not certain. The details around this second election in 588 are scarce. It was necessitated by Agnes' death. Leubovera won the majority – some 200 nuns against perhaps 40-50 in favour of Clothild. There was some attempt to settle the dispute internally, but in the end the nuns in the minority marched out of their abbey, even out of the city, to make an appeal at the court of Clothild's relative, King Guntram, in Orléans.

On the way, the nuns first arrived in Tours where they sought sanctuary in the church of Saint Martin. It is at this point in the story that one of our key historical witnesses became involved. Gregory of Tours, who was in the process of writing his *History of the Franks*, met with Clothild, he tells us, on the first day of March. The few dozen women had walked just over a hundred kilometres to reach his church. They had received no food or shelter from anyone on their route. On the last day of their march, which was perhaps three or four days in total, it apparently rained so heavily that the water was ankle-deep on the roads. This perhaps explains both Gregory's bit of patience and Clothild's impatience.

Clothild explained why she and her fellow nuns had arrived on Gregory's footsteps. She had come to pay her respects to the well-known bishop, but also to ask for a favour:

> 'I am going to my royal relations' she said, 'to tell them about the insults which we have to suffer, for we are humiliated here as if we were the offspring of low-born serving women, instead of being the daughters of kings!... Do me a favour, saintly Bishop, and keep an eye on these nuns, who have been greatly humiliated by their Abbess in Poitiers'.[7]

Gregory attempted to convince Clothild to return to Poitiers, and to seek out guidance from her own bishop, Maroveus. She refused and not without good reason. Before Clothild had led the march from Sainte-Croix, the bishop had come to discuss the results of the election with both parties. It did not go well. Later, at the princesses' trial, he included in his testimony that the women had knocked him to the ground and literally marched over him to lead their fellow nuns out of the abbey.

Yet, even before this assault, the relationship between Bishop Maroveus and the women in Sainte-Croix had been tumultuous, at best. The bishop had even feuded with Radegund herself. The feud between Radegund and Maroveus is well-recorded in the three contemporary biographies of the saint. The dispute was expressed primarily in Maroveus' persistent refusal to perform the liturgical formalities requested and required by the fledgling convent. It seems the nuns were frequently forced to call on the bishops of Tours to fulfil both pastoral and sacramental needs. Maroveus also expressly refused to consecrate the arrival of a chip from the True Cross sent from Constantinople by Emperor Justin II and Empress Sophia. Finally, when called upon to preside over Radegund's funeral, he left town, pleading more important pastoral business elsewhere.[8] For this, Baudonivia labelled the bishop a 'satellite of the Enemy of humankind'.[9] Gregory worried that 'something which I cannot understand lingered in his heart'.[10]

Radegund expressed similar sentiments in a letter to several bishops.[11] When she wrote to her bishops to submit Agnes, her spiritual daughter, as abbess, her anxiety for the physical and material security of her nuns was palpable. The object of the letter was to install an abbess, but the text is overwhelmed with concern for internal and external threats that would unravel the abbey. Radegund reminded the bishops that Agnes had been consecrated by the bishop of Paris himself and that they had been witnesses to it. She recalled the abbey's founding donation from the deceased Clothar and asserted that she had 'obtained confirmation by the authority of the most excellent lord kings Charibert, Guntram, Chilperic, and Sigibert', all four of Clothar's living heirs.

Radegund's appeals were forceful in their pleading but subtle in their distinctions of authority. To the kings, Radegund entrusted the whole convent, placing it 'under their protection and word, that they permit nothing pertaining to our abbey or our oftmentioned abbess, be harmed, or disturbed, or diminished or changed'.[12] If anyone did disturb the abbey in any way, then Radegund requested that 'it not be displeasing, in order to repel and confound the enemy of God, to have recourse to the king … for no Catholic king may permit such wickedness … nor permit to be undone what was confirmed by the will of God, me, and their kings'.[13] To the bishops, Radegund entrusts nothing:

> 'And you also, blessed pontiff, and your successors, whom I diligently take as patrons in the cause of God if, may it not be, there should be one who would attempt to do something against this, let it not be displeasing, in order to repel and confound the enemy of God, to have recourse to the king who shall oversee this place at that time, or to the city of Poitiers, for the thing commended to you before the Lord …'

This letter, which is transmitted to us by Gregory, and Radegund's feud with Maroveus foreshadowed this violent uprising in her abbey. So, despite Gregory's shock and disapproval, it should not have been a surprise that the nuns of Sainte-Croix could and would seek out the aid and authority of their royal kin over that of the men of the church, particularly their own bishop. Still, Gregory pleaded with and persuaded Clothild to wait in Tours until the weather had improved and tempers had cooled. As they waited, spring flowed into summer and Clothild's patience eroded. Finally, she went to Gunthram's court and secured his promise of support. He would order a council of bishops to convene and oversee a settlement between Clothild's nuns and Leubovera. Clothild returned to Tours, feeling secure in her position, sure that within the year she would be the abbess. This feeling would not last long as she waited with her nuns in Tours.

Gregory tells us that even before Clothild returned from the king's court, 'a number of the nuns had given in to circumstances … and had accepted the offers of marriage which were made to them'.[14] Apparently, as we are told later in his history, the 'circumstances' for some of the nuns included pregnancy. So, as the women waited, their numbers dwindled. After an unspecified amount of time, when no bishops or other representatives of the king arrived, the remaining nuns returned to Poitiers. Though they had lost several sisters, the princesses' entourage did not shrink in size. They replenished, even increased, their ranks with hired swords and began their conquest.

When the contingent arrived, they first attacked St. Hilarius, the cathedral and seat of the bishop. This became the headquarters of the rebellion for the next several months. Violence summoned the council of bishops much quicker than waiting in Tours. Maroveus and three other bishops were led by Gundegisel, the metropolitan of Bordeaux, who attempted to negotiate terms with the princesses. The women were insistent that Leubovera, the abbess, be dismissed and invoked their royal prerogative: 'We are queens and we will not set foot inside our nunnery until the abbess has been dismissed'.[15] Frustrated and out of ideas, the metropolitan excommunicated them on the spot. Enraged and out of options, Clothild ordered her men to attack. Gregory of Tours describes a bloody and chaotic scene of fleeing priests and deacons. One bishop even rode his horse into the Clain river to escape.[16]

Clothild did not let this first successful attack go to waste. She had taken the cathedral, expelled Maroveus, and chased him and his clerical reinforcements from the city. Thereafter, it was easy to take control of the abbey's estates in the surrounding countryside. Gregory tells us, at this point, that King Childebert (d. 595), the nephew of King Guntram, ordered that the count of Poitiers put down the revolt.[17] It is unclear where the count had been in the several weeks leading up to this conflict, and it is apparent that he took his time dealing with it even after receiving orders from his king. In the meantime, Maroveus requested that the bishops try again to meet with the nuns occupying his cathedral. This request was denied. Letters from the bishops, from Clothild, from Leubovera, and likely from several other people of high standing in Poitiers reached Guntram and Childebert. Finally, 'tired of the never-ending stream of complaints' Childebert sent a trusted priest, Theuthar, from his court to attempt to bring the nuns together to discuss the dispute.

Theuthar went first to Clothild in Poitiers, summoning her and her nuns to meet with him on neutral ground in the city. They refused to appear before him, demanding that they first be 'received back into the Church', and that their excommunication be lifted.[18] Theuthar then travelled to the bishops, likely staying in Tours, but perhaps as far away as Bordeaux. The bishops, some of them likely still bearing wounds from the nuns' attack, refused to lift the excommunication. So, Theuthar returned to Poitiers and finally to the kings – either in Orléans or Metz. Though he likely travelled by horse, his journey, crisscrossing the Frankish kingdoms, would have taken weeks. Indeed, by the time it was clear that no agreement could be reached between the two factions of nuns and the bishops, winter had begun. And still, the count of Poitiers had not arrived to quash the rebellion.

It is perhaps not surprising that the count of Poitiers did not prioritize this rebellion in his city. Given the drawn-out nature of the conflict, the back-and-forth exchange of letters and bishops and priests, it did not really seem like anyone's priority. In fact, around Poitiers and throughout the Frankish kingdoms there were several other issues, many of them significantly more violent, to deal with. In choosing Poitiers as the site of her abbey, Radegund had placed herself and her nuns in the eye of the Merovingian storm. The city had been surrounded by violence for decades.

The year before King Clothar had agreed to fund Radegund's abbey, the city had been sacked and severely burned by one of his sons. The construction of the abbey, as well as some refurbishments made at the tomb of Saint Martin in Tours, were likely acts of penance by the aging king. When the king died in 561, the kingdom was again plunged into the divisive wars of family drama, primarily between his sons Sigibert and Chilperic, father to the rebellious princess Basina. Following his father's death, King Chilperic and his mistress, Fredegund, allegedly murdered Chilperic's wife, the older sister of King Sigibert's wife. In 575, this violence reached a climax when Sigibert was assassinated; his widow married one of Chilperic's sons who was rebelling against him. This son was then hunted through Poitiers and fled to Tours, where he was assassinated.

While Poitiers and the surrounding region devolved into a battleground, Sainte-Croix quickly became a refuge for Merovingian princesses, both legitimate and natural. Gunthram Boso, a local count who was at war with Chilperic and Fredegund, placed his two daughters in Poitiers. The count of Poitiers deposited one daughter at Sainte-Croix and another in Tours. None of the contemporary sources explicitly mention this daughter's involvement in the rebellion, but if she was among the nuns occupying the cathedral with Clothild, this could explain the count's hesitation. Fredegund, the murderous mistress of King Chilperic, sent her stepdaughter, Basina, to the abbey in 580. Five years later, Basina's father – after a vicious campaign that saw the whole area between Poitiers and Tours plundered – was assassinated, and her half-sister, Rigunth, was robbed of her wedding trousseau in the countryside of Poitiers – en route to the Visigothic court in Spain.[19] Around the same time, Berthegund, a cousin of Basina's, had retreated to her estate outside the city following a controversy that involved her mother, Ingitrude, a somewhat infamous nun, and the bishops of Tours, Bordeaux, and Poitiers, and resulted in armed men sacking her villa.[20] Poitiers was a town embroiled in near-constant violence. A few dozen nuns occupying the cathedral and roughing up a few bishops was hardly a priority. If anything, it might have been seen by the nobility as an extension of the feuds between the kings.

The women placed in Sainte-Croix came from warring families, and several questions spring to mind: were Gunthram Boso's two daughters enemies of Basina, the daughter of Chilperic? Did the count of Poitier's daughter resent the daughters of the men who had sacked and burned her home city? Did these worldly divisions influence the outcome of the election of the abbess? Our sources do not answer these questions directly, but the rebellion itself makes it clear that tensions were rife in Sainte-Croix. Over the course of the conflict, it also became apparent that the ties binding the rebellious nuns were not particularly strong. Several had already abandoned the cause in Tours in order to marry local men. Gregory tells us that throughout the winter, even more women left Poitiers:

> 'Some went back to their own homes, others to their relations, and quite a few returned to the religious houses where they had previously lived. They could no longer live as a community, because lack of fuel made them unable to bear the winter cold. However, a few remained behind with Clothild and Basina. Even these few kept on quarrelling with each other, for each one of them wanted to lord it over her companions'.[21]

It was under these circumstances, as winter melted into spring and Easter approached, that Clothild ordered her mercenaries to storm the abbey and abduct the abbess in the middle of the night. Everything went according to plan. The convent was now under Clothild and Basina's control, and was defended by their mercenaries, who were paid and fed from the income of the Sainte-Croix estates. When Maroveus sent a messenger to negotiate for Leubovera's release, his threats fell flat:

> 'Free your Abbess from her imprisonment and let her go', he said. 'You know what season it is. Unless you order her to be released from the prison in which she is locked up, I shall refuse to celebrate our Lord's Easter ceremony, and no one being given instruction for baptism will receive it in this town. If you refuse to do what I say, I will rouse the townsfolk and free her myself'.[22]

It is easy to imagine how these threats must have amused Clothild. The count of Poitiers had yet to arrive or send any soldiers. Winter was over. She had taken Sainte-Croix into her possession along with all of its estates. She called the bishop's bluff. When Easter came, the bishop neither cancelled the ceremony nor roused the townsfolk. He sent another messenger to offer 'to pay over a sum of money as a surety if the Abbess were allowed to at least watch the baptismal ceremony'.[23] It is unclear if Clothild agreed to this or not. Our only source for this moment, Gregory, writes very vaguely:

> 'It happened that Flavianus, who had only recently been appointed as one of the King's officials, was in Poitiers at this time, and with his help the Abbess was released and carried into Saint Hilary's Church'.

Later, when recording the princesses' trial, Gregory writes that 'no persuasion or entreaty had been of any avail' in reference to the bishop's messages and offer of money. These are not necessarily contradictory statements. Clothild rejected the offer. Flavianus rescued the abbess. It likely would not have required a Bond-esque mission to break the abbess out of a house in town. Guards can be bribed. If Clothild would not take the money, this does not mean one or more of her mercenaries would not. Guards also sometimes shirk their duties or fall asleep on night watch. It would also not be unbelievable that Flavianus, with some assistance, could storm the house and take the abbess back by force. This is assuming the abbess had not been moved to the abbey after it had been fully sacked and secured by Clothild's forces.

Gregory also writes that while Flavianus was freeing the abbess, chaos was erupting in town. Men guarding Radegund's tomb were killed and a riot erupted outside the shrine at Sainte-Croix. It is possible that these attacks at the abbey and the tomb were crowds of roused townsfolk which would make a good distraction for the rebels while the abbess was allowed to attend the Easter ceremony. The bishop likely would not, or at least could not, publicly approve of the violence on Easter, but a young upstart royal official like Flavianus might take advantage of the moment.

Perhaps as the abbess was being escorted by guards from Sainte-Croix, the crowd began its assault. With possible reinforcements distracted, Flavianus could have led his own soldiers in a quick fight against Leubovera's guards and then escaped to the cathedral. It is also possible that the abbess was still being held in a townhouse closer to the cathedral. In this case we might imagine that the abbess was escorted from her prison to the cathedral by several guards. The distraction in this instance would be an attack on Radegund's tomb. The saint had been buried in a church just outside the city walls, about a mile away from the cathedral. The presence of mercenaries in the tomb seems the most likely reason for violence to take place there. This serious assault by the townspeople could have strained the rebel defences. Perhaps someone was sent to gather reinforcements, the nearest of whom were guarding the abbess. The division of the forces or the distraction of debating what to do would have provided an opening for the royal official to attack.

Regardless of how the abbess was rescued, the damage was done to Clothild's rebellion. Her fury at this setback was unmatched. The days following Easter were bloody and chaotic. Clothild unleashed her mercenaries on the town. According to Gregory, as the situation deteriorated, Clothild and Basina began to quarrel. He imagined Basina's regret:

> 'I committed a sin when I behaved in the same arrogant way as Clothild', she said to herself. 'I am in revolt against my Abbess all right, but that doesn't seem to stop me being despised by Clothild'.[24]

Somehow, during the days of violence, Basina went to the cathedral and threw herself on the mercy of the abbess. There was allegedly a brief peace between the two women, but this quickly fell apart following a brawl between the servants of Leubovera, Basina, and Clothild. Gregory tells us that the fight was started by Clothild's gang, but when the dust settled one of Leubovera's servants had stabbed one of Basina's. The truce between the two nuns fell apart and Basina retreated into her own part of the city. It was at this point, when there were then three rival factions of nuns, and 'scarcely a day passed without someone being murdered, scarcely an hour without some quarrel or other, scarcely a minute without some person or other having cause for sorrow', that the kings once again wrote to the count of Poitiers to order him to intervene. They also wrote to the council of bishops who had excommunicated the princesses to reunite for a trial.

Finally, after a year of assaults, abductions, and riots, Macco, count of Poitiers, gathered his forces and marched on Sainte-Croix. Clothild ordered her forces to ready themselves, shoulder to shoulder, to defend the abbey. It had been easy to fend off bishops and townsfolk, but the trained soldiers of a count made quick work of the mercenaries. As the tide turned against her, Clothild retrieved the piece of the Cross. Whereas Leubovera had prayed before the relic for protection from her kidnappers, Clothild held the piece of wood aloft and cried out, 'I warn you! Do not lay a finger on me! I am a queen, the daughter of one king and the niece of another! If you touch me you can be quite sure that the day will come when I shall have my revenge!'[25] Clothild experienced the same result as Leubovera. After her mercenaries were cut down or tied up, she was dragged from the abbey and carried off to the cathedral to stand trial.

Based on Gregory's account, the tribunal seems to have begun immediately. Clothild and Basina were allowed to state their case first and laid out a laundry list of accusations against Leubovera. They alleged she had failed to provide adequate food and clothing, treated them too harshly, enjoyed too many privileges, played backgammon, 'enjoyed the company of guests', organized parties, used donated goods for her own ends, and had disguised a lover as a female servant so that he might come and go at will.[26] The princesses' complaints about the quality of food and clothing were quickly dismissed. The asceticism of their abbey's founder was legendary, and the expectation of monastic life was supposed to be austere at its most luxurious. Against the more egregious charges, like taking a lover and disguising him as a woman or using abbey funds to buy presents for her niece, Leubovera defended herself with the testimony of several witnesses, including a local physician and the count of Poitiers.

The assembled bishops then asked Clothild and Basina if they had any other accusations to level at Leubovera before the trial moved on to their charges. It is difficult to imagine that the bishops' tone was not sarcastic when they asked the princesses if they wanted to instead accuse their abbess of 'sexual promiscuity … or homicide perhaps, or witchcraft'.[27] Clothild, likely fuming, and Basina, perhaps a bit red with embarrassment, replied 'that they had no such charge to make and that their case rested on what they had already said about her having broken the Rule'. Though they pointed out that several nuns from the abbey were now pregnant, it is unclear if they are speaking of the nuns who had left with them the previous March – accepting marriage proposals in Tours over the summer – or if nuns who had remained with the abbess and were without adequate supervision in the months of violence, had also abandoned their habits and vows. Either way, the bishops dismissed this charge against the abbess and seem to have even taken a laissez-faire approach to the now married and/or pregnant nuns:

> 'In our opinion this was not their fault. The poor girls had been left to their own devices for so many months, with their nunnery gates broken down and no control possible by their Abbess, and as a result they had sinned'.[28]

It is unclear whether the other forty or so nuns who marched out of Sainte-Croix were charged or convicted of anything. In Gregory's copy of the court proceedings, it is only Clothild and Basina who were named, who both accused and were accused, and when they received their punishment, they are specifically named together. The list of their crimes was long: disobeying both their abbess and bishop, assault, leaving their nunnery and encouraging others to do the same, rioting, arson, vandalism, theft, kidnapping, and murder. The mercenaries who aided them in these crimes were taken into the custody of the count and were executed or maimed. The princesses, falling under the authority of canon law, were excommunicated for a third time and told to return the property stolen from the abbey and cathedral. Until they had done this and 'proper penance', they were to be excluded from communion and their community at the abbey. After the sentence had been handed down, Clothild and Basina were released, and Leubovera returned to Sainte-Croix.

Throughout the scandal of the rebellion, the greatest crime committed by the nuns, from the perspective of the bishops, was their violation of the Rule of the abbey, particularly the rule of enclosure. When the nuns had arrived in Tours, Gregory had fretted over the fact that they had gone outside the walls of their abbey. The fact that the nuns had been outside the confines of their abbey was used to excuse the actions and consequences of all but the two ringleaders. When these two were punished, it was not for the actions of their mercenaries but for the fact that 'they had broken locks, burst open gates, started a revolt, and then escaped' from Sainte-Croix.[29] When they did this, Gregory tells us, one of the nuns who escaped with them had been enclosed in a cell – a penance she had undertaken after having previously escaped by lowering herself over the abbey walls with a rope.[30] The first item of the Rule was that nuns were not to pass beyond the walls of their abbey, and, as the princesses had pointed out in their accusations against the abbess, men were almost entirely banned from coming within the walls. However, when we look at the activities and letters of the abbey's founder and first abbess, it is easy to see how Clothild and Basina might justify their departure.

In theory, the abbey of Sainte-Croix operated under the *Rule for Virgins* written by Caesarius of Arles (d. 542) for the convent he founded and had built for his sister, Caesaria (d. c. 530). This was the first set of rules written for nuns and was nearly contemporary with the famous *Rule of Saint Benedict*, the former written in 512 and the latter in 516. The purpose of both was to organize the hierarchies and schedules of monks and nuns. Among the rules set down by Caesarius there are several worth mentioning in the context of Sainte-Croix. The nuns should never leave their abbey, or even enter the areas of the abbey with doors to the outside. The exceptions to this are the abbess and the prioress, who must entertain visitors, negotiate with wool merchants, and oversee the receipt of letters and rents from the abbey estates. Any woman taking on the nun's habit had to give up all her property to the abbey. They should share living quarters and chores – though Caesarius exempts the abbess and prioress from kitchen duty. They should go about their day mostly in silence, speaking only when 'the necessity of work requires it' or when it is their turn to read from the scripture during meals or work. All communication with the outside world should go through the abbess, whether letters from family, work orders for mending or washing clothes, or gifts of food to the poor.

In practice, Sainte-Croix operated under the Rule of Radegund. In some ways, this was a more severe approach. In a letter to Radegund, Caesarius' niece, Caesaria the Younger (d. c. 560), gently reproaches the future saint for going too far in her asceticism, abstaining too much and risking illness.[31] The queen's biographers both emphasized this asceticism: wearing hair shirts and iron circlets around her wrists, holding burning hot brass plates to her chest, hardly eating or sleeping. Both also detail her works of service, emphasizing that she herself fed, bathed, and met with the sick and poor. She also took on chores in the kitchen and bathrooms – chores from which she was likely exempt according to Caesarius' Rule.[32] The fact that Radegund was a deaconess, technically outside of the typical conventual hierarchy, makes it difficult to know what could be or would have been expected of her. As mentioned, this deaconess status made Radegund unique in her era, but she seems to have used it to pursue a more fervent asceticism.

On the other hand, she continued to have a personal maid, though one biographer insisted that she 'would not allow her maid to minister to her because she was anxiously bustling about being a servant herself' and received guests.[33] Perhaps this allowed her to put off her own enclosure for an indefinite period.[34] Both her biographers describe Radegund's enclosure as happening in phases, with her first lasting through Lent one year.[35] When the queen finally did go into her cell, it was a major event in town. We learn again from Fortunatus that there were 'such great gatherings of people … that those who could not be contained in the streets climbed up to fill the roofs'.[36] This scene is mirrored in Gregory of Tour's book, *Glory of the Confessors*, when the nuns, not allowed to leave their abbey to attend the funeral, gathered atop the walls of the abbey to watch Radegund's funeral procession.[37]

Prior to her enclosure and later death, Radegund stretched the boundaries set by the Rule by maintaining several connections with the outside world. As I mentioned before, she wrote frequent letters to the kings and nobility who were constantly warring with one another. She also patronized the arts and supported the famous poet and one of her biographers, Venantius Fortunatus. The latter was a frequent recipient of gifts from both Radegund and Agnes, the abbess. Several of his letters to the women and poems about them have survived. In these, he praises the generosity and piety of both women, but he is particularly complimentary of Agnes – so much so that rumours began that the poet and abbess were entertaining some sort of romance.[38] Fortunatus lamented the harm of the rumours in a letter to Agnes:

> 'Mother to me in rank, but sister sweet in love, whom I cherish with piety, faith, in breast and heart, with heavenly affection, not with any bodily crime: not the flesh, but what the spirit desires is what I love. Christ is witness to this, Peter and Paul ministers, with her pious comrades holy Mary sees [it], that you have been to my soul not with other eyes than if you were Titania, a sister from the womb, and I was as if in one birth mother Radegund had borne both, from her chaste innards, and that the dear breasts of the blessed one had nourished the two of us equally with one flowing milk. Alas, I sigh for the harm, lest perhaps with a thin whisper hurtful words impede my meaning; but yet I have the spirit to live with a similar wish, if you wish me to be cherished by [your] sweet love'.[39]

It is also apparent from the surviving letters that Fortunatus did not simply receive gifts sent by the women but must have also gone to the abbey himself. In one letter, he blames the 'excessively rainy air' for his absence. In another, he complains that he is 'closed off' from the abbey and instead finds himself going from house to house for company – perhaps in the time when he was keeping his distance to put the romance rumours to rest.[40] Many of his letters thank the women for sending 'feasts': honey, berries, savoury things, and wine – lots of wine! A strict reading of the Rule would have prohibited the nuns from providing a meal – or any gifts besides 'blessed bread' – in any fashion to Fortunatus, but some of his letters, which refer to the three of them sharing a table, seeing one another and hearing one another, imply that he was also sometimes physically present at the abbey.[41]

When Clothild and Basina accused their abbess of hosting meals and parties they would have known the Rule as well as the rumours, possibly giving some credence to this part of their accusations. The abbess' defence to these charges was interesting. According to Gregory, she replied that 'as far as the meals were concerned, she had done nothing new but had acted just as they used to do under the Lady Radegund: she had offered the bread of oblation to Christian souls, but it could not be shown that she had ever eaten with them'. In response to the accusation that she had hosted an engagement party for her niece, the abbess defended herself by describing a gathering of several people, including 'the bishop himself, the clergy, and some of the town notables' to witness the acceptance of a marriage portion.[42] There were provided in the Rule circumstances and spaces in which the elder nuns, the abbess and prioress, enclosed in the abbey, could meet with people from outside the abbey. For instance, workmen, under the watchful eye of a bishop, priest, or deacon, could enter the abbey to do repairs. The relatives of nuns, even male relatives, were also allowed to visit so long as an elder nun acted as chaperone. Given the poor relationship between Radegund and Maroveus, who was bishop of Poitiers for the last two decades of her life, as well as her status as deaconess, we might wonder if Radegund chose to ignore parts of the Rule which required a more daily involvement of religious men. Regardless of the extent to which the Rule may have been stretched or even broken by their elders, the accusations of Clothild and Basina did not stand and only they were excommunicated.

For their secular crimes, the bishops sent this message in their report to Kings Guntram and Childebert:

> 'For the rest, it lies within your piety and power, if you are prepared to exert your royal authority, to order restitution to its proper place of all property belonging to the abbey … which has been stolen and carried away … You have, then, to decide whether or not you will allow them to entertain some hopes of returning eventually, or if you will forbid them ever to be readmitted to the place which they have ransacked so wickedly and profanely, for fear that even worse things may happen'.

One of the kings, the young Childebert, residing in Metz several days' journey away, decided he would entertain the princesses' hopes. Clothild and Basina likely arrived in Metz sometime early in the summer and sought an audience with the king. When they came to his court to plead their case, they must have taken the same roads as the bishops' messenger; the same roads that had been taken by the priest, Theuthar, the previous autumn when Childebert had sent him to negotiate a peace between the abbess and the princesses, and by a royal messenger to the bishops to form a council and try the rebelling nuns. Now those nuns stood before him, telling him that their abbess had not only been sneaking lovers into the abbey, but that those same men had been spies for Queen Fredegund. Clothild pressed exactly the right button to convince the king to take her claims seriously. Only a few days earlier, an assassin sent by Fredegund had made an attempt on the king's life.[43] The men named by the princesses were arrested and investigated, but 'they were found to have done nothing wrong and they were sent home again'.[44] Still, Childebert seems to have welcomed the now-disgraced nuns into his court as they were still there in the autumn when a Bishop Egidius was tried for forgery and treason.

In the final episode of the drama surrounding Clothild and Basina, they were invited by the king to attend a council of all the kingdom's bishops to oversee the trial of one of their own. The bishop had been accused of conspiring with assassins to kill both Childebert and Guntram, forging royal documents, and taking favours from a hostile king, Chilperic I (d. 584), who was also the late father of Basina – perhaps a bit awkward for her in the audience! After the trial, when the bishop had been found guilty on all charges, stripped of his office, and removed from the priesthood, Basina 'threw herself at the bishops' feet and begged for forgiveness'.[45] It would have been an interesting scene in the cathedral at Metz with dozens of bishops gathered in their finest clothes, pale and tired, and a woman prostrate at their feet, weeping. We might imagine her in her nun's habit – milk white in accordance with the Rule – as a show of her devotion and desire to return to the fold. Or, perhaps, in deference to the Rule's ban on laywomen wearing the habit, she may have been dressed in the simplest noble garment she could find, a pale-coloured wool with only simple embroidery along the wrists and hem. Meanwhile, Childebert and Clothild looked on.

When Basina had finished her apologies and made promises to 'live in peace with her Abbess' and obey the Rule, the king asked that both women be pardoned and 'received once more into communion'.[46] Gregory refused to write the bishops' affirmation. He simply writes, 'Basina went back into her nunnery'. Clothild, on the other hand, still insisting that Leubovera was not the rightful abbess, retired to an estate outside Poitiers and ruled as an independent countess.

This stalemate with the bishops and abbess on one side, Clothild and her royal relatives on the other, is a revealing example of the fraught relationship between the religious and royal powers. Beginning with Radegund's demand that she be consecrated as a deaconess and ending with Clothild's refusal to bow to the bishops' threats and excommunication, Sainte-Croix had provided a position from which former royal captives and illegitimate daughters could make demands for respect and power. Throughout the abbey's early years, it was unclear under whose authority it fell. The local bishop, because of his long-simmering feud with Radegund, had ceded control to the nuns in her abbey. Her former status as queen and the royal dramas that swirled around Poitiers kept the abbey closely tied to the kings and queens. The complicated web of royal relations between the nuns and their lay relatives compounded this issue. Yet, when rebellion erupted, it was hardly a priority for the warring monarchs. From their view, it was a problem internal to the church to be handled by the bishops, but excommunication was their only weapon and even that was undercut by royal requests for pardons.

The results of the rebellion also exposed the variety of desires among the women given over to the church. Radegund, a captive princess turned queen, had fled and fought for entrance into the religious fold. Her devotion and ascetic piety, as well as that of women like Agnes and Leubovera, appear to have genuinely inspired dozens of women to follow in their footsteps; the majority of the nuns at Sainte-Croix had remained loyal to their abbess during the rebellion. Other women in Sainte-Croix, like Clothild and Basina, the unnamed runaway, and those who accepted marriage proposals over the summer in Tours, obviously did not enjoy the religious life. In a reverse of Radegund's fight to enter seclusion, the rebellious nuns fought to escape it, or at least to alter it, and though their rebellion was an extreme response, it is indicative of the contested and complicated history of religious women.

Chapter Two

'Mothers of the Fatherland'

In the year AD 738, a woman from Wessex pulled her black hood tightly around her face and huddled closer to the other nuns as their boat made the day-long trip south across the English Channel. Even in the early summer sun, the spray from the water would have chilled their bare hands and faces. Yet, the thrill of the adventure that awaited must have warmed them. They were on their way to Saxony to aid the Christianizing mission of Boniface, a future martyr and saint. Leoba, the woman leading these intrepid nuns and monks, had written to Boniface, a relative of hers, a few years before to remind him of his ties to her and his old friendship with her deceased father. She asked him not to forget her or her grievously ill mother. Boniface did not forget Leoba. When he wrote to the abbots and abbesses of England, he included Abbess Tetta at Wimbourne and specifically requested that his relative be allowed to leave her monastery.

Leoba's biographer tells us that Tetta was 'exceedingly displeased at [Leoba's] departure', but recalling a dream Leoba had as a young woman, she granted her permission. When Leoba had completed her studies and had disciples of her own, she had dreamed of a purple thread. She pulled the thread from her mouth, pulling and pulling until she formed a ball of the thread. An older nun at the monastery interpreted this dream, declaring that Leoba 'by her teaching and good example' would improve the lives of many people 'in other lands afar off'.[1] If this story is true, we might wonder if Leoba was thinking of it as she peered out over the choppy waters between England and the continent. Perhaps she thought of her father, who had been dead fourteen years when she set sail, and her ill mother, who may not have survived the six years between Leoba's letter to Boniface and her voyage. Perhaps she pondered the recent book from Bede, *The Ecclesiastical History of the English People*,, which posited that the Angles and Saxons had come to conquer Britain as divine retribution for the Britons' failure to preach the Word to their trading partners along the shores of the North Sea.[2]

Leoba (c. AD 710–782) hailed from the recently converted kingdom of Wessex in England. Though the queen of Wessex went on pilgrimage to Rome the year before Leoba's voyage, and a previous king had allegedly abdicated in AD 726 to do the same, the kingdom was still a blend of Christianity and traditional religion as well as a site of continuous debate over the actual practice of the new religion. It is then little wonder that Boniface sought out his fellow English clergy to aid his missionary efforts in the only nominally converted Saxony.

In the same year that Leoba sailed with her fellow nuns and priests to the continent, the *Annals of Quedlinburg* tell us that 'Charles [Martel] once again invaded Saxony and forced the Saxons to pay tribute'. His son, Pepin, would do the same in AD 758.[3] These years, AD 738 and 758, were merely punctuations at the end of a decades-long campaign into Saxony. Throughout these campaigns, with each victorious push into the east, the warriors were followed by missionaries who oversaw mass – often forced – conversions of the Saxons to Christianity.[4] Resistance to invasion and conversion persisted. In AD 754, Boniface was murdered along with several others while on a mission in Frisia to the north. In AD 772, Charlemagne oversaw the destruction of a Saxon holy place, Irminsul. In AD 774, 778 and in the year of Leoba's death, AD 782, there were uprisings against Carolingian rule and the annals record 'a great number of crimes inside the churches and against saint virgins'.[5] A final revolt in AD 793, which lasted three years, was attributed to the Saxons 'losing their faith'. It was put down in AD 796 when Charlemagne 'laid waste' to the region.[6]

None of this comes through in Rudolf of Fulda's biography of the saint. By the time Rudolf, a Saxon monk born sometime around AD 800, was writing, Saxony had been truly conquered. The violence of the conquest and the threat of pagan banditry had dissipated, and the deceased Charlemagne could be hailed as the 'apostle of the Saxons'.[7] Rudolf then could focus on other topics in his biography of the saintly woman interred at his monastery. Two new dangers took priority: laxity among female religious and natural disasters.

In the time since Leoba's death, the church hierarchy in Saxony had stabilized and no longer required the flexibility that had been granted to missionary women on a forested frontier. When Charlemagne was named Holy Roman Emperor on Christmas Day in AD 800, the symbolic unity between the Church and the Empire was complete. The teachings of the church, diffused by nuns and priests, became the 'fundamental tool to unify' the empire.[8] This meant a stricter adherence, or an attempt at a stricter adherence, to the religious life as laid out in the traditional Rules – like those of Caesarius and Benedictine, mentioned in the previous chapter. In his work on Leoba, Rudolf attempted to reconcile the reality of this itinerant and commanding abbess with the ideals of a reforming age. It was not an easy task. In many ways, Rudolf actually highlighted the great variety among women in monasteries, both in Saxony and Leoba's native England.

By the time he set quill to parchment, Leoba and all those who had known her personally were deceased. Rudolf was forced to rely on a disorganized collection of notes made by men, also deceased, who had met with four of Leoba's disciples: Agatha, Thecla, Nana, and Eoloba. Many of these notes, Rudolf complains, are too short and, in some cases, unintelligible because they were written in shorthand unique to their authors. Still, he persisted 'in obedience to the command of [his] venerable father, Abbot Rhabanus', one of the most famous theologians of his time. Just as Rudolf is deferent to his own teacher, he introduces Leoba through her 'spiritual mistress and mother', Tetta.[9]

Tetta was the abbess at Wimbourne, a double monastery that had been built by kings, and Tetta herself was the sister of a king, according to Rudolf. The monastery sat on the bank of a stream so clear and sweet that the place had at one time been called 'Winestream'. There, nuns and priests alike were ruled over by this noble abbess. Rudolf insistently tells his reader – repeating himself half a dozen times in two paragraphs – that the nuns never left the cloister and that Tetta never allowed any of the nuns to approach or be approached by men; even bishops were denied entrance into the community. Yet, even here in the thick of his insistence, Rudolf must qualify his statement. A nun could leave 'if there was a reasonable cause and some great advantage accrued to the monastery'.[10]

Rudolf goes on to tell two stories from Tetta's life to demonstrate the woman's piety. In one, she lightly scolds and prays with several younger nuns who danced on the grave of a strict older nun. In the other, she leads the nuns in prayer after one of them loses the keys to the church before locking up one night. Both are stories meant to highlight the piety of Tetta and the miraculous power of prayer, but they also highlight the gaps between the ideal and the real. The reader can catch glimpses through the cloister window into the community behind the walls. There, young women, many of whom had likely been gifted to the church as children, chafed under the severity of religious life. Elder nuns tasked with teaching and supervising the young ones might abuse their authority. Others, anxious to correct mistakes like lost keys, might get out of bed early to pace back and forth over the monastery grounds, searching by the light of a lone candle before dawn.

Rudolf's description of Leoba's childhood, in a similar way, is meant to highlight her virtue and foreshadow her saintliness but also reveals details about life at Wimbourne. Leoba was born to parents who had for many years worried that they were barren. When they finally did conceive, her mother, Aebba, dreamed that she pulled a ringing bell from her chest – a clear sign that her future child, like the bells in the church tower, would summon the masses to God. So, after the young girl was weaned from her mother, she was given over to the nuns. Rudolf tells us that from her earliest years, Leoba was 'fired by the love of Christ' and 'fixed her mind always on reading and hearing the Word of God'. She did not care for 'aimless jests' or 'girlish romances'. She turned away 'dainty dishes', preferring moderation and simple fare. She also 'worked with her hands' though she preferred to dedicate her time to reading. The intent of Rudolf's work is to set Leoba apart from her fellow nuns. Indeed, he makes her an amalgam of all their best traits: 'the continence of one, the cheerfulness of another, copying here a sister's mildness, there a sister's patience'.[11] Whether a reader does or does not believe that Leoba was such a model of virtue, they can peek around this ideal to find a lived reality. Wimbourne was home to approximately fifty nuns in Leoba's youth, according to Rudolf. Given the lineage of Tetta,

Leoba – and of other known nuns in their time – most of the women living there, and the men in the adjoining monastery, were from noble families. Some, like Leoba, took well to their conditions and found a passion for religious work. Others, like the young girls who celebrated the death of a cruel prioress, did not. Instead, they might have preferred the jests, romances, and dainty dishes that Rudolf criticizes.

However, Rudolf throughout his work is also clearly trying to emphasize the uniqueness of Leoba, a woman so devout and virtuous that she was even granted entrance into his monastery at Fulda, 'a privilege never granted to any woman either before or since'.[12] This is a necessity for his argument because as he comes to Leoba's later life, the dissonance between the doctrinal ideal and the real necessitated by the sudden addition to Christianity of the Saxons who had been converted en masse becomes even more pronounced. In the most obvious way, Leoba and the several women who accompanied her from England to the Continent did not remain permanently within the walls of their cloister. They walked, rode, and sailed their way over hundreds of miles, travelling between towns, residing in several different monasteries along the way, before finally arriving in a foreign country where they were expected to educate the converted elites of Saxon society.

They did not cease to move about when they arrived. Leoba was made the superior abbess over all convents in Saxony. She was based in the town of Tauberbischofsheim, but her role over the convents required her to roam. She also became a favourite of Queen Hiltigard and was often summoned to the court at Aachen, even in the final years of her life. Rudolf writes,

> 'The princes loved her, the nobles received her, the bishops welcomed her with joy … But her deepest concern was the work she had set on foot. She visited the various convents of nuns and, like a mistress of novices, stimulated them to vie with one another in reaching perfection'.[13]

Leoba was a special case. She was in a particularly high position on the frontier of Christendom and the empire, which required her to move about significantly more than could be expected of a typical nun.

However, Leoba was not the only nun who moved around.[14] By AD 741, two years after Leoba and her companions set sail for the continent, Boniface had settled at least two of them with their own abbeys. Leoba, as mentioned, was in Tauberbischofsheim. Her disciple, Thecla, was made a teacher at the abbey in Kizzingen.[15] Yet, in a letter written by Boniface sometime later in the 740s, we find that Leoba, Thecla, and a third woman, Cynehilda, who oversaw a school somewhere in Thuringia, were all together. It is unclear where the women were gathered, but Boniface wrote to them with an urgent request for prayers to 'strengthen [his] heart with the spirit of a ruler, so that when the wolf comes [he] may not flee like a hireling…'[16] At an unknown point after AD 741, we again find Thecla away from her abbey in Rudolf's tale of one of Leoba's miracles.

A storm had swept over Tauberbischofsheim, bringing 'terrible lightning and falling thunderbolts [which] struck terror into the stoutest hearts'. The townspeople had initially gathered their families and animals into their individual houses, but 'when the danger increased and threatened them all with death', they fled to the church. Leoba went out to the people, urging them to be calm and patient. When the storm did not pass quickly but instead lurked over the town, tearing roofs from houses, the wind howling and the sky as dark as night, Leoba gathered the terrified crowd around her at the altar and led them in prayer. It must have been a dramatic scene, the sanctuary dimly lit by candles, casting shadows over the faces of men and women, children clinging to their mothers, the nuns clustered around Leoba. The whole crowd turned to watch as Leoba fell to her knees before the altar. Outside, lightning crackled, and the thunder rattled the walls of the church.

Rudolf paints a picture of strained panic: 'The mob, unable to endure the suspense any longer, rushed to the altar to rouse her from prayer and seek her protection'. We might imagine the nuns stepping between their abbess and the 'mob', holding them off long enough for Thecla to kneel down, touch Leoba's shoulder, and gently say, 'Beloved, all the hopes of these people lie in you: you are their only support. Arise, then, and pray to the Mother of God, your mistress, for us, that by her intercession we may be delivered from this fearful storm'.[17] At this, Leoba stood and turned to the crowd, which parted before her as she went to the door of the church. As the storm continued to rage, the abbess pulled open the doors of the church and flung off her cloak as she stepped out over the threshold. Instantly soaked, wool now heavy and sticking to her skin, she made the sign of the cross and lifted her hands to the sky. After thrice invoking the protection of Mother Mary, 'suddenly God came to their aid'. Like the sea before Moses, the darkness parted, and the storm retreated.

In a similar fashion, a frightened mob of townspeople rushed to the abbess one day when a fire broke out. Rudolf says she had been sitting with her disciples to begin a lesson. When the townspeople told her about the fire, she ordered them to bring her buckets in which she sprinkled some salt 'which had been blessed by St. Boniface'. The buckets were then used to carry water to put out the fire. Tales like these are intended to demonstrate the holiness of their subject, Leoba, but they also highlight her role, not only as a religious leader but also as a civic one. It is to her that the town turned when in need of shelter or direction in a crisis.

It was not only when Leoba was on the move that these exceptions to the rule of enclosure appeared. In the administration of her own abbey at Tauberbischofsheim, Rudolf describes two instances of nuns going home and, in one, the community coming onto the monastery grounds, even crowding around Leoba and her nuns. In the first instance, an unnamed but ill nun from the small convent of Williswind, was granted permission to return home to her parents. When Leoba heard of this, she wrote to the parents offering her aid, which they attempted to refuse. They asked only for prayers that their daughter would die peacefully. Leoba certainly set some of her nuns to this work of prayer, but she went to the home of this ill nun to personally pray over her. By Rudolf's account, the woman was already considered dead when Leoba arrived and fed the woman blessed milk from a small spoon of hers. Within a week, the nun had fully recovered and went on to outlive the abbess who had cured her.

In a more sinister instance, the absence of a nun, Agatha, who 'had been summoned to her parents' house on urgent business, resulted in accusations of child-murder. In a story clearly meant to highlight the risks of allowing nuns to leave the monastery, Rudolf recounts the tragic tale of a disabled girl who spent her days begging along the path to the monastery. The girl secretly gave birth and afterwards tossed the baby into a nearby creek. The ensuing drama played out publicly before the town when a woman found the baby and raised the hue and cry:

> 'Oh, what a chaste community! How admirable is the life of nuns, who beneath their veils give birth to children and exercise at one and the same time the function of mothers and priests, baptising those to whom they have given birth... Now go and ask those women, whom you compliment by calling them virgins, to remove this corpse from the river and make it fit for us to use again. Look for the one who is missing from the monastery and then you will find out who is responsible for this crime'.

When the absent nun returned, Rudolf tells us that she 'fell on her knees and gazed up to heaven, crying' for mercy for her fellow nuns to be spared from these false accusations and 'filthy rumours' caused by her sins (leaving the monastery). Leoba, assuring the poor nun that she was believed and innocent, ordered that a procession be undertaken. The nuns were to sing through the whole psalter of their order three times a day, then make a round of the monastic buildings 'with the crucifix at their head, calling upon God to free them, in His mercy, from this accusation'. On the first day, upon the third procession, Leoba prepared the altar of the church and led a prayer before the public. Rudolf tells us that when the prayer was complete, the 'wretched little woman' who had committed the crime was surrounded by flames and confessed. Though the reputation of the nuns was saved and 'praise was showered on them in every place', an infant was dead, and a young woman was 'for the rest of her life ... in the power of the devil'. This tale is clearly intended as a warning against departure from the monastery. Yet, in telling us of the mob's response and the nuns' public penance, Rudolf again betrays the lack of a boundary between lay people and religious women as well as the gap between the ideal and the real.[18]

Though he was the only one to write about Leoba, we are not forced to rely solely on Rudolf to learn about her – or the other nuns on the move in Saxony. Unfortunately, only one letter written by Leoba survives: that letter to Boniface asking him to remember her. However, there are three letters addressed to her that survive. The first, the letter from Boniface to Leoba, Thecla, and Cynehilda, has already been mentioned. The second, another letter from Boniface, is short but illuminates Leoba's role as a teacher and her deference to Boniface's opinion about who is admitted to the convents' schools. Boniface assures Leoba 'that whatever [she] may see fit to do' has his approval.[19] The final letter, which was sent by Boniface's successor, Lul, sets a different tone.[20] Lul seems to scold Leoba, perhaps reacting to terse words in the letter she had sent him. He tells her that she must not suppose that he is ignoring her, but that he is 'occupied by the crafty wiles of the devil'. He signs off with a complaint about good help being hard to find and the crush of 'ever-increasing perplexities'.

Lul, bishop of Mainz, represents the shifting tides in Saxony. Whereas Boniface had relied heavily on the religious women around him, Lul adhered to a stricter conception of religious life. According to Rudolf, prior to Boniface's departure for Frisia, he had summoned Leoba to him and before Lul and the other elders of the Saxon church, he gave her his cowl and 'exhorted her not to abandon the country of her adoption and not to grow weary of the life she had undertaken, but rather to extend the scope of the good work she had begun'. In other words, he was promoting her to his own position, and he ordered Lul and the others 'to care for her with reverence and respect'. If there was any doubt that he saw Leoba as his equal, Boniface also reiterated his wish that after their deaths they would be buried in the same tomb 'so that they who had served God during their lifetime with equal sincerity and zeal should await together the day of resurrection'.[21] In this context, Lul's letter is not only curt, but practically impertinent.

In another letter by Lul we find a similar tone now directed at a woman who did not have the protection of Boniface's cowl. Abbess Switha, another pupil of Boniface's, had allowed two nuns 'to go freely into a far region'. For this, she and 'all [her nuns] who committed this crime of negligence by consenting to it' were excommunicated. Switha's response is not recorded. We do not know what monastery was under her supervision or why two nuns were permitted to go beyond its walls. In his letter, Lul refers vaguely to the 'arrogance and desire of laymen'.

When he informs Switha of her excommunication, he also states that the two nuns, upon their return to the monastery, should be kept outside, 'doing penance in bread and water'.[22] The expectation then was that the women would return, so what had they set out to do? When we look at Leoba's life – the exemplar by which the nuns of Saxony would have lived – the possibilities are varied. Perhaps they had gone to work as teachers, to oversee the care of an ill relative, or to speak on religious matters in a noble court. Notably, the nuns had gone together as a pair – each supervising the other in much the same way that Leoba herself had travelled with an entourage of women. But as we saw with sister Agnes, who was a nun in Leoba's convent, a nun might be granted leave to go on her own when summoned by her parents. Bishop Lul clearly did not agree, but he, like Rudolf, was fighting a losing battle. The nuns of Saxony would continue to go on pilgrimage, travel to and with the imperial court, and even act as regents for the empire.

> 'I fear, too, that I shall be accused of temerity and that I shall encounter the reproaches of many … If, because of its crudeness, I should wish the work to be shown to none, should I not deserve the blame of all?'[23]

Hrotsvit and her anonymous counterpart in Quedlinburg were not interested in Leoba – perhaps surprisingly, at first, but their intent was not to record women's history – or even religious history. Instead, the women writers of the tenth and eleventh centuries in Saxony were participating fully in the broader project of writing Saxon history. Consequently, the English missionaries and the Frankish invaders were mentioned only when necessary. Boniface, a martyred saint credited with instilling Christianity in Saxony, is only mentioned in passing. The focus of the nuns' historical works is instead their nobility and military victories – the ascension of the Ottonian dynasty, which replaced the flagging Franks when Otto I took on the mantle of God's emperor. Hrotsvit, the earlier writer, insistently repeats that it is beyond her talents and propriety as a woman to write about emperors and war, yet this is her most prominent topic. Even her plays, which are ostensibly about piety and virginity, feature caliphs, Roman governors, and political intrigue that results in trials and executions. The anonymous annalist of Quedlinburg does not qualify her writing. The history of her monastery, the prominence of its princess-abbesses, Matilda and Adelaide, and the centrality of the city in the pomp of the Ottonian court demand that she write about imperial politics.

In many ways, their histories are typical of the time. They describe comets, famine, and brilliant visions of light and saints. The Quedlinburg annalist begins her history with the creation of the Earth and a summarized genealogy of humanity. The trope of ancient Trojan origins, theological arithmetic, and an abundance of classic references settle *The Deeds of Otto* and *The Annals of Quedlinburg* firmly in the medieval historical oeuvre. Yet, there are also many intimate moments, particularly when the historians focus on their own monasteries. The nun in Quedlinburg informs us over several years of certain nuns joining the 'heavenly entourage'.[24] In this way, the work is both typical and atypical. We are told the names of several women like Riksut, Bertalis, Erispa, Burgared and many others.[25] Recording the death of one's fellow religious devotees is typical, but to read the names of so many women, particularly women who are not members of a royal family, is a thrilling novelty in medieval histories. The mingling of nuns' pilgrimages, vows, and deaths with the battles and deaths of counts and emperors is a clear statement: we are a part of this history.

A noteworthy example of how these historians emphasized the position of their female subjects is the description of women's funerals and the periods of public mourning observed for them. In the *Annals of Quedlinburg,* the death of Otto I may have been elaborately described, but this portion of the annals was lost before a copy was made in the sixteenth century. The death of Otto II is similarly lost, and the annals only begin again with the abduction of the young Otto III. At last, with the final Ottonian emperor, a record is made of him being 'taken on the hands of angels', but his death is overshadowed by the ongoing battle with Roman soldiers and the public grief of his soon-to-be replacement, Henry. Otto, as 'he was given to the earth', is lauded simply as 'a great consolation for his subjects'.[26] The annals then move on quickly to the various elections to make Henry king and then emperor.

In contrast, the deaths and funerals of Empress Adelaide and Abbess Matilda occupy several pages. Their deaths are presaged by fiery omens and prophetic inclinations. The funerals are attended by massive crowds, and the grief is felt throughout the empire; 'around the villages, squares, crossroads, and wastelands, wherever that news of [Matilda's] death came, people beat their breasts and tore their hair … they filled the air with soul-rending shouts'.[27] A similar contrast is found in the work of Hrotsvit when she describes the impact of Queen Edith's death in AD 946. Hrotsvit writes that 'the whole race mourned her' both because of and despite the obvious sanctity of the queen – the comfort of knowing the queen had gained heaven could not soften the blow dealt to the empire. The Gandersheim historian lightly scolds the past mourners for grieving when they should have been rejoicing in the knowledge that 'the rest eternal without end will… speedily be granted [to Edith]'.[28] Throughout her works, Hrotsvit also tends to describe the deaths of men through their connections to their female heirs. In *The Deeds of Otto*, when King Lothar dies, he 'rightly leav[es] the kingdom of Italy to be ruled by the will of the eminent queen whom he had made his wife'.[29] In her poem on the foundation of Gandersheim, she mourns that the founder, Liudolf, 'had scarce attained the warmth of middle age' before being 'stricken by the baleful doom of our common mortality', but comforts her reader with the knowledge that Liudolf 'entrusted the whole weight and responsibility of the momentous undertaking' of founding and constructing the abbey to his 'dear surviving wife', Oda. The success of the abbey is then tied to the success of Liudolf and Oda's daughter, Liutgard, in persuading her royal husband to be a generous patron.

The grief for these eminent women was likely sincere. In the case of the *Annals of Quedlinburg*, the annalist who described Abbess Matilda and Empress Adelaide may very well have known both women. Yet, there was also a political consciousness in these works. For Hrotsvit, both her history of Otto I and that of her abbey are reminders to their readers, particularly those at the imperial court, that their ancestors were intimately and zealously linked to this foundation. Her history of Gandersheim ends with the birth of Otto I, 'first king of the vigorous Saxons, and likewise Augustus of the mighty Romans'.[30] The deaths and births of Frankish and Saxon kings are interwoven with the lives of Gandersheim's first abbesses who were sisters of Queen Liutgard and Duke Otto, the namesake for the future emperor. In a way, Hrotsvit suggests that the birth of the Ottonian dynasty and the birth of Gandersheim, as well as their fates, were interwoven. As mentioned above, Hrotsvit's history of Otto I, commissioned by Gerberga II, his niece and daughter of a part-time rebel, had the clear intention of rehabilitating the historical image of Gerberga's father and appealing to the mercy and generosity of Otto's heir, Otto II. A similar tactic is used by the annalist in Quedlinburg, and with the same motive, to appeal to Adelaide and Sophia's cousin, Emperor Henry II. The death of his predecessor is respectfully but quickly recorded with greater attention paid to Henry's grief and his quick election to the throne – perhaps a reminder of the abbess-sisters' involvement in his success. Many of the deaths in the Gandersheim and Quedlinburg histories are also paired with general statements about the benefits and liberties lavished on the communities. In this way, the histories are again typical, functioning as a statement of authority and inheritance with the intent of maintaining the abbey's independence and possessions.

They are also much more than this. These histories are creative works. Both of Hrotsvit's histories are written in verse. The Quedlinburg annals – particularly those after AD 984, when the author is writing from personal experience and memory – paint vivid pictures of imperial politics and of the state of the empire. Hrotsvit tells us the story of Queen Adelaide's daring escape from imprisonment in Italy, digging a secret tunnel from her cell and fleeing through the wilderness and hiding in grain fields.[31] The annalist at Quedlinburg records 'fierce and extremely bloody quarrels', and 'victorious … winners in the glow' marching home from wars with the Slavs.[32] They record events but also tell stories for the sake of models, just as Rudolf did for Hathumoda, and, as Hrotsvit writes to the young Otto II, for amusement.

The success of the Carolingian campaign and the tandem work of the Bonifacian missionaries was apparent in the proliferation of religious houses, particularly for young women. The tradition of female houses took root in the eastern portions of the empire. It made sense to the locals to entrust women with the care of souls, the memories of families and the empire, and with the education of children.[33] Leoba and her peers, Thecla most notably, were all involved in the creation or maintenance of monastery schools, which were attended by both girls and boys from elite families. Much like the female monasteries in sixth century Gaul, which were discussed in the previous chapter, these religious houses in Saxony were founded by and filled with the widows, sisters, and daughters of counts, dukes, and kings. Unlike their Gallic fellows, however, the women of imperial abbeys did not relinquish their secular authority or power. In fact, the abbesses of several houses would rival princes.[34] This is particularly true for two prominent religious houses of the tenth century, Gandersheim and Quedlinburg.

The founding of the abbey of Gandersheim is recorded in two literary sources – a brief biography of its first abbess, Hathumoda, by a monk, Agius of Corvey, and a long poem, *The First Days of the Cells of Gandersheim*, by a nun of the abbey, which describes the series of Liudolfing sisters who ruled over the abbey.[35] Hathumoda, the first abbess, was the twelve-year-old daughter of Liudolf, count of Saxony, and his wife, Oda, who were also patrons of the abbey at Fulda. One of the extant versions of the *Life of Leoba* was dedicated by Rudolf to the young abbess. The Liudolfing establishment in Gandersheim would provide a home and occupation for two of Hathumoda's four sisters and for her mother, Oda, in her widowhood. One of the daughters who did not take the veil, Liutgard, married a man named Louis, who would go on to become king of Saxony and Bavaria. One of their brothers, Otto, would be the namesake for his grandson, Otto the Great, the first Holy Roman Emperor of the Ottonian dynasty. As a direct result of these royal and imperial connections, this house of canonesses became particularly powerful in the early years of Saxon Christianization, and at the turn of the tenth century, it would even be ruled over by a daughter of the emperor. [36] There, in the dense woodland of central Germany, several women would make their mark on history as holy women and stalwart princesses – and some of their stories would be recorded by one of their own, Hrotsvit, the first female playwright and historian of the medieval era.

What we know about Hrotsvit comes from her own work, which means we know very few biographical details.[37] She was likely noble, given her presence in an imperial abbey closely linked to the royal family. She was older than her abbess, Gerberga II, who was born c. AD 935.

In one of her presumably earlier works, a collection of stories about Christ, saints, martyrs, and a devout Frankish knight, Hrotsvit tells us that she was not 'mature in age' when she began her writing, meaning she was not yet sixteen. Yet, she was already well-versed in the seminal texts of her era and demonstrated an interest in the far-flung corners as well as the imperial centre of her world. In later works, when she was older and more self-assured, she positioned herself as a Christian rival and alternative to the ancient playwright Terence. Though her plays are her most famous work, Hrotsvit also composed two historical epics in verse, the aforementioned history of her monastery's foundation and a much longer poem dedicated to her abbess and presented to a young Otto II shortly before he became the emperor (c. AD 970).

The Deeds of Otto is, on the surface, a history of the reign of Otto I and the ascendancy of the Ottonian dynasty. It is presented by Hrotsvit as a deserved gift to an illustrious emperor's heir from an unworthy nun. Her abbey was the work of Ottonian ancestors; the grandmother of Otto I had spent her final years enclosed at Gandersheim. When Hrotsvit wrote her history, the situation for Gandersheim had changed. Nearly thirty years had elapsed between abbesses from the imperial family. Consequently, the growth of the abbey had stalled, and imperial generosity had shifted to other religious houses. Gerberga II was Otto I's niece, a first cousin of the intended audience of Hrotsvit's work. Gerberga's father, Henry, had died while on good terms with his brother, but for many years the two had quarrelled over the throne. Much of the early parts of the history reads as an apology for Henry and his past rebellion, emphasizing Otto's mercy and generosity when pardoning his brother. Hrotsvit highlights Henry's later devotion, like his involvement in the wedding between Otto's parents, Otto I and Adelaide, while consistently painting Henry's former allies as malicious influences who used seductive speeches and threats of force, including taking one of Henry's sons as a hostage.[38]

Hrotsvit's descriptions of Henry are emotional and compelling, certainly a result of discussions with his daughter, her abbess. They appear to have had a positive effect on Otto II. When his daughter, Sophia, was four years old, he placed her at Gandersheim for her education rather than at her aunt's abbey in Quedlinburg. This is especially impressive considering that Gerberga's brother, Henry II, had attempted to overthrow Otto II several times during his short reign, and had been imprisoned for a second time in the year before Sophia went to Gandersheim (AD 978–9). Gerberga had directed Hrotsvit well, despite the historian-nun's concerns about her skill and sources, and imperial attentions had been redirected to Gandersheim. In Sophia's adolescence, the abbey benefited greatly from her imperial connections. In AD 987, when she officially took the veil at thirteen, she refused to be consecrated by the local bishop and chose instead the archbishop of Mainz, a clear sign of the independence of the abbey, achieved through its proximity to the emperor. When her mother died in AD 991, Sophia inherited several estates and archives related to her mother's administration and properties. After her brother came of age and was acting as emperor in his own right, Sophia frequently appears in his official documents, particularly as a beneficiary.[39] When Sophia herself became abbess at Gandersheim in AD 1002, she would begin nearly a century of rule by princess-abbesses.

Emperor Otto II was dead. Only twenty-eight years old, he unexpectedly succumbed to malaria in the summer of AD 983 while visiting Rome. With him were three women who would become known as the 'mothers of the fatherland': his mother, Empress Adelaide, his wife, Empress Theophanu, and his sister, the princess-abbess of Quedlinburg, Matilda. His three-year-old son, also named Otto, was at Aachen, under the care of two archbishops. Fortuitously, the boy had been elected and crowned as King of Germany only a few weeks prior. This was a typical move made by emperors to publicly declare their heir in an attempt to minimize disputes over the throne. The stability of the empire and the security of the heir likely put the imperial women at ease. While Otto's body was prepared for his funeral, they would have concluded any imperial business with the pope and the nobles of Rome. The honour of burial in St. Peter's Basilica was not granted to any other Holy Roman Emperor. According to one legend, the lid for the emperor's tomb was taken from the tomb of Emperor Hadrian. The original casket for Otto was made of marble and adorned with serpentines of gold. The funeral, even with the city in the grip of disease, would have been a spectacle. The emperor's body was escorted from the palace to the basilica, his mother, widow, and sister following behind him, weeping beneath long black veils, while on either side of the street, peering down from balconies and out from doorways, the city watched and prayed.

The funeral is not described by the anonymous annalist from Quedlinburg. The perceived security of the empire was shortly thereafter disrupted, and the ensuing conflict demanded the annalist's full attention. A cousin of the imperial family, Henry, the sometimes duke of Bavaria, had been released from prison when word of Otto's death reached Germany. He rushed to Aachen where he took custody of his young cousin, claiming to protect the boy from corrupt advisors. Word would have been sent to Rome immediately, a series of messengers on horseback pressing their steeds to the limit to warn the empresses. Henry had allies throughout southern Germany, and the imperial retinue would be in danger as they hurried back over the Alps and into the heart of the empire. Henry had taken his young cousin from the imperial capital and established a base at Quedlinburg, a strategic point with a strong fortress turned abbey, but also home to the tomb of Henry the Fowler, the first Ottonian emperor and this younger Henry's namesake and great-grandfather. It was at Quedlinburg, in the early summer of AD 984, that the empresses and Henry, earning his nickname 'the Quarrelsome', disputed the imperial inheritance before an assembly of nobles and clerics.

Much like Gandersheim, Quedlinburg was a darling project of the imperial family. It was founded in AD 936 by Queen Matilda, mother of Otto I, to memorialize her husband, who was buried there. The widowed queen and her noble nuns took up residence in what had been an imperial fortress.[40] The town had been founded sometime in the early ninth century as a base of operations for campaigns against the Slavs to the east. The fortress stood atop a broad hill with the River Bode curling around it. As an abbey, it continued to serve the imperial court as a meeting and resting place. During Otto I's reign alone, the court would reside there on at least seventeen occasions, including several Easter celebrations.[41] In AD 973, the abbey played host to an international conference with imperial guests from as far as Byzantium, including Otto I's new daughter-in-law, Theophanu, who was introduced to the court at this event – perhaps a nostalgic nod to the fact that Otto had married his first wife, Edith of England, there in AD 930.

Otto's mother retained control of the abbey for thirty years until her granddaughter, also named Matilda, was old enough to be consecrated as its abbess. The young Matilda, in AD 966, was eleven years old. The ceremony that accompanied her consecration was lavish and unprecedented. The entire imperial family had gathered in Quedlinburg: Emperor Otto I, his second wife, the beloved Empress Adelaide, the young Otto, heir to the throne, Matilda's uncles, the dukes of Saxony and Bavaria, and perhaps even her aunt, Gerberga, Queen of the Franks, who had come to Saxony in AD 965 to celebrate both her brother's coronation as Holy Roman Emperor and the marriage of her son to his step-daughter. Besides these individuals and their entourages, the town was filled with bishops and priestly retinues. Rather than the typical consecration by the single bishop who oversaw the local diocese, the young abbess was blessed by each German bishop in turn.[42] It was April, and the whole town would have been prepared with the first blooms of spring, budding trees, birds and choirs singing, and a crowd of hundreds clothed in black wool and white, gold, and purple cloth and silk. At the centre was an eleven-year-old girl, looking out from under her veil as one bishop – perhaps William, the Archbishop of Mainz, her own half-brother – slipped the ring signifying her marriage to Christ onto her little finger and another bishop handed her the crozier signifying her role as a holy shepherd on Earth.

Abbess Matilda was a force to be reckoned with. She was the sixth child of Emperor Otto I, born to his second wife, Adelaide. All her elder siblings, except William, had died before she became abbess; her only sister, Liutgarde, had died the year before her birth. When Matilda's brother became Emperor Otto II in AD 973, she was his only living sibling. The granddaughter of a soon-to-be saint, the daughter of an emperor and a famous queen, Matilda had been raised and educated to be confident and intelligent. Even as a child, it would not be inaccurate to envision her with her head held high, an imperial stare unnerving even for grown women and men. By the time she was an adult, her position in the world and the years of personal trials had moulded her into a woman who struck her peers with awe.

Right away, she was thrust into the centre of the imperial drama. In her first year as abbess, she hosted an imperial synod. Only a few months after her consecration as abbess, her father, Otto I, was pulled to Rome to deal with the fallout from his unpopular choice for pope. In AD 968, Otto's regent, his eldest but illegitimate son, William, the archbishop of Mainz, died. Otto had been successful in putting down the Roman opposition, going so far as to have his son crowned by the pope as co-emperor on Christmas Day AD 967, but he had opted to remain in Rome for several more years to secure the situation; this had been his third military campaign in Italy in fifteen years. While the two Ottos were in Rome, after William's death, Abbess Matilda was the only core member of the imperial family living north of the Alps.[43] In the same year that her half-brother, the regent, died, Matilda received *The Deeds of the Saxons,* a history in three books, written by the monk Widukind of Corvey. Much like Rudolf of Fulda's dedication of a copy of his *Life of Leoba* was intended to provide a religious model for a young abbess, so Widukind's history was intended to provide models of governance to a young princess-abbess. His preface to the first book makes this clear:

> 'To the virginal flower with imperial majesty and singular wisdom, the striking Lady Matilda ... For with our labour, you will read the things done and handed down in memory of your most powerful father and most glorious grandfather, from which you may become from best and very glorious, better and more glorious'.[44]

In the preface to the second book, Widukind addresses Matilda as 'mistress of all Europe and wherever in Africa and Asia the power of [her] father extends' – perhaps a nod to the ongoing dispute and marriage negotiations between Otto and a string of Byzantine emperors who were also involved in affairs on the Italian peninsula. We should not overestimate or exaggerate the role in imperial politics played by a thirteen-year-old abbess. Otto had left other elder statesmen, like Herman Billung, in charge of the day-to-day governance. Yet, we should also not discount the symbolic power of the young woman, residing in her fortress-abbey at a major crossroads in the empire as the sole living daughter of the emperor. As Widukind's prefaces demonstrate, Matilda was expected to learn from her forefathers and through their example become an even greater leader. When her father returned triumphantly from Italy in AD 972, it was clear that Matilda had honed the 'masterly talent of her grandfather and father'.[45]

The return of the emperor was a celebration and cause for a grand gathering. Otto had left Germany in August 966, only a few months after Matilda had become an abbess. In the interim six years, she had gained the managerial experience necessary to hold court for hundreds. Quedlinburg was a mother-abbey to at least half a dozen smaller houses and oversaw the management of several dozen estates and small villages.[46] By the end of AD 973, both her father and his most prominent statesmen were dead. The empire was now in the hands of the eighteen-year-old Otto II, who was bolstered by the sage wisdom of his older sister who, unlike Otto, had been developing her own sense of authority, separated from their parents, and living in her own role as abbess. Otto bestowed several more estates on the abbey. Matilda became his intermediary among the clergy and in AD 980 even accompanied him to Rome. They remained there until Otto's death in AD 983. Otto bequeathed nearly a quarter of his treasury to Matilda and her abbey, upon his death.[47]

The annalist from Quedlinburg describes Matilda returning to her abbey, flanked by two empresses, at the head of a small army of 'the most eminent persons in Italy, Gaul, Swabia, Franconia, and Lorraine … the Saxons, the Thuringians, [and] the Slavs'. Like her father's triumphant returns to the city in AD 965 and 972, now Matilda was 'welcomed with the songs of the clergy … as well as God's people and those serving Christ's virgins, being jubilant at that long-anticipated arrival of this ecclesiastical mother'.[48] The 'grandmother, mother, and aunt', as they are repeatedly styled in the Quedlinburg annals, had successfully won the allegiance of the empire and secured custody of the young Otto III.

The details of the grand meeting of nobles and the dispute between Henry, duke of Bavaria, and the three empresses are sparse. According to the annalist from Quedlinburg, the confirmation of Otto III as king and the rightful regency of his mother, Empress Theophanu, was heralded by 'the star of the ruler … shining brightly in the middle of the day'.[49] Frightened by the omen, several nobles who had supported Henry changed sides, and Henry was stripped of his titles and briefly sent back into exile. In the following year, he would return 'wearing penitent garb, fold[ing] his hands in a begging gesture, also in the presence of the empresses taking care of the affairs of the kingdom'.[50]

With the succession dispute settled, the three empresses returned to their respective positions in the empire. Abbess Matilda remained in Quedlinburg, celebrating her achievements, and dedicating her victory to God through a series of building projects. In AD 986, the annalist at Quedlinburg records that a new monastery on the hill had been 'raised, in the name of memory of the only and beloved Matilda's brother', Liudolf, whose wife also died that year.[51] Empress Adelaide, mother of Otto III, returned to her own estates and, for the most part, left the governance of the German portions of the empire to her daughter-in-law. Empress Theophanu, as the emperor's mother and a niece to an emperor herself, retained the bulk of the administrative and military power. For several years, she kept her son by her side as she oversaw a war against the Slavs. Her regency was a success. The Ottonian administration was maintained and there were no more quarrels with Henry the Quarrelsome. There were successful military campaigns beyond the borders of the empire and a general peace within. When Empress Theophanu died suddenly in AD 991, power shifted seamlessly to the remaining empress and empress-abbess.[52]

Matilda was addressed in several ways throughout her life: *domina, abbatissa, metropolitana, augusta* and *domina imperialis*; lady, abbess, overseer of bishops, majesty, and imperial mistress.[53] In the final eight years of her life, she ruled an empire from her abbey-fortress in Quedlinburg. Her nephew, Otto III, was still only eleven when his mother died. Her mother, Otto's grandmother, Empress Adelaide, returned to the court in Aachen to accompany the young king and fulfil the secular duties of the regency. Empress Adelaide, consequently, is more apparent in the historical record with many of her letters, charters, and coins surviving. Yet, it was Matilda who was chosen by Otto III to act as regent in AD 996 when he went to Rome; a fact memorialized in her epitaph: 'the emperor, Otto, her nephew, put her at the head of Saxony as a matriarch when he was away in Italy'.[54] She and her mother both died in AD 999, having led the empire through the final three decades of the century.

The grief for the two women is nearly palpable in the *Annals of Quedlinburg*. The annalist explains that their deaths were foreshadowed by a terrible earthquake and 'two fiery stones fall[ing] from the sky'. She likens the strikes from the stones to deadly strikes to the head, causing the whole world to '[lose] its entire desire to live'. The empress-abbess's funeral took place in the basilica first constructed by her grandmother, Saint Matilda, mother of Emperor Otto I. Matilda was buried beside her grandparents before an audience of nuns, bishops, monks, and dukes. When the news reached Rome, Adelaide and Otto grieved terribly. Shortly after, Adelaide herself passed away, leaving a grief-stricken emperor alone in the holy city. The annals describe his return home as a swift march, 'forc[ing] the hard way through the Alps', to be with his sisters, Sophia and Adelaide.

Sophia would soon be abbess in Gandersheim. Another sister, Adelaide, had been consecrated as her aunt Matilda's replacement by the time Otto was back in Quedlinburg. They mourned their losses while celebrating Easter at the abbey. After this, Otto quickly put his sister Adelaide in his aunt's former position and she accompanied him on a tour of the other imperial centres, Mainz, Cologne, and Aachen, before returning to Rome.[55] Otto would die without an heir two years later. Perhaps, if he'd had a child, the two abbesses could have settled an arrangement much like their aunt and mother had in AD 983. Instead, the empire was inherited, after some dispute, by their cousin, Henry IV of Bavaria, son of Henry the Quarrelsome. This was in no small part due to the influence of Sophie and Adelaide at court.

There are some hints in the *Annals of Quedlinburg*, which were compiled in the early years of Henry's reign as emperor, that Abbess Adelaide may have felt some pressure to re-emphasize the importance of Quedlinburg, not only to the Ottonian branch of the family, but to the Bavarian branch as well, through the patronage of Saint Matilda, their great-grandmother. Her sister had been consecrated as abbess of Gandersheim during the coronation ceremony for Henry's wife, Cunigund, which would have clearly and publicly linked the imperial couple to Gandersheim.[56] Whether the annals were compiled in response to courtly pressures or not, Quedlinburg did not suffer at the expense of Gandersheim. The new emperor continued the tradition of frequently granting estates and daughter-houses to Quedlinburg and when Henry also died without an heir in AD 1024, Sophie and Adelaide were again instrumental in the elections of the next two emperors.

The two abbeys are often described as rivals.[57] While this is not untrue, by focusing on rivalry, we lose sight of the greater significance, and overlook the fact that after Sophie's death in AD 1039, the abbesses of Gandersheim and Quedlinburg were frequently the same woman.[58] Gandersheim and Quedlinburg were only two of several prominent imperial abbeys. Rather than seeing the rivalry as a zero-sum competition for imperial favours we find two abbeys that by the turn of the tenth century, were both headed by daughters of the emperor. Both abbeys housed relics, imperial archives, and scriptoriums. Each had repeatedly assured its independence from local bishops and maintained the right to mint coins and raise defensive armies. They were not alone; of note was the abbey of their cousin, Matilda of Essen, who amassed a major library which included one of the earliest Latin copies of the *Anglo-Saxon Chronicle*.[59] Saxony was home to a thriving network of female monasteries that not only recorded and protected imperial history but also actively participated in and shaped it.

Chapter Three

Nuns and the Crusades

A November chill hung over the town of Clermont, but it was not felt by the crowd in the streets. Several hundred deacons, priests, bishops, and archbishops of France and Italy had gathered to discuss a call for aid from the east. For decades, the Byzantine Empire, centred around Constantinople, had been in decline. The new Seljuk Empire had been nibbling at the Byzantine borders, seizing cities one by one until all of Anatolia (modern-day Turkey) and most of the Levant (modern-day Syria, Lebanon, and Israel-Palestine) were under its control. In 1073, Seljuk forces seized Jerusalem from the waning Fatimid Caliphate to the south. The ensuing conflict between Byzantine, Fatimid, and Seljuk soldiers made pilgrimages to Jerusalem riskier and more expensive. European Christians had returned home to report that the way was dogged with tolls and bandits, the holy city filled with Gentiles and Muslims, and the presence of the Holy Spirit was under threat. These reports filled the noble and papal courts of Europe with indignation. It was in this spirit that so many had gathered in the south of France to hear Pope Urban II (d. 1099).

Besides the religious men, throngs of noble and common people had also flocked to the city. There, in the public square, the pope took to the pulpit. Those who knew what this speech was about watched with bated breath. Others, perhaps drawn to the city for the spectacle, the once-in-a-lifetime chance to see the pope, or for work, to care for the horses, to sell wares to travellers, to hear the pope's message in order to convey it back to the smaller towns nearby, whispered amongst themselves as they stood along the edges of the crowd. Wives had come with their husbands, children in tow, clinging to their mothers' skirts.

The details of the speech vary, but that November day in Clermont, Urban II laid out the sins of his fellow Christians – murder, greed, war among the faithful – and then presented a means of absolution: a pilgrimage of knights. He described the plight of their fellow Christians in cities like Antioch, Damascus, and Jerusalem. The Turks, 'an accursed race, a race utterly alienated from God',[1] had seized the holiest sites and allegedly used them as stables. Some of the accounts of Urban's speech add gruesome details, invoking ancient tortures and martyrdoms, describing Levantine Christians being eviscerated, flogged, circumcised, and enslaved – their blood used to fill baptismal fonts. Slightly less polemical accounts focus on the possibility of a global Turkish conquest:

> 'They have occupied more and more of the lands of those Christians, and have overcome them in seven battles. They have killed and captured many, and have destroyed the churches and devastated the empire. If you permit them to continue thus for a while with impurity, the faithful of God will be much more widely attacked by them … O what a disgrace if such a despised and base race, which worships demons, should conquer a people which has the faith of omnipotent God and is made glorious with the name of Christ!'[2]

It is no wonder then that the crowd listening to Urban was moved to tears. Some wept, others cried out for vengeance and blood. Many took the cross that very day, approaching the papal pulpit, kneeling before Urban II, and pledging themselves to the liberation of the Holy Land. And it was not just the bishops and the knights. Though some wives insisted that their husbands stay and some shed tears while urging their husbands to go, there were several thousand daughters, wives, unmarried women, and nuns who joined the flood of people marching east. Contemporary descriptions of women's participation in what we now call the First Crusade are what you might expect from medieval authors. When the pilgrimage and the sieges were going well, the women were pious helpers; they washed clothes, cooked meals, brought water to resting soldiers or stones and slings to fighting ones. On the other hand, when a siege failed, or famine seized the army then women were condemned as lascivious distractions that dragged men into sin. In these moments, the women were expelled from the army, forced to seek refuge in hostile towns along the way. Though the First Crusade was arguably the most successful – the crusaders stormed the city of Jerusalem in 1099 and would hold it for nearly a century – women bore the brunt of the blame for the campaign's faltering moments.

In the years following the First Crusade, the stories told about women on the pilgrimage are clearly intended to discourage female participation. In one famous tale, a woman in Germany is convinced that a goose has been filled with the Holy Spirit. She and the goose join a gaggle of pilgrims, persuading many of the woman's belief. Unfortunately for the goose, at some point on the trip to the Holy Land, its crowd of followers are struck by hunger. The goose was roasted and eaten, bringing an end to any belief in its religious power. It is possible this is a true story – people have believed sillier things – but it is certain that the inclusion of the story in a chronicle by Guibert of Nogent is intended to deride the intelligence of common folk, particularly the 'wretched woman' who led the goose's march.[3] In less condescending descriptions of women on the crusade, the focus is almost entirely on their suffering. Infants suckle at the breasts of mothers dead from heat, famine, or slaughter. Young women die of thirst or are taken off into the desert. Some of those who were abducted never returned. We are told they were either killed or sold to the highest bidder. In one brutal description, Albert of Aachen describes a lost battle of 1096. When the crusaders fell, the Turks swept through their camp at Civetot:

> 'entering those tents they found them containing the faint and the frail, clerks, monks, aged women, young boys, all indeed they killed with the sword. Only delicate young girls and nuns whose faces and beauty seemed to please the eye and beardless young men with charming expressions they took away'.[4]

If some authors are to be believed, these 'delicate young' Europeans most often ended up in the harems of caliphs and emperors, sometimes persuading their captors to convert like ancient female martyrs. Others returned to the army, either escaping or having their ransoms paid, but to return was not always a relief. In fact, women who returned from captivity were often pressured to take the veil as it was assumed that they had been sexually assaulted and were therefore undesirable as a bride. This was the case even for Yvette, a daughter of King Baldwin II of Jerusalem (r. 1118–1131). The young princess was traded as a political hostage after her father had been captured in 1124. Though she was only four years old when she was a captive, it was implied by one chronicler that her virginity was considered questionable after her captivity. Her older sister, Melisende, would become queen of Jerusalem, but Yvette was forced to enter the Convent of Saint Anne shortly after her return from the enemy's court.[5] This is how we encounter most of our crusading nuns – women who had participated in the crusades as pilgrims, captives, and fighters before retiring to a convent because their participation had rendered them 'questionable'.

For captive women who had already taken the veil, of whom we find very few explicit examples, there was even less sympathy. One chronicler of the First Crusade records a story of a nun from Trier, Germany who was taken prisoner by Turkish soldiers in 1096. The nun had been a pilgrim in the Peoples' or Paupers' Crusade which was led by Peter the Hermit (d. 1115/1131). Though there may have been some trained soldiers and nobility among them, this so-called army was characterized by its distinct lack of training and supplies. It was this arm of the crusader pilgrimage that was responsible for the massacres of Jews and Hungarians en route to the Holy Land. The throng of men, women, and children – numbering an estimated 15,000–20,000 – had made it as far as the rural outskirts of Nicaea before they were captured or scattered by Turkish soldiers. In the following year, the trained crusaders arrived at the city and began their siege. It was a month-long struggle, but the Christian army prevailed. A tower in the city wall collapsed and Sultan Kilij Arslan's wife and two children were captured as they attempted to flee. An exchange of hostages was made following the city's surrender. Among these hostages was the unnamed nun of Trier.

When she was returned to the Christian army, she tearfully recounted her experience as a prisoner and how 'she had been taken in a vile and detestable union by a certain Turk and others with scarcely a pause'. Among the noblemen listening to her, she recognized a German count and 'appealed to him to come to the aid of her purification'. He did come to her defence, 'employing diligence and every argument of pity he could'. She was 'granted forgiveness for her unlawful liaison … and her repentance was made less burdensome', though we are not told what repentance she was expected to make. We might assume that it was still quite burdensome as, according to the chronicler, she fled the Christian camp and returned to her 'abominable husband' the very next day. The chronicler claims she did this 'for no other reason than because her lust was too much to bear'. Yet, he includes the detail that the Turkish man had sent a messenger to the nun, promising to convert to Christianity and keep her as his wife once he was ransomed from the army.[6] It is difficult to know how true this story is. It could easily be intended, like many stories told about the mostly anonymous women on the First Crusade, to discourage women's future participation or to enflame Christian men's rage against an enemy who captures and either rapes or seduces Christian women. The nun is not named though the German count, Henry of Esch, is. Throughout the crusading era both Christian and Muslim sources recount marriages, both forced and willing, which cross religious lines. However, it is very rare to find mentions of religious women, particularly in such a situation. If the story is true, then we might grant some overdue sympathy to the anonymous nun who saw more hope in returning to captivity than seeking forgiveness among her own countrymen.

It is in the shadow of stories like this that Thomas of Froidmont encouraged his older sister, Margaret, to join a convent after her return from Jerusalem at the end of the twelth century. Margaret of Beverley – she is named after her hometown in England, while her more famous brother is named after his monastery in France – began her life on pilgrimage. Her parents had made the journey to Jerusalem after discovering that Margaret's mother was pregnant. Perhaps their hope was to relive the experience of Mary and Joseph. The journey was a success, and the girl was born in the holy city. It seems that she longed to return there most of her life, but tragedy kept her from returning as soon as she was able. When she was eleven her brother was born and only a few years after this both their parents died. The care for the young boy was left in the hands of his adolescent sister. She had been raised to be brave and tough.

Thomas records a story told to him by Margaret, perhaps recounted several times while she raised him. On the return from Jerusalem the little English family had encountered a wolf. Margaret describes the wolf as 'thirsty for carnage', prowling from its lurking spot in a shadowy hill to terrorize them. Her mother, cradling the infant Margaret, was astride a donkey led by her father. All of them were tired and weak from the journey, the heat, and the scarcity of water. Yet her father remained brave, determined to protect his wife and newborn child. He grabbed a branch from a tree, swiping it back and forth along the ground 'as if playing with the wolf'. When the wolf moved forward, her father swung the branch at the animal. The wolf fled 'without hurting anyone'. This was clearly an important story for the family, particularly for the young orphans, and its inclusion in the beginning of Margaret's tale sets the tone. This was a devoutly religious family of courageous travellers who would defend their own.

Margaret saw to her brother's education – by what means is unclear though we may assume that the family was not poor given the successful pilgrimage – and she was able to place Thomas in a school where he excelled to such a degree that he was later employed by the archbishop of Canterbury. It is thanks to his career as a writer that remnants of his sister's story survive. The whole poem – Thomas recorded his sister's life in verse – has not survived to the modern era. In fact, the original manuscript was lost sometime between 1642 and 1829. In 1642, a French historian recorded several portions of Margaret's story from a manuscript in Clairvaux, but by 1829 when another historian followed up on the matter, the manuscript could not be found: a tragic, and common fate of medieval manuscripts. So, we are forced to rely on bits and pieces. Still, Margaret's story is one of our fullest examples of a woman actively participating in the crusade movement.

We do not know how Margaret provided for her younger brother. We do not know what she did with her time between his entrance into the monastery at Froidmont sometime in the 1160s and the siege of Jerusalem in 1187. Perhaps Thomas included this in the original manuscript, but if he did it was deemed uninteresting by the seventeenth-century historian who copied it. Margaret's story resumes on the ramparts of Jerusalem as the army of Saladin laid siege to the city. Much had changed since 1099 when the first crusaders had stormed the city and rejoiced at how they filled the streets with blood. The political fractions in the region which had catalysed the crusaders' victory were no more. A new dynasty, the Ayyubid, had begun in Egypt and Syria with Saladin as its founder. At nearly the same time that Thomas had entered a monastery in France, Saladin had been sent to Fatimid Egypt to protect a young heir to the caliphate. He had been more than successful, ultimately installing himself as sultan in 1174. His success was driven by his military acumen. His adult life had been dedicated to shoring up Islamic power in the south and driving out the Christian invaders to the north. We might wonder if Margaret of Beverley was already in Jerusalem when Saladin made a truce with King Baldwin IV of Jerusalem in 1180. Or did she feel compelled to go to Jerusalem because of the failing crusader position?

Regardless, she was there in 1187 and ready to defend the city to the last moment. She paints a desperate scene of civilians, women included, arming themselves with whatever was available. For a helmet, she told her brother, she used a small cauldron. The siege lasted fifteen days. The summer heat had continued into late September – another year in a long series of years full of drought. Saladin's army flung stones and Greek fire. One stone – Margaret thought it may have been the grindstone from a mill – struck the wall near her as she brought water to soldiers. Fragments of stone struck her. She was stunned and bleeding, but 'she learned to conceal her weakness' and continued with 'the air of a warrior'.[7] She armed herself with a sling and hurled bits of rock right back at the enemy soldiers below. When the city fell and a truce was signed, she cursed the misfortune, paid her ransom, and began her journey home. We do not know how long she had been away from England, but it would still be many years before she returned.

Only a few days' march outside Jerusalem, Margaret's band of refugees was attacked, and she was enslaved. It was not the harem fate described by earlier chroniclers. Instead, Margaret spent fifteen months digging moats, chopping wood, and hauling stones. Her brother records her suffering in detail:

> 'I was beaten with rods. I endured the blows, the threats, the heat, the cold, in silence. My chains rusted from my tears. The work and the slender diet tired my limbs. The long days were boiling hot and rest was rare and brief'.[8]

Despite this abuse, Margaret was allowed to keep her one prized possession, a psalter. This small book, likely small enough to fit in a pocket, would have contained psalms, prayers, perhaps a saint's life or two. Psalters were incredibly personal and important items in the medieval era. Considering Margaret's likely comfortable origins, the psalter may even have been illuminated with colourful letters at the beginning of songs or little motifs of vines along the edges of its pages. It must have been her only source of comfort in this time of suffering. She describes it as 'my one companion in the midst of this wilderness'. After her freedom was purchased by a local Christian man who had recently had his first son, she describes the book being briefly stolen from her by a thief on the road. He sneaked up on her, leaping out from behind a tree, and snatched her psalter away. Weakened by her sparse diet and heavy labours, she could not put up any resistance. Escaping with her life was enough of a miracle though the loss of her psalter was heartbreaking. She began to leave, head down, shoulders heavy with despair, but then the man returned. He chased after her, throwing himself at her feet, and begging for her forgiveness. Had her time as a slave taught her some of his language? Apparently not. She describes him as a Turk, but he clearly recognized what the psalter was as he returned it to her, repentant. Was he a Christian? Margaret did not know. As she continued on her way, squeezing her psalter close, she wondered, 'What had caused this barbarian to submit himself to me?'[9]

Margaret continued her journey, 'alone, troubled, lost'. She avoided towns, abandoning the marked roads to avoid crowds. Hiding among the rocks and trees, she clung to her psalter, her frail body wrapped in rags. She had set off into freedom with a single loaf of bread. She made it last five days. The past fifteen months had taught her how to stretch food, to subsist off as little as possible. After the bread ran out, she resorted to eating the roots of plants. This might refer to the wild asparagus and fennel that grows in the region if the season was right and assuming Margaret knew how to identify them. She may have resorted to stinging nettle and wild chicory, the roots of a purple flower.[10] As she scavenged for plants, she progressed north through the hills, hoping to reach Antioch. She describes treacherous paths through the wilderness and having to ford a dozen rivers. All the while, Margaret was driven by her hunger and her fear – fear of captors, of thieves, and of 'ferocious beasts'.[11]

By the time Margaret reached Antioch, a city that she had assumed would be a haven for Christian refugees, a Turkish army was camped outside its walls. Once again, she was taken prisoner, accused of stealing a knife. She tells her brother later that she only found the knife. Regardless, the image is pitiable: a half-starved woman, stumbling from the wilderness after at least two weeks' journey, dressed in a slave's rags, standing in an enemy camp, accused of petty theft. But Margaret was a lucky woman. She describes her escape from another close encounter with death thus:

> 'Around me are sentinels, no door is open. I'm afraid of everything, the looks, the words, of those surrounding me. I don't understand any Turkish words. Not knowing what to do, seized with the greatest sorrow, I pronounce the name of St Mary. At this name the chief of the Infidels is amazed, this faithless man becomes benevolent and pious, and turns towards the others. "See", he says, "She invokes Mary". He orders me to return. This order displeases the others, but I am only a little scared. I leave and give you thanks, O Virgin Mary'.[12]

After this, she was allowed to enter Antioch and seems to have remained there for three years until the peace treaty was settled between Saladin and Richard I in 1192. She was able to safely visit Jerusalem again, returning to the holy places that had drawn her family there so many years before. Once this was done, after an unspecified amount of time, she returned to Europe on a crusader ship. Again, our source has been redacted by the seventeenth-century copyist, but he tells us that the poem recounts a European pilgrimage for Margaret. She visited Santiago of Compostela, Rome, and finally went to France where she 'learned that [her] brother had become a monk'.[13] When she arrived in Froidmont, asking after Thomas, he did not recognize her. What an anxious end to her journey, sitting in a church sanctuary or the courtyard of a monastery, more than one monk chaperoning this meeting between their brother and a female stranger. Margaret must have wanted to hold her baby brother, to finally feel the comfort of the familiar, but he looked at her with confusion, perhaps even suspicion while she explained:

> 'My father had three children. You see in me the only daughter he had. The other brother was taken to heaven soon after baptism. Why do you hesitate any longer? It was Sybilla who gave us to the light of the day; she was our mother. Hulnon was our father'.

Finally, he believed her, bursting into tears. It had been nearly thirty years since they had seen one another. She recounted her journey, showed him her scar from the millstone crashing near her in Jerusalem, while 'he broke out in sighs'. When she was done, we might imagine him gently taking her hands in his, commending her for her bravery, thanking God for her survival. They must have prayed together, wept together, and then he advised his sister to take the veil. Thomas had been successful in his monastic career, and he was able to secure the funds to support her entrance into a monastery in Laon. Shortly after, he copied two books as gifts for Margaret and she spent the rest of her life living quietly as a nun in northeastern France.

In the same year that Margaret was slinging stones from the walls of Jerusalem, a young monk in Germany was returning from the Holy Land. He was accepted into a monastery in Schonau as a novice. Brother Joseph quickly caught the attention of his fellow monks. His voice had not broken. He had a soft chin and an attractive face. He asked odd questions about the consequences of a woman being found in the convent or whether a body was undressed before burial. In the year that he resided at the monastery, he grew weaker and weaker until, finally, he fell ill, collapsing in the courtyard. On his deathbed, he told his confessor his life story.

As a child, Brother Joseph's mother had died, and his father had decided that they should go on a pilgrimage to Jerusalem. Together, with a single servant, they set off from Neuss in central Germany. Tragically, on the way, Joseph's father fell ill and died in Tyre – a coastal city in modern-day Lebanon. It is possible he died before their ship even entered the port. He entrusted his child to his servant, but the child awoke the next morning to find that the servant, along with all their money and supplies, was gone. The young orphan whose age is unclear had been abandoned in a foreign city. He did not know the language and had nothing to sell. Despite this, Brother Joseph told his confessor that he was able to earn enough to eat and to take the occasional lesson at the local schools. Eventually, presumably after learning the language and finding work, he was able to fund a trip to Jerusalem where he briefly joined a military order.

The Knights of the Temple of Solomon, known simply as The Knights Templar, were a military religious order established in 1119 to defend the pilgrimage routes to and through the Holy Land. These men took in the young Joseph, and he travelled with several knights, perhaps as a squire, from holy site to holy site for at least a year. Eventually, Joseph met a German pilgrim, perhaps one who had known his father, and was offered safe passage back to his homeland. There, he was recommended into the service of the archbishop of Cologne as a courier. It is through these connections – the Knights Templar and an archbishop – that Joseph was allowed to enter the monastery at Schonau, despite his inability to speak or write Latin and his lack of liturgical training. The young novice was granted a tutor and began the rest of his short life as a monk.

Upon his death on 20 April 1188, it was discovered that Brother Joseph, in fact, was a woman. The shock – and potential scandal – rocked the monastery. The abbot, a man named Gottfried, immediately announced the revelation, and declared it a miracle:

> 'Do you see, brothers, the body placed before you? It is not, as we thought, the body of a man, but of a woman.

> Omnipotent God wished to have a person among us who was completely unknown to all of us until this very hour … Let us give thanks to him, therefore, who left behind such a welcome treasure for us and wanted us to have such a patroness in heaven'.

This was a far cry from the outraged answer Joseph had received when inquiring about the possible discovery of a woman in the convent. When he had asked, he had been told that any woman who donned the clothing of men and sneaked into a monastery must be 'impudent, wanton, insane'.[14] Had Joseph's sex been uncovered in life, the consequences would have been extreme, but in death the anonymous woman could be interpreted as a miracle. She had overcome the fragility of her sex to take on the strength of a man in pursuit of Christ. This was not an uncommon trope in the lives of female saints; Saints Athanasia, Marina, and Eusebia – to name only a few – are good examples of girls and women who were either disguised by parental figures or of their own will.[15] Often the disguise was intended to provide protection on a pilgrimage. The publication of the female monk's story was clearly meant to add to this genre. The earliest version of the story was included in an example book for nuns.[16] The young woman, whose name was not known in the earliest version of her story, is lauded for her bravery and strength though the author tells his feminine readers that her example is not one to be followed, simply admired.

Clearly the female monk was admired by her contemporaries. Five different versions of her story have survived – four in prose and one in verse. The poetic version, *Vita Hildegundia metrica*, was still being recommended to students a century after its composition.[17] What marks Joseph's story as different and perhaps adds to its contemporary popularity is his disguise not just as a monk, but perhaps as a monk-soldier. This detail was added in a later (c. 1191) version of his story, but the anonymous author of this version claims to have been a fellow novice who knew Brother Joseph personally.[18] It is a tantalizingly short detail:

> 'And he was led back to Jerusalem. He remained there for a year, received in a house of the Templars, and, traversing

> back and forth, he saw all the holy places… Then, the strongest wrestler, a renowned warrior, a soldier dear to God … without a loss to his integrity, believed he would be happier in his native land …'

It could be argued, based on the first part, that Joseph was received simply as a lay brother, but then this might have required him to remain at one house, attending to the menial labours that kept a religious order operational. The description of Joseph 'traversing back and forth' implies the possibility that he was fulfilling the main role of a Templar: escorting pilgrims from one holy site to another. The description of Joseph as a wrestler, a warrior, and a soldier leaves no room for doubt. He had served as a guard for pilgrims. It would also explain his experience after the year in Jerusalem. He was allowed to return to Germany. In most versions, including the official one published by Caesarius of Heisterbach in his book on miracles, Joseph was provided passage on a ship home by a generous German pilgrim.[19] Was it possible though that he was escorting the pilgrim and others as an official guard?

Upon his return to Germany, inexplicably if we assume that he was not associated with the Templars but merely an orphan returning from Tyre, Joseph entered the employ of the archbishop of Cologne. There had been a disputed election in the nearby town of Trier and a message reporting the issue to the pope needed to be sent. Caesarius of Heisterbach writes that the young monk was chosen as a courier because a young man, travelling alone on foot, would gather less attention than an older one travelling on horseback.[20] Unfortunately, this was a poor assumption, and several calamities befell Joseph on his way to the papal court. Before he was even out of Germany, somewhere near Augsburg in the southern part of the country, Joseph unknowingly began to travel with a thief, who had very recently run off with a bundle of stolen goods.

Shortly after encountering Joseph on the road, the thief worried that his pursuers were coming upon them. He, 'pretending that he was compelled to retire, gave the girl [Joseph] his bundle containing the stolen goods, and hid himself in the thicket'.[21] The thief's instincts were correct. The people chasing him arrived soon after and arrested Joseph who was dragged before a tribunal and sentenced to be hanged. Though the monk attempted to defend himself, the evidence was damning. The stolen goods were in his possession and his insistence that he wanted to return them accomplished nothing. All hope seemed lost until Joseph was allowed to meet with a priest for confession. In a panic, he told the priest everything, even showing him the letter he was carrying to the pope, fetching it out of its hidden compartment in his staff. With the priest's aid, Joseph was able to persuade the court that the real thief could be found. Men were sent with hunting dogs and nets to comb the woods. When the thief was found, both he and Joseph were brought back before the court. The thief accused the monk who again insisted that he wanted to return the stolen goods to their proper owners. At the priest's suggestion, the two underwent the trial by red hot iron and Joseph's hand remained unburnt – the first miracle in his story.

Dangers remained. A friend of the thief, incensed at Joseph's acquittal, followed him down the road. Attacking the monk, he dragged him to where the thief had been hanged, cut down his dead friend, and strung Joseph up instead. This, according to Caesarius, was the second miracle in Joseph's life. Rather than hang, the innocent monk was suspended in the air for two days, listening to the songs of angels, until some shepherds cut the body down. Rather than fall to the ground like heavy body should, the monk was gently set upon his feet and then miraculously transported within three miles of Verona where he dutifully delivered the letter to the pope.[22] After this, Joseph returned to Germany unmolested and entered the monastery at Schonau, apparently with the help of a certain well-known, but unnamed recluse.

The monks of Schonau, both during Joseph's year living there and after his death, did not know what to make of the situation. While retrospectively they expressed suspicions or recalled telling moments, they seem not to have questioned the authenticity of their brother, though one did note his 'womanly chin' and another wondered at his attraction to his fellow monk: 'This brother of ours is either a woman or a devil, because I have never been able to look at her without temptation'.[23] Yet, Caesarius writes:

> 'When she entered upon her probation, she put her hand to the hardest tasks. She slept among men, with men she ate

> and drank, with men she bared her back to the scourge. And though she was a maiden of serious habit, yet that her sex might not be discovered, she sometimes made displays of levity among her companions …'[24]

Joseph, who after his death was found to be Hildegund, had travelled, fought, fasted, and prayed as an equal to his peers. For this, he was provided with a tomb in a new chapel in Schonau. When the chapel was consecrated, the story of Hildegund was recounted to the crowd and they gathered around the tomb, praying to its inhabitant for intercession in heaven:

> 'Let all men marvel at the life of him, of her, who lies within this tomb. Living, she seemed a man, but death revealed her sex, for death makes plain what life can hide. The Book of Life contains Hildegund'.

The problem with the lives of Margaret of Beverley and of Joseph/Hildegund von Schonau is an obvious one. These religious individuals, while they were likely real, have been embellished; Margaret's story perhaps less so because it seems to have produced no public interest. Joseph/Hildegund, as evidenced by the final scene in their life, became an object of fascination and perhaps even a minor cult. Their story grew with each retelling, attracting pilgrims to Schonau and obscuring the reality of a girl who was wrapped up, first by necessity and then by choice, in the life of a man. It can seem then that we are forced to rely on tropes and moralizing fables to find women in the crusades. Fortunately, this is not the case. Unfortunately, the unembellished women are more difficult to find and their experiences, discovered in fragments, must be generalized.

Despite the contemporary obfuscation in the sources, there can be no doubt that women went on crusade. In the first, they accompanied husbands, brothers, uncles, and cousins. In later crusades, particularly after Jerusalem was taken back by Saladin's forces in 1187, we find a major shift in the treatment of women in our sources. Rather than discourage women from participating, they are actively sought out as donors, recruiters, and even leaders. The beginning of the thirteenth century especially provides several pieces of evidence that women themselves were taking the cross.[25] A papal decree from 1200 not only granted explicit permission to women to accompany their husbands on crusade in hopes of encouraging men to take up the flagging cause but also granted wealthy women the right to lead their own soldiers. The use of the Latin verb *ducere* – to lead – cannot be ignored.[26] In 1216 in Genoa, Jacques de Vitry, a bishop and crusade preacher, was on his way east to Acre. He was forced to delay his trip in Genoa when his horses were commandeered by local soldiers. As he waited in the city, he preached the crusading message. The noblewomen there were inspired by the preaching and many of them made oaths to take the cross. When their husbands, brothers, and sons returned with the bishop's horses from the local skirmishing, the women encouraged the men to make the same oaths. Jacques de Vitry then writes in his letter to his followers in Acre that he spent several months in Genoa preparing ships and soldiers for travel to the Levant. All of this at the instigation of the local noblewomen.[27] In the same year that the women of Genoa were organizing a crusading campaign, Pope Honorius III (r. 1216-1227), granted dispensations to women who had taken the cross, but were no longer personally able to travel east. Instead, like their male counterparts, they too could fund able-bodied soldiers in their place.[28]

Modern historians often – almost exclusively – dismiss descriptions in medieval sources of women warriors as fiction.[29] There are valid reasons for this. Many descriptions seem to copy classical sources with constant references to the Amazons and one of their queens, Penthesilea. Though this is a typical literary flourish which medieval authors use to describe any event or person, it is used against women to mark their moments as fiction. It is also argued that the larger, though still relatively small, presence of women warriors in Muslim sources is intended to demean Christian armies. In some cases, this intention is clear. The presence of women operating siege engines or taking up knives and slings to defend themselves is situated in contexts of crisis and desperation. The inverse is also true of Christian authors occasionally describing Muslim women dressed for battle or armed with bows. In one infamous depiction, these women are accused of accompanying their men for the purpose of conceiving children whom they promptly abandon when the crusaders take the victory. Instances of this nature are clearly polemical, but it seems drastic to extend the intention of these depictions to every single mention of a woman in battle.

Perhaps we can chalk up some examples like the battalion of wives who entered the fray in a twelfth-century poem about the siege of Antioch during the First Crusade to hyperbole or fiction[30] – likely dramatizing the real role of women who provided water and arrows or perhaps helped carry wounded soldiers off the field – but there are less fabulous examples like those described by the twelfth-century Kurdish author, Baha al-Din ibn Shaddad. He describes a female archer upon the walls of Acre in 1191. According to his source she was wearing a green mantle and was equipped with a wooden bow. This bow was presented to the sultan after the woman was finally 'overpowered by numbers'.[31] He also off-handedly mentions that soldiers had seen four women engaged in battle. Al-Din saw two of their corpses and was informed the other two had been taken prisoner. These women were described separately from the other women taken captive who were discovered in the crusaders' camp. While he mentions a sense of wonder at the female archer, the presence of female warriors is of little note, and he moves on quickly to another topic without making any moral judgments.[32] But must we find these and more examples of women on the battlefield to argue that they played a martial role?

Historians of the crusades cannot restrain themselves from reiterating the caveat that women in battle were rare, even exceptional, after every example of female presence on or near a battlefield or in a position of martial leadership. Though the symbolic importance of a duke or king leading his soldiers into battle is obvious it does not mean that leadership is acquired only through direct action on the battlefield. There are several examples of women commanders which simply cannot be ignored or credited to authorial imagination, either flattering or derisive. The fact that women did not personally enter the fray should not be used to discredit or minimize their influence and role in warfare. It will be helpful now to turn to some of these examples of secular noblewomen to grasp not only the possibility, but the necessity of women in military settings.

Our earliest examples predate the crusading era by a handful of years, but indicate the possibility that women, like their male peers, were also participating in the increasing militarization of culture that culminated in the crusades. The three women discussed below are also connected either directly or through marriage to the growing Norman world. The Norman conquests in Europe – of England and of Sicily – are quite famous. It is no surprise then that Norman warriors also participated heavily in the First Crusade campaigns. Their women were no less violent. We have only to turn to the female relatives of William the Conqueror to see evidence of this; like his daughter Adela, who is famous for her literary patronage and her public insistence that her husband, Stephen of Blois, return to the crusade he had abandoned; or his granddaughter, Empress Matilda, who oversaw a twenty-year civil war in England. Orderic Vitalis (c. 1075–1142), a chronicler writing at the turn of the eleventh century, tells us that Matilda's sister, Juliana, was also no stranger to battle. In a dramatic episode, which Orderic treats with great disapproval, the English princess fired a crossbow from the walls of her castle, attempting to strike her own father, who had blinded her daughters.[33]

Orderic also tells the story of two lesser-known Norman women who 'dominated their husbands and oppressed their vassals' in pursuit of their own feud.[34] These were the countess Helwise of Evreux and lady Isabel of Conches. The latter's husband, Ralph of Tosny, had accompanied William the Conqueror at the Battle of Hastings in 1066, a fact that would help him and his wife in their cause. Orderic does not give us any specifics of the women's feud, claiming the small war was rooted in 'some slighting remarks … suspicions and quarrels of women'.[35] The conflict lasted three years, according to Orderic, and involved several other local lords and their supporters, eventually garnering the attention of the king himself. Orderic's support, like the king's, clearly sided with Isabel and Ralph, possibly due to the pillaging of a Conches monastery by some of Helwise's nephews.[36] This support is reflected in his respective descriptions of the women. Countess Helwise is 'clever and persuasive, but cruel and grasping'.[37] On the other hand, lady Isabel is:

> 'generous, daring, and gay, and therefore lovable and estimable to those around her. In war she rode armed as a knight among the knights; and she showed no less courage among the knights in hauberks and sergeants-at-arms than did the maid Camilla, the pride of Italy, among the troops of Turnus. She deserved comparison with Lampeto and Marpesia, Hippolyta and Penthesilea and other warlike Amazon queens …'[38]

Lady Isabel and her husband ultimately prevailed and their eldest son, Roger, was named the heir of Helwise and her husband to settle the peace.[39] One of their other children, a girl named Godehild, would later marry a future crusader king, Baldwin I of Jerusalem, though she herself died en route to Jerusalem in 1097.[40]

The third woman from this era immediately preceding the crusades, Sikelgaita, was the second wife of Robert Guiscard, a famous Norman conqueror, who overtook Sicily and most of southern Italy at the end of the eleventh century. Sikelgaita was a Lombard princess who was married to Robert as part of a political alliance made in the hope of staving off his conquests. This was a vain hope. The two were a perfect match: ambitious, bellicose, and by all accounts tall and handsome. Anna Comnena, a Byzantine princess and historian, writing a few decades after their deaths, described them as a new Achilles and Athena.[41] Since Anna Comnena was only a child when both Robert and Sikelgaita died, she must have relied on others' reports. Also worth consideration is the hostile relationship between Robert and Anna's own people in Constantinople. She had incredibly negative things to say about Robert, describing him as a rascally barbarian who was intent on inventing some cause to go to war with the Byzantines.[42] The point of contention between the two forces were the Byzantine lands in Italy which bordered Robert's own. They were the only thing standing between him and complete domination over southern Italy. On the other hand, Anna seems to have respected Robert's wife, perhaps even admiring the woman for her freedom and power.[43] She claims Sikelgaita was a voice of reason in Robert's court warning against 'starting an unjust war', particularly against fellow Christians.[44] Ultimately, however, Sikelgaita was convinced of her husband's cause. Anna writes:

> 'Robert … stayed for a few days waiting for his wife Gaita. She went on campaign with her husband and when she donned armor was indeed a formidable sight. She came and he embraced her; then both started with all the army again for Brindissi …'

Later, at the battle of Dyrrachium (1081) on the coast of modern-day Albania, Sikelgaita was still in her husband's company. Though Anna Comnena describes her as 'another Pallas, if not a second Athena', she does not go so far as to have the duchess entering the battle. Instead, she was where we might expect her, armoured and armed with a spear at the back of the army. When the tide of the battle began to turn against the Normans, some of Sikelgaita's and Robert's men began to flee:

> '… seeing the runaways and glaring fiercely at them, [Sikelgaita] shouted in a very loud voice: "How far will ye run? Halt! Be men!" – not quite in those Homeric words, but something very like them in her own dialect. As they continued to run, she grasped a long spear and charged at full gallop against them. It brought them to their senses and they went back to fight'.

This scene is one of those classical comparisons that is dismissed by modern historians as a fantasy. Yet, Anna Comnena herself acknowledges that she has replaced the actual words of Sikelgaita with a Homeric quote, indicating that at the time the composition was made the author was aware that some might interpret the instance as unreal because of this quote. It has also been argued that this scene is meant to demean the Normans as effeminate and weaker than their female leader – an inversion of the typical derision directed at Byzantines by western authors.[45] This could be, but Anna Comnena clearly admires Sikelgaita and, in the end, the Normans win the day. If, in this moment, Anna Comnena is effeminizing the Normans, then she is consequently making the statement that the soldiers of the Byzantine army must be even more effeminate. This is possible, but it is also possible that Sikelgaita really was an effective leader who was able to encourage her troops in a moment of panic. When we look to western depictions of Sikelgaita, she is a fierce, even frightening, woman who is suspected of instigating wars and is accused of poisoning her husband. This is a stark contrast to the image presented by the Byzantine Anna Comnena who depicts the duchess as a peacekeeper who held her husband's hand as he passed. Sikelgaita appeared frequently beside her husband in charters and following his death (1085), on more than one occasion, styled herself as duke rather than duchess.[46] In a truly powerful political move, she was able to have her son, Roger, rather than her husband's eldest from his previous marriage, Bohemond, named as heir to all of Robert's possessions. Bohemond was then forced to pursue his fortune as a crusader, eventually becoming lord of Antioch (r. 1098–1111).

When we turn to the crusades, we continue to find women in command of troops, fulfilling all the roles required of a military leader. They made plans, procured supplies, swore and received oaths, marched alongside their troops, and lived or died alongside them too. One of the most prominent of these women was Ida of Austria, the widow of Margrave Leopold II of Austria. In 1101, she joined a band of princes and dukes on their way to reinforce the crusader victory in the east. It is likely her husband had taken the cross in the initial wave of crusade preaching but had fallen ill and died before he could begin his journey. So, it was Ida who led a part of the alleged 160,000 'cavalry, infantry and of the female sex' who departed from the Austrian borderlands.[47] She is listed alongside Prince William of Poitiers and Duke Welf of Bavaria as leaders who 'became bound to [Emperor Alexios] by an oath of loyalty' and received 'very many gifts of necessary provisions and the licence to buy supplies'.[48]

The crusade of 1101 was short lived – made apparent by its name. After a few small victories, the army was ambushed outside the town of Heraclea in modern-day southern Turkey. Prince William and Duke Welf 'only just evaded enemy hands'. The prince earned a reputation for recklessness and failure, eventually returning to Poitiers where he became better known for his support of troubadours. The duke died only a few months later in Cyprus. Ida, on the other hand, did not flee.

> 'Countess Ida was either captured and taken away, or was torn limb from limb by the hooves of so many thousand horses; to this very day her fate is not known, except that they say she was carried off among the thousands of women into the land of Khurasan in eternal exile'.[49]

A later myth, falling in line with tropes of Christian noblewomen in captivity, claimed that she had become the concubine of a Muslim prince and was the mother of Zengi (d. 1146), an antagonist of the Second Crusade. The more likely reality was that Ida of Austria met the same fate as the 'very many thousands of Swabians, Franks, and Gascons' who died on the field that day.

Other women had better luck. Matilda of Tuscany, also called 'of Canossa', is most famous for her intercession between the Holy Roman Emperor and the pope in the 1070s. In this role, she is depicted as a traditional noblewoman, attempting to bridge a religious and political divide to create peace among Christians. Beyond this, however, she was a powerful landholder in northern Italy, who oversaw a court known for its jurists, chroniclers, and artists. Her biographer, an Italian monk named Donizo, describes her also as a formidable general who in 1061, at the age of fifteen, led her soldiers in pursuit of antipope Honorius III from the borders of Tuscany all the way to Rome.[50] Obviously, Matilda's biographer should not be taken at face value; he was writing while Matilda was still alive and clearly wanted to impress her importance upon any readers at her court. Yet, we should not completely dismiss his claim that 'all her noble deeds of arms … would outnumber the stars'.[51] Matilda ruled alone for most of her life. She had two unsuccessful marriages which both ended in mutual separation and disinterest. So, it fell to her to lead her soldiers in several recorded battles: a victory at Po (1077), a defeat at Volta (1080), a victory at Sorbara (1084); and all the while able to retreat to the safety of her triple-walled fortress at Canossa.

Similar examples are found in the Viscountess Ermengarde of Narbonne who led soldiers alongside her uncle, an abbot, at the 1148 siege of Tortosa, a city in Spain held by the Almoravid Emirate.[52] There was also Countess Alice of Blois who took up the cross when her husband, John of Chatillon, died. Alice led 'a large body of troops' to Acre in either 1286 or 1287. Her forces met with some success as she was able to march further south into Syria and then Palestine, erecting towers and funding churches along the way.[53] It would be remiss not to also mention Marguerite of Provence, queen of France, who, following her husband's capture on the Seventh Crusade (1248–1254), directed troops and organized supplies while recovering from giving birth to her sixth child.

The stories of these women are caught in the trappings of authors' moral judgments and political motivations, but this does not render them entirely fictional. And the fact that their moments as leaders are often treated only briefly should not undercut their importance. When taken as a whole they cannot be dismissed. There were women who directed battles, commanded troops, and wielded the same kind of hard, military power as their male peers. In this role, it is not unrealistic to imagine them astride their steeds, protected by armour, and urging their soldiers on through shouted orders and encouragement from the back of the ranks. It is, then, not surprising to find that many noblewomen were supportive of, and involved in, the military-religious orders that were formed during the crusading era.

The most famous of these orders are the Templars, of whom a little has already been said, the Hospitallers, and the Teutonic Order. The first two were established earliest, growing out of debated origins in the 1110s; the Teutonic Knights developed later (c. 1190), following the fall of Jerusalem to Saladin. Many other smaller, 'national' orders followed in their footsteps, particularly in the Baltic kingdoms and the Iberian Peninsula. The appeal of these orders was obviously rooted in the general enthusiasm for the crusading movement, but their popularity was also bolstered by their welcome attitude, in some places, to retiring married couples. In some orders, like the Order of Santiago, a man or woman could even arrive single and request that a spouse be supplied for them.[54] And in some houses, widows lived with their children, who could join or not, as they pleased.[55] This was permissible because of the orders' unique status outside of the ecclesiastical hierarchy with their leaders answering directly to the pope. It may also have been possible because of the Orders' sizes. Compared to the more traditional monastic orders, the military-religious orders were quite small, particularly in the European kingdoms where there are several recorded houses with only a handful of members at any given time.

Despite these smaller numbers, we find in the houses of these orders, both in the east and the west, a proliferation of religious titles a woman could obtain, ranging from a salaried wet nurse for children raised in the orders, to full-fledged nuns, and several stages of lay sister in between. There was also a great variety of the types of houses with some composed of an almost entirely male membership with a handful of women serving as labourers; others were more co-ed with varying degrees of separation between the sexes; and then there were fully separate female houses. These women served a variety of roles in the houses: cleaning, washing, cooking, praying, tending crops, caring for the ill and injured, occasionally witnessing or recording charters and wills, and, in some cases, particularly in the houses of Spain, taking command. The evidence tends to favour the Hospitallers, who maintained the most and the longest-lived houses for women, and the Order of Santiago, which at its height maintained half a dozen female houses, all in the Iberian Peninsula.[56]

A curious example from Prague demonstrates the extent to which women could dictate the fate of their house. In 1180, a man named Peter joined the Hospitallers along with his mother, his wife, his aunt, and his niece. He turned over all his possessions to the order and then took the cross. While he was in the east, the women received papal approval for the construction of a chapel. Peter never returned from the holy land. When news of his death reached his female relatives, his widow was removed from the convent by her father and Peter's mother quickly recruited several other women (and their possessions) to the cause. Together, they removed the Hospitaller brother who oversaw their house; it is not clear by what means. Peter's mother then applied for a substantial loan from the Hospitallers. When she had received the money, she and several of the other women swore oaths to travel to Jerusalem. Instead, they summoned Peter's brother and began selling off Hospitaller properties, leading to a protracted legal battle over those properties as well as the fifteen villages Peter had initially granted the order in 1180. Though the women's house was obviously dissolved after this, it is unclear whether any of them experienced any legal consequences for their brief real estate scam.[57]

A longer-lived, and perhaps more sincerely inspired, female house of Hospitallers was founded in southern Spain, initially adjoining a male house in the town of Cervera. There, in 1245, a widowed noblewoman, Marquesa de la Guardia, used her inheritance to endow a house that supported her and six other sisters, including her daughter, Gueralda. This was the case for most Hospitaller houses. They, like their monastic counterparts, were founded by noblewomen, often widows, even though some of the orders allowed married couples. The women's house would then follow a blend of the Hospitaller Rule and the Rule of Saint Augustine; each essentially laying out a schedule for prayer, reading, and some sort of labour, either related to lace or manuscript production, or agricultural work. The largest Hospitaller women's houses were capped at thirty-nine fully professed sisters. The women elected an abbess or prioress from among their own. This nun then answered to, or worked alongside, a male commander who was himself often selected by the abbess or prioress; even in cases where he was appointed by an external male superior, the women maintained the rights of refusal and dismissal.[58] This granted the women substantial control over the workings of their monastery and was particularly true in the case of Marquesa.

We do not know exactly how much Marquesa granted to the Hospitaller commandery at Cervera, but it must have been substantial. The founding charter for her women's house granted her the right to house herself and six sisters in addition to the small group of lay and semi-professed women already residing at the male house.[59] Despite the small size of the house, under Marquesa's command, they were allowed to expand to a second location in Alguaire by 1252. From there, Marquesa ruled as commendatrix while a male lieutenant oversaw the day-to-day functions of the male and female houses in Cervera.[60] Over the course of the next decade, Marquesa transferred some of the convent's operations to her daughter, Gueralda, who she was setting up as her successor. While Gueralda filled this position, Marquesa continued to operate in the secular world, managing family estates and intervening in local politics. A series of lawsuits plagued the Hospitaller women at Cervera and Alguaire as relatives complained that the women had granted too much family property to the order, taking the income with them. Marquesa seems to have steered her houses through these controversies well. When she retired from the house in the 1270s, she was granted a life pension by her *fratrisse,* 'female brethren'.[61] This was not a unique situation in the female Hospitaller houses of Spain. A Hospitaller house in Sigena, established by a queen, maintained a similar level of authority, using the incomes from dozens of royal and noble estates to fund nearly forty sisters as well as continuous building projects and art collection. A Templar house in Barbara was also led by a woman, Ermengarda d'Oluja. She had entered the house with her husband in 1196. Following his death, she took vows as a full sister and became preceptrix over both the male and female houses there.[62] At the same house, a generation later, a woman named Berengaria of Lorach appears on several legal documents as a witness and is 'recorded as giving counsel to the commander'.[63]

The situation in Spain may have been particularly conducive to noblewomen taking over the leadership of houses, particularly in the military orders. Much like the Crusader Kingdoms in the east, the kingdoms on the Iberian Peninsula were on uncertain ground. Alguaire had only been wrested from Muslim control in the 1150s and though a series of shrinking caliphates had been pushed to the southernmost extreme of the peninsula by the end of the thirteenth century, violence remained a threat. As late as the 1380s, there was trouble from pirates along the southern coasts of Spain, preventing at least one convent from placing a house in La Rapita.[64] Still, despite the threats and the relatively small number of women involved in the military orders, the houses, particularly of the Hospitallers and the Order of Santiago, became prosperous bases of operations for noblewomen. They were able to capitalize on the growing crusade movement, which granted much more variety in the manner of religious life. The more traditional ideals of chastity, enclosure, and prayer-centric routines were even harder to enforce in these houses along frontiers of war zones. Women entered houses with their husbands or to find one, as in the case of the Order of

Santiago. Once there, they were able to exert substantial authority over their own houses and the houses of men, particularly lay brothers. Several of these houses would last into the fifteenth and sixteenth centuries, gaining a reputation for luxurious living and artistic patronage.

This chapter is a reflection of the changes wrought in the medieval world by the crusading era. The borders of the European imagination had never really collapsed, but they had become dimmer and seemed further off. With the call to crusade in 1095, those borders were suddenly a brightly illuminated goalpost. Tens of thousands of people poured out of their villages and towns, flooding the roads to the east to Jerusalem and to the west into Spain. The absence of men in the west provided new opportunities for the women left behind to maintain and reimagine their lives and their livelihoods. In the east, there was a sporadic stream of warrior men, building up new kingdoms which required constant defence. The consequently high mortality among men carved out space for female inheritance, new forms of political alliance, and chances for women to join the fight as commanders or emergency combatants. It was a similar situation in Spain where Christian conquest moved slowly south over two centuries, cementing religious and political presence through the establishment of religious houses. Whereas women of the previous chapters were forced to rely exclusively on ancient allusions – apparent in the way they were described by medieval contemporaries, even in the crusading era – after the twelfth and thirteenth centuries, the chronicles and poems could not ignore their presence in every facet of political, religious, economic, and even military life. In the coming centuries, women would continue to expand their presence in the courts, the markets, and the histories.

Chapter Four

The Burned Beguine

For more than a year, Marguerite Porete had not spoken. At least, she had not uttered a word in her defence each time she was summoned before the inquisitor in Paris. It is, consequently, difficult to know what she thought of the accusations levelled against her, of the condemnation of her book, and of her conviction as a relapsed heretic. Turning to her book, *The Mirror of Simple Souls*, we might assume that she had surrendered herself entirely to what she must have assumed was either the will of God or a quick route into His presence. Regardless, on the first day of June in 1310, she was escorted from her prison cell and out into the public square, the place de Grève, in front of what is now the Hotel de Ville. Her sentence was passed in front of a crowd the previous day, condemning her as a particularly stubborn and rebellious heretic who had strived to lead simple people away from God. Those who had heard the sentence returned, likely accompanied by an even larger crowd of curious Parisians. The burning of books and people had become tragically common over the course of the thirteenth century, but this was the first time someone would be burned within the city limits. It was also the first time an author would be burned for, and likely with, their book.[1]

Marguerite was not alone that late spring morning. She had acquired one outspoken defender in the course of her trial, Guiard of Cressonessart. He had also been charged with heresy, with defying papal bans on lay people dressing and behaving as clerics, and for presuming to call himself the 'Angel of Philadelphia', an apocalyptic figure from the book of *Revelation*. Yet, in the final hour, Guiard had acquiesced to his inquisitor's demands. To escape the pyre, he took off his clerical accessories, promised to forsake his chosen title, and accepted, instead of execution, a lifelong prison sentence. We can only wonder what crossed his mind and weighed on his spirit as he watched Marguerite ascend the pyre, as her executioners tied her to the stake, and as the embers flickered to life and began to burn. Accounts of the execution are manifold, but vague. They refer to Marguerite as a heretic, a pseudo-woman, a beguine, a 'clergesse'. Some say she was burned for writing an anti-clerical book, others for preaching a theology that allowed depravity without shame. One describes the reaction of the crowd:

> 'As she died, she nevertheless showed many signs of repentance both noble and devout, by which, as the eyes of those who saw it witnessed, many were piously and tearfully moved to sympathy for her'.[2]

The execution of Marguerite Porete remained in the collective memory of Paris for years, even as her name faded into obscurity. For centuries, the connection between her and her book was also forgotten. It was not until 1946 when the historian Romana Guanieri tied *The Mirror* to its tragic author by identifying the two excerpts included in the trial documents.[3] Since Guarnieri published a critical edition and translation of Porete's book in the 1960s, interest in the text and its author have bloomed. Yet, we know very little about Marguerite Porete herself. She included essentially no biographical details in her work. To do so would have flown in the face of her theological arguments. The self is nothing and the goal of spiritual progress is to be completely subsumed in the divine. Consequently, we must rely on the scant records of her trial and some speculation. It is assumed that Marguerite was of middle- or upper-class origins. It is certain that she was literate, well-read, and possessed a self-confidence more commonly found among medieval elites. She had several connections to university clerics, local priests, and other public figures, evidence of a vast network that she was able to maintain through consistent travel or written communication between places. According to her trial records, she made several copies of her book, a costly and time-consuming process. Yet, it is noteworthy that her last name, Porete, was something that she was '*dicta*' or 'called', and not a formal family name.

While Marguerite's biographical details are obscure, her theology, for which she was burned, is not. Thus: In the beginning, there was God and He was nothing. This nothingness was not a lacking thing, but instead a sort of transcendent being that existed beyond or outside human understanding.[4] Creation, then, was made by God separating a piece of His will from the vast nothing and placing this will inside something: first Adam, and then every human after. This piece from God is understood by Marguerite as the free individual will that every person possesses. The natural state of this will is to seek to be reunited with its original nothingness, a complete reunification with the divine will. Unfortunately, according to Marguerite, the individual will must struggle against worldly desires and distractions. This struggle is an orthodox idea. It agrees with the concept of 'original sin'. The orthodox response to this struggle is to dedicate oneself to piety and virtue while having faith that divine grace will absolve this original sin upon death. Marguerite argued, instead, that the annihilation of the personal will and, consequently, the shame of original sin, was possible for the living. It was this line of thinking that earned her the ire of the leading clergy of France. Marguerite argued that the annihilated or liberated soul was freed from the virtues. In other words, an individual who believed themself to be completely given over to the divine will was no longer beholden to the virtues or required to perform good works. At least, that is how Marguerite's judges interpreted her book – or, more accurately, the fifteen sentences of her book that were provided to them by William of Paris, the man in charge of the trial.

The Mirror of Simple Souls is a long book with 140 chapters. In it, Marguerite presents an extended dialogue between many characters, including Soul, Reason, and Love. Throughout the book she includes several poems of various lengths to celebrate what Love has done for the Soul. While the dialogue can be difficult to follow and delves into intense theological discussion, the poems are clearly intended for a simpler listener. An excerpt of mixed text and verse found in Chapter 122 illuminates what Marguerite meant when she claimed that she was freed from the virtues:

> 'And when Love saw me think about her, on account of the Virtues, she did not refuse me, but instead she freed me

from their petty service and guided me to the divine school. There she retained me without my performing any service, there I was filled and satisfied by her.

Thought is no longer of worth to me,
Nor work, nor speech.
Love draws me so high
(Thought is no longer of worth to me)
With her divine gaze,
That I have no intent.
Thought is no longer of worth to me,
Nor work, nor speech'.[5]

The institutional response to this message was to denounce Marguerite as insane, to label her a heretic, and to have her and her book destroyed. Marguerite was not surprised by this. In fact, she expected it. In her book, Reason repeatedly wonders if Soul has gone mad or lost her senses, exclaiming things like, 'For the sake of God! What are you saying?'[6] Over the course of dozens of chapters, Love patiently explains to Reason that there is a way of being beyond the virtues where Soul, because it ceases to possess its own will, is no longer burdened with the fear of sin. Marguerite writes,

'Now listen, Reason, says Love … This Soul has no thought nor word nor work except the practice of the grace of the divine Trinity. This Soul has no anxiety about sin which she might have ever committed, nor about suffering which God might have suffered for her, nor about the sins or anxiety in which her neighbors remain … For her thought is at rest in a peaceful place, that is, in the Trinity … From this place, no one falls into sin, and any sin which was ever done … is as displeasing to her will as it is to God's'.[7]

This is only one of the ways in which Marguerite explains that to cede to God's will is to live a virtuous life, free of the anxiety of failing to fulfil those virtues. Instead, the liberated soul believes completely that grace will be granted to the soul that strives to know divine love. In the meantime, the soul will still pursue good and virtuous things because God wills these things. However, the inquisitor and canon lawyers charged with judging Marguerite and her soul interpreted this as an abandonment of virtue entirely. Despite their harsh treatment of her, we should imagine Marguerite pitying these men. From her perspective, they were shackled to reason, slaves to the virtues, and incapable of experiencing the fullness of God's love. She would have described them as 'lost souls', tragically stuck on one of the lower four stages of spiritual progress.

In the opening chapters of *The Mirror*, Marguerite lays out a path that takes the soul from languishing in despair down into the 'abyss of love', a place where the soul can rest and be one with God. There are seven stages along this path. At the start, the soul is touched by grace and acknowledges that it is wretched and debased. Throughout the following two stages, the soul dies its first deaths, the deaths to sin and then to nature. These deaths are enacted by dedicating all the soul's energy to the virtues and to good works.

> 'So you can and must grasp everything about the Virtues … For at first this Soul did whatever Reason taught her, whatever the cost to her heart and body, since Reason was the mistress of this Soul. And Reason constantly told her to do all that the Virtues wished, without resistance, until death … and this Soul was truly obedient to all that was commanded, for she wanted to live the Spiritual life'.[8]

In the medieval era, the virtues (chastity, temperance, charity, diligence, kindness, patience, and humility) were often represented as seven beautiful women. Under their feet, conquered and defeated, were the seven deadly sins, the inverse of each virtue (lust, gluttony, greed, sloth, envy, wrath, and pride). These virtues and sins had been established hundreds of years before but had become particularly important over the course of the eleventh and twelfth centuries. During that time the sins began to be ranked, ordered by severity and how forgivable they were so that priests hearing confession might assign the appropriate penance. Parallel to this sort of legalistic development of the sins was a growing idolization of the virtues. This coincided with the rediscovery of Aristotelian works, particularly his writings on ethics which were adopted and popularized by thinkers like Thomas Aquinas. In these arguments, the Virtues were not only morally laudable, but also politically vital. To be virtuous was to be a good citizen and vice versa. Without strict adherence to the virtues, enforced by both ecclesiastical and secular oversight, society itself might collapse. In this context, when Marguerite Porete wrote that she was taking leave of the virtues, it sounded to her critics as if she was taking leave of well-ordered society.[9]

Marguerite argued in her book that this anxiety surrounding the virtues, good works, and the desperate panic to live rightly in order to reach God was itself a barrier between the soul and God. Only when a person gave up the idea of reaching God through virtue could they experience the 'ecstasy of love'. This fourth stage on the path of spiritual progress is described in a dialogue between Love and Reason:

> '[*Reason*]: Now, Love, says Reason, I still have a question, for this book says that this Soul has taken leave of the Virtues in all respects and you say that the Virtues are still with these Souls more perfectly than with any other…
>
> Love*:* Let me calm you, says Love. It is true that this Soul takes leave of the Virtues, insofar as the practising of them is concerned. But the Virtues have not taken leave of her, for they are always with her, but this is from perfect obedience to them… this Soul has gained and learned so much with the Virtues… This Soul has within her the mistress of the Virtues, whom one calls Divine Love, who has transformed her completely into herself, is united to her, and which is why this Soul belongs neither to herself nor to the Virtues.
>
> Reason: To whom does she belong then?
>
> Love*:* To my will, says Love, which transformed her into me… I am God, says Love, for Love is God and God is Love, and this Soul is God by righteousness of Love …'[10]

Marguerite Porete follows this dialogue by comparing the soul, which is now liberated from nature and the virtues, to an eagle flying 'higher than any other bird because she is feathered by Fine Love'.[11] This flight moves the soul to the fifth stage of progress. Once Soul has taken leave of the virtues by becoming Love, and thus Virtue itself, then Soul can focus on the 'meditation on Pure Love'.

> 'Meditation on Pure Love has only one intent alone, which is that the Soul love always loyally without wishing to have anything in return. And the Soul can do this only if she is without herself, for Loyal Love would not deign to have any consolations which might come from her own seeking... Meditation on Love knows well according to the better part that she must not excuse herself from work, which is to will perfectly the will of God. She allows God to work and to do what is according to his will'.

Again, we see that Marguerite is not making an argument for the total abandonment of works, but rather an argument for a blending, perhaps a back-and-forth movement, between works and meditation. Throughout her work, she insists on the importance of an interior focus on the divine. For her, and for many of her contemporaries, this divine is personified as Love, Lover, or Beloved. The sixth stage of Marguerite's path of spiritual progress is the most difficult to achieve, and to understand. It requires a complete loss of self in the divine. At different points, she compares it to swimming in a sea, to burning in a fire, to melting like wax. The soul, in Marguerite's understanding, is forever moving between the fifth and sixth stages. The sixth stage is too difficult to maintain because it is to become one with divinity, to be annihilated. Curiously, this annihilation, this unbecoming, is not accompanied by visions or revelations, which was the most common way for medieval mystics to legitimize their works. Finally, the seventh stage, is unknowable until the soul dies the third and final death, the death of the spirit. In this stage, presumably, the soul is permanently rejoined to the vast unknowable nothingness of God, the individual soul will seamlessly fuse to the divine will.

Marguerite's theology is complex and she is aware of this. It is likely for this reason that she repeats herself so many times in her book. At the end, she apologizes for the length of the book.[12] She, also, in a final poem, remarks that she knows that her thoughts will be rejected and condemned.

> 'O my Lover, what will beguines say
> and religious types,
> When they hear the excellence
> of your divine song?
> Beguines say I err,
> priests, clerics, and Preachers,
> Augustinians, Carmelites,
> and the Friars Minor,
> Because I wrote about the being
> of the one purified by Love.
> I do not make Reason safe for them,
> who makes them say this to me.
> Desire, Will, and Fear
> surely take from them the understanding,
> The out-flowing, and the union
> of the highest Light
> Of the ardor
> of divine love'.[13]

This poem, and the last several chapters of the book, which are thought to have been added in a sort of second edition following the book's first condemnation, re-summarizes Marguerite's main points. She then ends the book with a chapter that modern translators title, 'The Approval'. Here, Marguerite includes the names and qualifications of three clergymen who had read and approved the publication of her book: Brother John, 'a Friar Minor of great fame, life and sanctity'; Dom Franco, a Cistercian monk who 'proved through Scripture that truth is what this book speaks'; and 'a certain Master of Theology named Godfrey of Fontaines'. This last man was a renowned master at the University of Paris. His conditional approval of the book is likely why the inquisitor in Paris felt it necessary to call together twenty-one canon lawyers and theologians to condemn Marguerite. She tells us in the final sentences of *The Mirror* that,

> 'He said nothing unfavorable about the book, as little as the others did. But he did indeed counsel that not many should see it, because, as he said, they could set aside the life to which they were called in aspiring to the one at which they will never arrive. And so in this they could be deceived, because, as he said, the book is made from a spirit so strong and ardent that few or none are found to be like it. Nevertheless, he said, the soul is not able to arrive at divine life or divine practice until she arrives at the practice which this book describes. All other practices are inferior to this, said this Master, they are human practices; this alone is divine practice and nothing other than this'.[14]

A similar qualification was written in the margins of an early fifteenth-century copy of *The Mirror*. Sometime around 1425, in a monastery in Tuscany, a Czech monk, John-Jerome of Prague (d. c. 1440) made a copy for himself, adding the note: 'To be read cautiously, and not by everyone'.[15] John-Jerome was not a man whom we might imagine reading and, even if cautiously, approving of a heretical text. Yet, the fact that he did reveals some of the complex problems surrounding Marguerite's execution a century earlier and the idea of heresy itself. John-Jerome, like Marguerite, was not fully satisfied with the state of the medieval church. A serious monk who dedicated his life to asceticism and reform, he saw something similar to his own works in Marguerite's. The concept of spiritual progress as a slow, but intense stripping away of the self to attain a closer relationship with the divine will complemented messages in his own work, *Linea*. So much so that John-Jerome thought it worthwhile to draw a monk, perhaps himself, smiling and contemplating a book in a large 'A' in his copy of *The Mirror*. This small figure makes his copy the only version of Marguerite's book with decoration.[16]

John-Jerome's was not the only copy of the book. Obviously, he was working from another version, but there are several more that have survived to the modern era. In fact, dozens of copies have been identified in several languages: Old and Middle French, Italian, Middle English, and Latin. It was not only religious men who owned these books. One copy was included in a book list in the will of an apothecary from Dijon who died in 1482. Another was found in a convent in Ghent. *The Mirror* was also included in a list of books for sale at a shop in Tours. The surviving copies vary in size (30-158 pages) and some, like the one owned by the apothecary, were not impressive books. The apothecary's copy was written on paper and its cover made of parchment – light and easy to carry, but not very durable or expensive.[17] All of this is to say that when separated from its convicted author and taken out of its immediate context, the book was popular, and was enjoyed by a great variety of people. In fact, it has been argued that, if Marguerite Porete had been a sworn member of an approved order, she and her book might not have been deemed heretical at all.[18]

The theology preached by Marguerite was radical, but it was not entirely new. She had cultivated ideas that had origins among the beguines, a movement of religious women in which Marguerite had begun her spiritual journey. This is why she was often described as a beguine, though she wrote in her own work that the beguines thought she erred. In fact, she had likely been expelled from a house of beguines in Valenciennes, a small town about two-days' walk northeast of Paris.[19] When an inquisitor was investigating the women there in 1323 – part of a much larger inquisition into women's houses – he asked if any women there had ever disputed the basic facts of the faith or 'spread opinions incompatible with the Catholic faith'.[20] The beguines responded:

> '... with a humble and unanimous devotion, that this was the case with only one of them, called Margonette, who while she lived with them, they said she had been punished for her faults, according to what justice demanded, but nevertheless, this Margonette had never had, among them, even a single follower of her errors'.

As Marguerite knew, she had been so completely disavowed by her own movement – or at least this house – that they did not even properly remember her name. Given the unusualness of the name 'Margonette', but its obvious similarity to 'Marguerite', and the fact that Marguerite is the only beguine, former or otherwise, to have been so publicly punished, the assumption is that Margonette is Marguerite.[21] It is also generally accepted that it was the trial and execution of Marguerite Porete that instigated the next generation of inquisitions and persecutions of beguines throughout western Europe. But what was a beguine?

There have been several proposed etymologies for the word 'beguine' itself. Some have traced the term back to a priest in Liège, Lambert le Bègue. Others have connected the word to the Old Saxon verb, *beggen*, meaning either 'to beg' or 'to pray'. Some beguine women themselves, hoping to add some legitimacy to their movement through ancient origins, traced their name back to Saint Begga, a seventh century abbess who was the grandmother of Charles Martel. All of these have been dismissed over the last century of historical work, leaving the origin of the name obscured in uncertainty. Their critics would likely have pointed to the Old Saxon roots. The wandering, begging woman, living outside of an order without a rule, was derided by contemporaries in the thirteenth century as, at best, silly, and at worst, an impudent or insane burden on society. Yet, one of their most ardent supporters, Robert of Sorbon (d. 1274), connected the name 'beguine' to the Latin word *benigna*, meaning 'kind' or 'good'.

In Robert of Sorbon's view, beguine women performed a vital service to their communities. They exhorted their families and friends to contemplate the religious life, to pray, and to attend sermons and Masses. More than this, because beguines lived in the world and did not enclose themselves in convents, they demonstrated how an individual could be in the world and yet not succumb to its influences. Robert also lauded, loudly and repeatedly, the beguines' strength in the face of public criticism. To bear the brunt of mockery and to uphold their devotion to God in the face of persecution was, to him, a sign of their sanctity and a fulfilment of the apostolic ideal.

For others, like Robert's contemporary Gilbert of Tournai (d. 1284), the beguines were an existential threat to society. They were women on the loose, posing as religious devotees, but actually, according to Gilbert, they spread heresy, cavorted with Dominicans, and became financial and spiritual burdens on their communities. He denounced the beguines as 'irreverent and impudent'. He complained that they had translated 'the mysteries of the scriptures in vulgar Gallic tongue' and, worse, the women took what they had read and discussed it 'in conventicles, in workhouses, in the streets'.[22] Guilbert's criticism of the beguines was part of a larger rebuke of a growing movement of lay religiosity. The friar considered it inappropriate, even an excommunicable offense, that lay people who had taken no formal vows were dressing in hair shirts, cutting their hair, wearing habits, and preaching in public. However, Guilbert was raging against a cultural force that he could not defeat. At the head of this growing religious fervour was the king himself. Louis IX (r. 1226–1270), who was canonized as a saint after his death, was publicly and zealously devout – so much so that some even griped that they were ruled by a monk and not a king. He organized two crusades, dying on the second voyage. When he was home in Paris, he oversaw the foundation or expansion of innumerable convents, chapels, monasteries, and other holy sites. While he was alive, though the debate over lay religiosity, particularly female lay religiosity, raged on, there would be no quelling the piety of the common folk.

King Louis IX was also sympathetic to the beguine movement for many of the same reasons as Robert of Sorbon. Louis, who had a habit of wearing a hair shirt and often woke in the middle of the night to pray, had spent his life trying to balance the duties of being king, a worldly and demanding endeavour, with his personal devotion to Christianity. His sister, Isabelle, in a similar way had remained at court, but scorned every marriage proposal in favour of zealously defending her virginity in the name of Christ. She, like her brother, was a supporter of religious institutions and founded her own house for Franciscan sisters where she was later buried and recognized as a saint by that order. Upon his return from his first crusade (1248–1254) – the seventh official crusade of that era – Louis turned his attention to the foundation of several religious houses in Paris. About this time, Robert of Sorbon entered the king's employ and quickly gained his favour. It was perhaps at his instigation, or with his help, that Louis selected a place along the right bank of the Seine to establish a royal beguinage.[23]

Even before Louis had founded the beguinage, there were several smaller beguine houses scattered throughout the city. And many of these smaller houses continued to exist and thrive in the bustling capital city. Despite their critics, an ever-growing number of women were devoting themselves, even if temporarily, to their faith. They took informal vows of chastity, met in groups to discuss religious texts, and attended sermons as often as they could. The foundation of a formal 'house' or beguinage by the king was, on the one hand, a clear show of support for this new wave of piety and on the other, a way to centralize this sprawling community of lay religious women. A fact of beguine life was that the women were allowed to maintain their own private property. So, a beguinage was a collection of properties. Individual beguines would rent out their houses, or rooms in their houses, to other beguines and lay women. If a beguine later chose to return to the world, usually by accepting a marriage proposal, her property would not be forfeited. This was one of many points of criticism from clergymen, but a major selling point for the women and their families.

Our clearest picture of beguine life in Paris comes from a series of tax rolls from the end of the thirteenth century during the reign of Louis's grandson, Philip IV (r. 1285–1314). In these records we find hundreds of women, living alone or in small groups, who were considered wealthy enough to pay taxes. Together they made up almost 14 per cent of the taxpayers listed between 1297 and 1300.[24] Within this group were the women who built up the silk industry in Paris. Beguines, in particular, worked as silk spinners, silk merchants, and other types of silk workers who specialized in making headdresses, hats, purses, and other embroidered goods.[25] The development of the silk industry in northern France had coincided with the swell of the beguine movement. Women had traditionally dominated in the textile industry working as wool combers, spinners, and weavers. Silk was an obvious evolution of this work. Beguines, especially those in Paris, were well-situated to take advantage of the new industry. The beguines who owned and operated workhouses had come from middle- and upper-class families who could afford the materials, tools, and training necessary to enter the silk trade. By the end of the thirteenth century, the tax rolls for Paris show more than 100 individuals or groups of beguines paying taxes on their silk-related businesses.[26] A demanding hierarchy of mistresses and apprentices developed around these women. An apprentice was

An early twentieth-century reconstruction of Saint Radegund's enclosure in Poitiers. (Elizabeth Quillen, *Radegund's Enclosure*, May 2015)

Above: Quedlinburg Abbey and Castle, Tilman 2007. (Wikimedia Commons)

Left: Hrotsvit presenting one of her works to Emperor Otto I. (Albrecht Durer, *Opera Hrotsvite,* 1501, photo of printed woodcut, Bridwell Library Special Collections)

Urban II calling for crusade at the Council of Clermont. *Roman de Godfroi de Bouillon*, c. fourteenth century, manuscript illumination. (Wikimedia Commons)

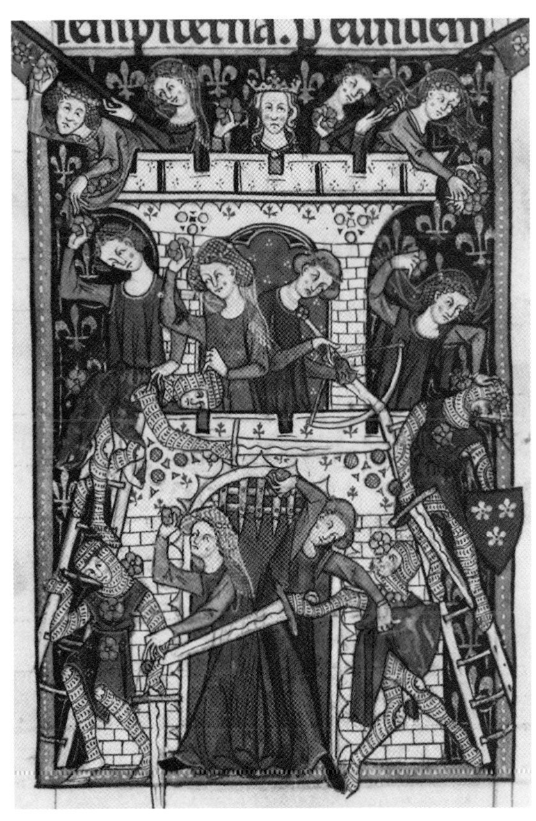

An allegorical depiction of women defending the 'Castle of Love' and fighting off suitors. One of the few medieval images of women fighting. KBR Ms. 9961-62, *Peterborough Psalter*, c. 1300–1325, manuscript illumination. (Royal Library of Belgium)

Hotel de Ville, formerly Place de Grève, where Marguerite Porete was publicly burned at the stake. (Tori Fullerton, *Hotel de Ville*, July 2024)

A twentieth-century depiction of a woman being burned at the stake. (Encylopedia Brittanica)

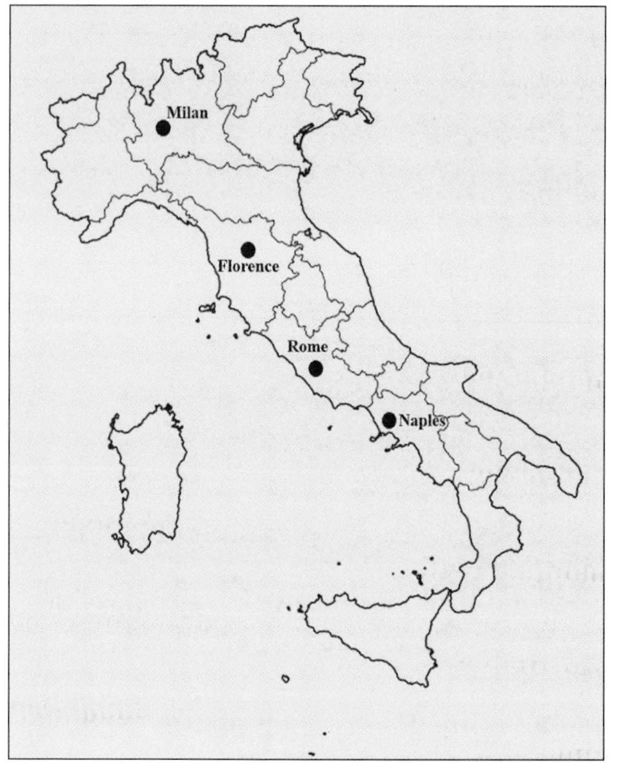

Above: A nineteenth-century photograph of the houses on the former Rubaconte Bridge over the Arno River in Florence. *Ponte alla grazie*, c. 1860. (Wikimedia Commons)

Left: Map of Italy. (July 2024, Elizabeth Quillen)

Right: Juan van der Hamen y Léon, *La monja alférez,* c. 1624-1626. (Wikimedia Commons)

Below: A depiction of the mining city, Potosi. Bernard Lens, *Map of South America*, c. 1715. (Wikimedia Commons)

Map of South America. (Wikimedia Commons)

required to work under a mistress for a decade and could not take on apprentices of her own until she had proven herself in front of a board of six judges.[27] Despite this, beguines were still often accused of laziness and of becoming burdens on society because some – the wandering ones – continued to live on alms.

Whether beguines lived in houses and worked, or wandered and begged, they pursued knowledge with a voracious appetite. It was their devotion in their time outside of work to religious study that set them apart from the other lay women in the city. The Paris beguinage frequently hosted masters from the University of Paris and the fledgling Sorbonne. Despite the beguines' close relationship with both the Sorbonne and the University of Paris, they often found themselves stuck between the two types of religious men who studied there: the secular clergy and the mendicant friars. The secular clergy – the typical priest or cleric who had taken religious vows but was not a monk – had almost immediately gone on the defensive when the new mendicant orders appeared on the scene in the early thirteenth century. The Order of the Friars Minor (Franciscans) and the Order of Preachers (Dominicans) were the most prominent of these orders though other smaller ones, such as the Carmelites, also developed over the course of the century. Named after their founders, the mendicant orders developed out of a reform impulse, a desire to return to the poverty and preaching of the original apostles, and in response to growing concerns of heresy throughout western Europe. The Dominicans especially devoted themselves to the education of the laity through the creation of fables, sermons, and other illustrative examples which communicated the basic tenets of the faith in a straightforward manner.

The secular clergy, at the beginning of the thirteenth century, were settling into an era of scholastic thought. Universities, of which the University of Paris was the most renowned, had sprouted up in the major cities of Europe over the previous century. Major philosophical thinkers like Peter Abelard, Thomas Aquinas, and William of Ockham had begun to set out detailed theories about creation, the divine will, and the soul. Wealth, like that generated by the crusades, from the expanded trade in the Mediterranean and new technological developments like the luxury silk industry, had flown into the coffers of the church. The secular clergy was reaching the zenith of its power, residing in the newly built Gothic cathedrals and monasteries, convening councils with hundreds of attendees, and dictating to the kings and emperors of Europe. The full power of the traditional church hierarchy was exemplified in the reign of Pope Innocent III (r. 1198–1216) and his decrees at the Fourth Lateran Council in 1215.

At this council, among many other decrees, it was decided that no new religious orders would be recognized. The Franciscans had received papal approval only a few years prior and the Dominicans were approved shortly thereafter. Yet, others would follow because of the popularity of the mendicants. These friars gained the love of the people because of their intimate proximity to them, moving from town to town, preaching publicly, and living noticeably austere lives, particularly in comparison to the secular clergy in their liturgical garments embroidered with silk. Repeatedly the secular clergy complained that the mendicants diverted the tithes on which they depended and encroached on their sacramental duties, like hearing confessions, administering last rites, or serving the eucharist. The dispute came to a head at the University of Paris where the secular clergy made their last stand against the encroaching influence of the mendicants, attempting to bar them from serving on the faculty. The mendicants, for their part, refused to acknowledge the authority of the secular clergy while using the protective rights of the university to openly criticize the church hierarchy. In the end, the mendicants were victorious, having the full support of Pope Honorius III (r. 1216–1227). Papal approval, however, did not smooth the tensions between the rival types of religious. In the middle of the century, the secular clergy attempted to expel the mendicant friars from the University of Paris, but were rebuked by another friar-friendly pope, Alexander IV (r. 1254–1261).[28]

The ways in which this complicated the lives of the beguines is exemplified in the career of William of Saint-Amour (d. 1272), a Master of Theology at the University of Paris in the 1250s and 1260s. William was a vicious critic of the mendicant orders. He had led the charge to expel the mendicant friars in 1253 and was furious when the pope rejected the secular clergy's complaints.[29] In retaliation, in 1256, he published *A Brief Tract on the Dangers of the Last Days*, a treatise that conjured up images of the end times while attacking 'pseudo-Apostles', who he clearly intended to be interpreted as the mendicant friars. In the treatise he laid out forty-one signs by which these 'pseudo-Apostles' could be identified. Some signs were obviously directed at the mendicant friars, like living by begging, ministering to congregations which, in William's mind, already belonged to parish priests, and preaching without the proper approval. Others included simple vices such as pride, boastfulness, deception, extortion, participating in worldly entertainments like drinking and feasting. Some accusations have an aura of irony around them: defying secular rulers, building ornate lodgings, courting worldly support, nepotism, and relying on logic and reason – this last one is particularly humorous given William's position on the faculty at the University of Paris. Other more serious accusations included extortion, teaching beliefs contrary to the scriptures, and entering women's private chambers.[30]

Shortly after this incendiary treatise was published, William was censured for attacking the mendicant orders who had the approval of the papacy. William defended himself by claiming that he was not attacking any approved orders.[31] Instead, he focused his defensive attack on the beguines, who had never been officially recognized by the papacy. Referring to them as 'silly little women', he could accuse the beguines of all the sins he would rather have thrown at the mendicants. The beguines, then, were loose, not only from enclosure, but sexually. He insinuated that while they first turned to the friars for confession, their admiration quickly devolved to lust. And, because the beguines were all, in his arguments, young and beautiful, how could the friars resist such temptations? The beguines were also guilty of sloth, according to William, because though they were young and able to work, they chose to live off alms which ought to have gone to 'deserving' poor.

Several friars, particularly from the Dominican Order, responded to William's accusations. In the year after his treatise was published, the pope ordered it to be publicly burned. William, still firm in his opposition to the mendicants, the beguines, and what he saw as a betrayal of the university by King Louis who had come to favour the friars, was also excommunicated and exiled from France. He would return to the kingdom after Pope Alexander IV died in 1266, but he does not seem to have regained his place at the university. With his career ruined, William retreated to Burgundy where he died in 1272. A small consolation, however, to this public scandal and exile was the support of the popular poet, Rutebeuf, who repeatedly satirized the beguines in a series of poems. The most direct of these, *Le diz des beguines*, specifically criticizes the fact that beguines could return to a worldly life, apparently with the full support of the king:

> 'If she laughs, it is amiability;
> If she weeps, it is devotion;
> If she sleeps, she is ravished;
> If she dreams, it is a vision;
> If she lies, think nothing of it.
> If the Beguine marries
> That is her conversion,
> Since her vows, her profession
> Are not for life…
> But do not speak ill of her.
> The king will not tolerate it'.[32]

Opposed to Willaim of Saint-Amour and Rutebeuf stood the founder of the Sorbonne, the previously mentioned Robert of Sorbon. Though he was a secular cleric himself, he agreed with the mendicant friars' call for improved theological education in the pursuit of better and more interpersonally effective pastoral care. Many of Robert of Sorbon's students frequented the beguinage, either observing him or other teachers preach to the religious women or practising their own preaching. One of those students, Pierre de Limoges (d. 1306), created a collection of sermons preached throughout Paris in 1272–1273. About a quarter of this collection is made of sermons preached at the beguinage, including those preached by the mistress, Agnes of Orchies (d. 1284), herself.[33] Pierre was not the only Sorbonne student to record sermons preached at the beguinage. We find other collections donated in the last wills and testaments of clerics like Jean of Essomes, and Godfrey of Fontaines, the Master of Theology who cautiously approved Marguerite Porete's work. These sermons and those preached at the beguinage provide another glimpse into the world of the beguines.

Some of the sermons preached to the beguines were obviously preached by clerics who were either wary or outright suspicious of the beguine lifestyle. For example, one preacher in the 1270s expressed his concerns to the women in attendance that because they were not 'properly' enclosed, they risked 'outside invasion'. Another exhorted the beguines to control their fellow religious women who 'wandered about the towns' and to insist that those women enclose themselves in both traditional religious garb and enclosed living spaces. Gerard of Reims, a secular master, seems to call the piety of the beguines into question in a sermon he preached at the beguinage. He tells a story of a beguine of noble birth, still residing in her own residence with family, who wanted to test her patience after hearing a sermon on the virtue. This noble beguine requested that one of her servants say something insolent to her. The nervous servant refused, at first. Later, at a dinner in front of others, the servant did what her mistress had asked at which point the beguine was outraged. A Dominican preacher of the same era recounted a conversation he supposedly had with a noblewoman in which he suggested to her that she commit her daughters to the beguinage. The noblewoman rejected this suggestion outright because of the beguines' 'bad reputations'. Yet, in the same story, this preacher claims that the noblewoman would instead place her daughters in convents 'because religious devotion was not expected in a convent'. Apparently, no house of religious women was above criticism in this Dominican's view.[34]

Other preachers came into the beguines' chapel in good faith. In one sermon, the beguines' freedom from enclosure was especially praised. A story that appears in more than one sermon about the beguines recounts how one of them, travelling from Cambrai to Paris, sought out a new book, William of Peraldus's *Summa on the Vices and Virtues.* After acquiring the book, the beguine took it to several other priests and canons throughout the region to allow them to make copies for themselves. It was this type of diffusion of knowledge through the beguines' dedication that earned them the adoration and support of the Sorbonne masters. A sermon from the collection of Pierre of Limoges, recorded sometime before his death in 1306, described an interaction between a beguine and a Parisian master at church. The master came upon a beguine weeping at the altar in a church. Shocked by her devotion despite her lack of formal education, the master asked her for advice on how he could also feel this type of emotional connection to God. The beguine chided him that her connection with the divine could not be learned from books or derived from reason. In fact, it is the master's over reliance on study and scripture that kept him at arm's length from God. In a similar vein, one of Robert of Sorbon's own sermons at the beguinage compared the holy women there to a treasure hidden in a field, a reference to a story from the gospel of Matthew. In this sermon, Robert criticized his fellow masters who were 'unable to find the treasure in the beguinage because they fail to recognize anything not found in study or reason'. Robert claimed the beguines or 'the little ones', as he styled them, were able to experience a deeper connection to the divine which confounded, sometimes even contradicted, reason. These are incredibly similar arguments to the ones put forward by Marguerite Porete in her work which she likely wrote sometime in the generation after Robert of Sorbon.

This rejection of reason in favour of love was maintained by at least some of the individuals who copied Marguerite's work later in the fourteenth century. A prefatory poem was added to her work, warning readers that what the book would ask of them would stretch the mind beyond reason and would not be easily understood.

> 'You who would read this book,
> If you indeed wish to grasp it,
> Think about what you say,
> For it is very difficult to comprehend;
> Humility, who is the keeper of the treasury of
> Knowledge
> And the mother of the other Virtues
> Must overtake you.
> Theologians and other clerks,
> You will not have the intellect for it,
> No matter how brilliant your abilities,
> If you do not proceed humbly …'[35]

Similarly, Robert of Sorbon and Marguerite Porete also compared the beguine devotion to that of Mary Magdalene. Mary Magdalene was a popular exemplar among the mendicants. Often conflated with Mary, sister of Martha, Magdalene was the perfect picture of repentance and devotion, saved by the merciful grace of Jesus. Marguerite, in the chapters at the end of her book, asks her readers to consider 'the sweet Magdalene'. Magdalene, like the mendicants who lived in apostolic poverty or the beguines who bore the weight of constant public criticism, loved Jesus 'for the sake of nothingness … not motivated out of need'. Marguerite emphasizes the humanity and tenderness of Mary Magdalene as well. Through asceticism and works of love, Mary 'worked by tilling the land which God had given her to cultivate … Truly was the intention pure which she directed toward God. When the intention is truly for the sake of the love of God, it is very difficult for it not to yield some fruit …'[36] Robert too made this connection between the humility and love of Mary Magdalene to the piety and public devotion of the beguines. In a sermon from the 1260s, he even referred to the beguines as the 'ordo caritatis', or 'order of love'.[37]

The theme of love was common in beguine works. In Agnes of Orchies' sermons, collected by Raoul in the 1270s, she tells her fellow beguines that 'God is acquired by loving'.[38] The theme of courtly love is also used frequently by beguine authors to describe the relationship between God and his believers. God and Jesus are often depicted as lords of manors, owners of vineyards, or charming princes who stalwartly defend and ardently love Christians. The first allegory in Marguerite Porete's work compares the believer to 'a maiden, daughter of a king', who hears stories of the legendary King Alexander and begins to pine for him.

> 'But this maiden was so far from this great lord, in whom she had fixed her love from herself, that she was able neither to see him nor to have him … When she saw that this faraway love, who was so close within her, was so far outside of her, she thought to herself that she would comfort her melancholy by imagining some figure of her love, by whom she was continually wounded in heart'.[39]

Other beguines also wrote about their longing for God, the distance between themselves and the object of their love.[40] Beatrice of Nazareth (d. 1268), who was herself a Cistercian, but was educated in a beguinage, wrote in her *Seven Ways of Love*, that 'the soul's great sadness is to have to be so far away and to seem so alien'.[41] She longed 'to be dissolved and to be with Christ'.[42] In Beatrice's seventh stage of love, like Marguerite's sixth stage of spiritual progress, 'the soul is united to the bridegroom, and is wholly made one spirit in inseparable faithfulness and eternal love'. Another beguine, Hadewijch of Antwerp/Brabant (c. thirteenth century), also foresaw Marguerite's mystical union in which the soul becomes transparent and completely united to the divine, and Hadewijch too hoped to melt into the divine.

> 'My soul melts away
> In the madness of Love
> The abyss into which she hurls me
> Is deeper than the sea;
> For love's deep new abyss
> Renews my wound'.[43]

This melting of the soul and the continuous or renewed wounds are indicative of the beguines' approach to an emotional and often inner spirituality. In another sermon by Agnes, the mistress of the Paris beguinage, she emphasizes this 'interior contrition'. She even goes so far as to invert the statement of an influential theologian from the previous century, Peter the Chanter. He had stated, 'Confession is the greatest part of satisfaction'. The mistress of the beguinage, foreshadowing Marguerite's rejection of the sacraments, argued instead that 'Confession is the least part of satisfaction'. Confession risked becoming habitual or performative. The true penance was performed internally and should be 'motivated by grief, given of one's own free will, and accomplished with alacrity, completeness, and purity'.[44] Continuing to emphasize the primacy of interior contemplation, the mistress also downplayed the need for ascetic living through fasting and physical punishment. And, like Marguerite Porete, she counselled her fellow beguines that 'good works should be done with good intention and on account of God alone'.

It was the will that mattered most. Without a well-intentioned will, based in love, all virtue was hollow, like an empty church.[45]

If the beguines were as popular in Paris as it seems, given their royal support and the close relationship not only to the Sorbonne but also with the University of Paris, and Marguerite Porete's theology, steeped in long-standing beguine traditions of love and mystical union, then why was she singled out for condemnation and execution? The answer to this lies in the larger political context of her time. As mentioned, if Marguerite had been a member of a recognized order or established house, perhaps the royal beguinage, then she might have evaded notice. With the tide turning against the beguines, their most outspoken supporters having died in the years prior to the turn of the century, a lone outspoken woman with big ideas was a risk. But even less lucky for Marguerite was the culmination of a century of growing inquisitorial power and centralizing royal authority.

Shortly before Marguerite's own arrest, the king, Philip IV, had called for the sudden and surprise arrest of every Templar knight in his kingdom. His motives have been a topic of debate ever since, but there is a general sort of agreement that Philip was motivated primarily by two things. One, the finances of the French kingdom and the Templars had become increasingly intertwined over the last half century with a great deal of royal treasure stored in Templar vaults. Two, Philip was in the midst of a long game for supreme authority with the papacy. The elimination of the Templars on the grounds that the group had become heretical deviants was a major blow to a martial arm of the papacy and was intended to bolster the king's own image as the 'Most Christian King'.[46] Marguerite was caught up in this political contest.

She first came to the attention of the ecclesiastical authorities sometime before 1306.[47] In Cambrai – a diocese to the northeast of Paris which included Valenciennes, where Marguerite was likely living – the bishop, Guy of Colmieu, had acquired a copy of Marguerite's book. It is even possible that Marguerite had provided the copy herself. As mentioned, she had sent out at least three copies to other clerics. While they had approved the book, Guy took issue with it. The issue at hand, more so than Marguerite 'taking leave' of the virtues was her suggestion in *The Mirror* that the Soul 'neither desires nor despises poverty, neither martyrdom nor tribulations, neither masses nor sermons, not fasts nor prayers'.[48] This was interpreted as a particularly anti-clerical message and as an outright rejection of the sacraments. Consequently, her book was burned and the bishop warned Marguerite that if she continued to write down and share these ideas, then she would be convicted as a heretic.

It is easy to imagine the offence taken by a bishop when reading a book that referred to him as a 'little one' or a 'lost soul' and to his church as 'Holy Church the Little'. Holy Church the Little, like Reason, is personified throughout the book and is in a near-constant state of confusion. It asks, repeatedly, how Soul has found peace and how Soul can know God or His will. Love and Soul, as always, patiently explain that Holy Church the Little must see beyond what Reason has shown it and return to love.

We might also imagine Marguerite's frustration in the face of the charges against her book. The effort alone of writing and copying a book in the thirteenth century was so demanding that to see all that work consigned to flame would be maddening. Doubly so for Marguerite who, in her own words, described the book as a gift from God; a gift she happily passed on to those in the little church.

> 'And for the sake of my memory of Him, He gave me this book, which makes present in some fashion His love itself … As for you little ones of Holy Church, says Love, I have made this book for you, so that you might hear in order to be more worthy of the perfection of life and the being of peace …'[49]

Undeterred, Marguerite made more copies of her book and, possibly, added several chapters at the end in an attempt to clarify her thoughts. When the work was complete, she again sent it out to men of high standing in the church, seeking their approval. Unfortunately, one of these men, the bishop of Châlons-sur-Marne, also considered the book heretical and turned it over to an inquisitor who oversaw Lorraine, the region in which Marguerite had been circulating her book. The official charges against her claimed that 'she had not only sent this book to this Lord [the bishop of Châlons-sur-Marne], but also to many other simple persons, beghards[50] and others, as if it were good'.[51] If this is true, and given the plethora of copies which were made in the century following her execution it does seem likely that Marguerite herself made several, we must wonder where and how she did this. She was apparently evicted from the beguinage in Valenciennes, as noted, but must have had access to the necessary materials (parchment, ink, a working copy of *The Mirror*) and space to continue writing. We will likely never know the details of who Marguerite's patrons were, but it is evident from her production that she had them.

Her case, deemed worthy of a trial by the inquisitor in Lorraine, was handed off to higher authorities in Paris sometime in 1308, only a few months after the arrests of the Templars. For more than a year, she was imprisoned somewhere in Paris, perhaps Châtelet. It is possible that her case dragged on for so long because the inquisitor in Paris, William of Paris, was busy overseeing the trials of the Templars. The interrogations in Paris had gone quickly, lasting only a few weeks in the autumn of 1307, but elsewhere they dragged on. Further from the king's authority, other inquisitors were less sure of how, or less keen, to press charges against the monastic knights.[52] Further complicating the conviction of the Templars was the growing ire of Pope Clement V (r. 1305–1314). The king had ordered the arrest of the Templars in his kingdom without consulting with the pope, bypassing a vital step in any heresy trial. For six months in 1308, the pope suspended the authority of the inquisitors in the French domains. It seems completely possible, in the shadow of this struggle between king and pope, that Marguerite's case was simply forgotten.

It was not until either late in 1309 or early in 1310 that William of Paris, in a political bind following the scandalous interrogation, trial, and execution of dozens of Templars, needed a clearer cut case to re-confirm his authority as the inquisitor in Paris. A single beguine whose radical ideas had already been condemned once in Cambrai should have been a quick trial. Instead, following her arrest, Marguerite resisted her second inquisitor at every turn. She steadfastly refused to swear any oath or even to speak to William or his subordinates. At least, this is what William claimed in his reports to the twenty-one theologians he had summoned to review Marguerite's book. Almost half of these men had also sat on a council 'concerning the trial of the Templars'.[53]

Most of them also served on the faculty at the University of Paris and were some of the most prominent theologians in the kingdom. The trial itself unfolded at the Church of the Mathurins, the administrative centre of the university.[54]

When Marguerite's trial finally began, it moved very quickly. In fact, inquisitions were supposed to move quickly. Typically, they were instigated by either widespread rumour or reputation. If enough people in a neighbourhood, town or parish church were whispering about someone's less-than-orthodox ideas or behaviour, then it was deemed necessary to investigate. If tangible proof of unorthodox or heretical belief could be produced, then this part of the investigation moved even faster. The accused would be arrested, and the inquisitor should inform them of the accusations against them. Then the accused would be asked to swear an oath to answer truthfully, either in defending themselves against the charges or confessing. However, it had become somewhat common practice to have the accused swear an oath before the inquisitor had read any charges at all. The accused would then be expected to explain why they thought they had been summoned. If they refused to answer, then they would be excommunicated and after a year could be charged as a heretic. This may have been what happened to Marguerite since she reportedly refused to speak to William of Paris, or even to take an oath, and then remained in prison for at least a year. However, it has also been argued that William of Paris was attempting to cover up his own bureaucratic failures and, in the process, convicted Marguerite twice for the same instance of heresy.[55]

Regardless of how the trial was handled, the outcome was a guaranteed conviction. Marguerite's book had already been condemned once. She had continued to write, expanding on the ideas in her first edition, and shared new copies with several people. Unafraid of, even seeking out, episcopal and mendicant approval, she had placed her book, and consequently her life, in the hands of individuals who had been waiting for a reason to suppress the growing problem of vernacular theology and lay preaching. Marguerite, as a result of her conviction, would also become a catalyst for the growing call within the church to suppress the beguine movement. In August of the year that Marguerite was arrested, Pope Clement V summoned a council in the city of Vienne, a short trip south of Lyon. Six of the twenty-one theologians who judged Marguerite were in attendance.

The Council of Vienne (1311–1312) first condemned the Templars, disbanded their order, and transferred much of their property to the Hospitallers, and retrospectively approved the arrests and trials ordered by Philip IV. The pope also issued the papal bull *Ad nostrum* which claimed that 'the perverseness of heresy' had been planted and nurtured by the 'faithless women, commonly called Beguines'. It then listed eight errors which were clearly influenced by the (mis)interpretations of Marguerite Porete's *Mirror of Simple Souls*. According to *Ad nostrum*, the beguines believed that an individual could 'acquire a degree of perfection that renders him utterly impeccable', and having become impeccable, it was 'not necessary to fast or pray', and 'that those who have reached the said degree of perfection and spirit of liberty, are not subject to human obedience nor obliged to any commandments of the church'. In the most obvious connection to Marguerite's work, the sixth error, attributed to the beguines as a whole, was 'that the practice of the virtues belongs to the state of imperfection and the perfect soul is free from virtues'.[56] Consequently, the beguines were condemned as a 'detestable sect' and the inquisitors of heresy in the regions where they lived were tasked with investigating and punishing them. Yet, room was left for 'truly pious women', causing a great deal of confusion in the course of the inquisitions.[57]

Over the next several decades, the papacy would issue a series of decrees and rulings targeting beguines, sometimes broadly and sometimes regionally, then making exceptions when inquisitions often revealed that the difference between beguines living in beguinages and more traditional nuns was merely the adoption of a formal rule. Over the course of the fourteenth century, beguines would slowly convert their beguinages into houses of the various orders.[58] The royal beguinage in Paris, where the demise of the movement had begun, held out longer than many others. Even after the Council of Vienne, it had enjoyed the support of the royal family, but by 1485, following decades of war and the loss of close ties to the royal family through the ever-changing and often absent monarchs, the beguinage had been converted into a house of Poor Clares, the nuns associated with the Franciscans.[59] As we will see in the next chapter, the fallout from these decrees was not limited to France or even to the beguines, but had a confining effect on independent houses of religious women across Europe.

Chapter Five

The Walled-In Women of Florence

A low boom resounded through the convent of Le Murate late one August night in 1530. Outside the convent walls, a magistrate of the Florentine republic had ordered his guards, armed with harquebuses, to fire on the locked convent door. Blasting through the locks and hinges, the guards pried the door from its jamb to reveal the distressed holy women inside. Abbess Bonifazia Risaliti blocked the magistrate's path, pleading with him to have compassion and to think on what he was doing by forcing his way into their cloister. Unbothered, he marched into the interior courtyard and demanded that the abbess hand over her convent's ward, the young Catherine de' Medici.

The eleven-year-old girl refused, 'resolving to cut her hair and put on [the nun's] habit', in the hope that this would force the magistrate to leave her in the convent.[1] The crowd of nuns surrounded the child. Some cried out with 'pious and tearful prayers', while others 'begged with such insistence and deep affection' that the magistrate would treat their ward with compassion. Abbess Bonifazia explained to the magistrate 'the girl's troubles and terrors, showing that she expected them to murder her cruelly'.[2] Unmoved, but unwilling to physically wrestle the girl from the protective grasp of the nuns around her, the magistrate retreated for the night.

The following morning, Silvestro Aldobrandini, the father of the current pope and an esteemed jurist for the republic's government, 'came to find the disconsolate girl, whom they got out of bed, not wanting to wait until she was dressed'. Catherine stood in front of him in her nightdress with a spare habit covering her freshly cut hair. The chronicler of Le Murate describes Silvestro as 'very displeased' upon seeing her this way. We might imagine him sighing angrily, hands raised up to God in frustration, as he ordered that the girl be dressed in her usual clothes, and she refused. Catherine insisted that if she was to be taken then she would remain in her habit 'so that everyone would see that they took a nun from the convent'. It seems that Silvestro won in the end as one local historian described the young girl 'bitterly crying all the while' as she was escorted from Le Murate, at the outskirts of the city, to the more central convent of Santa Lucia.[3]

Catherine spent less than a month at Santa Lucia, perhaps only a few days. The republican government had wanted to move her to this more secure location in the hopes of keeping her out of the hands of the imperial forces laying siege to the city. Others had argued that the young Medici girl should be left where she was – closer to the city walls and, consequently, the enemy's cannon fire. It mattered very little as a treaty concluding the siege was signed within a matter of days. The young girl returned almost immediately to Le Murate to wait out the tense change in government. She would remain there for almost a year before her life was once again uprooted for the political purposes of her cousins and uncles. Though her chances to visit the convent were incredibly rare after this, she never forgot the relative calm of the convent nor the protection of the nuns who lived there.

The history of Le Murate began in a similar way. For several years, a small group of devout women had lived together in a small house 'practically dangling there' on the Rubaconte bridge, which spanned the Arno, a river that cuts through the heart of Florence.[4] In 1410, a young woman, who took the name Filippa, entered this house 'to live and die among these holy women'. She lived there, peacefully, for three years before her fiancé arrived and 'violently forced her to leave'.[5] The ensuing drama of the aspiring nun and her resentful consort played out publicly in a series of court cases, both civil and ecclesiastical. Filippa had presumed that her fiancé, who had given her a ring and then disappeared for five years, was dead. This normally would have given her every right to enter a monastery, but the 'walled-in women' living above the Arno River had not taken vows to adhere to a specific Rule and were thus not officially recognized as a convent. So, to protect Filippa from her grasping betrothed, on 25 November 1413, the seven women 'took the white Benedictine habit ... and called themselves sisters'.[6]

The early days of the convent were marked by stories of young men prowling just outside the walls, lingering at the door, and scheming to either get into the convent or pull the women out. The most famous Le Murate chronicler, Sister Giustina Niccolini, describes two miracles in quick succession after the convent's acceptance of the Benedictine Rule. In the first, 'an Observant reverend father' at San Miniato, a small village about two-days' walk west of Florence, received a vision of the convent. As he prayed in the choir of his church, a hole appeared in the wall before him revealing 'a miraculous splendour hovering over the Rubaconte bridge'. That same day, he hurried to Florence to see the splendour for himself. As he approached the city gate, he spotted 'a dishevelled young boy' pacing anxiously at the edge of the bridge. The 'reverend father' instantly recognized the boy as the devil in disguise and inquired 'where he was going and whom he sought to harm'. The boy, 'full of rage', replied that he was trying to cross the bridge but could not 'because of the powerful force of those angry women'. He then scampered away to find another route over the river. The priest continued into the city to report his miraculous vision and his odd encounter with the devil-boy to 'the noble lords of the republic'. After this, the walled-in women were 'esteemed and venerated more than ever by everyone'.[7]

Several years later, after the convent was moved from the bridge and onto Via Ghibellina, another 'young man of horrendous appearance' was prowling around the walls of the convent. Mariano, an old man who often stayed in the church attached to Le Murate reported to the abbess that he had discovered the young man lurking at the convent door, muttering angrily about how 'he would master the place and its inhabitants'. When Mariano confronted him and demanded to know who he was, the young man replied that he was 'the devil of discord'. The abbess 'cautioned her daughters that they had been warned, because these were satanic dangers from which God was pleased to liberate them'.[8] These stories were passed down for several decades before Sister Giustina recorded them in her chronicle in 1598.

There are a few possible reasons why these stories were deemed important to the history of Le Murate. They are, of course, interesting moments laced with potential danger. We might imagine a nun occasionally, in a moment of boredom as she was spinning thread or preparing ingredients for a meal or a medicine, asking if anyone else recalled the time when the devil lurked at their door. 'Which time?' one of her sisters might have replied. The stories also may have been read aloud in the refectory as most mealtimes were accompanied by 'edifying readings' or 'a recitation of the convent rules or even the convent chronicle'.[9] There is also a motivational quality to the stories. The need for vigilant prayer to protect themselves from 'satanic dangers' is made clear. It may have also highlighted the other dangers of the outside world like ugly young men with angry schemes and devious desires, an unpleasant alternative to convent life.

These were exactly the arguments presented by Abbot Gomez, a Portuguese cleric who had been sent to Florence to reform several Benedictine monasteries and convents. Le Murate, initially, had not been among those Benedictines deemed in need of reform or supervision, but one day the abbot was walking across the Rubaconte Bridge when his attention was drawn to 'this small house with the church perched so low and in such great danger of being submerged easily by the Arno River'. Besides this, the small house was also on a busy bridge with several other houses, hermitages, and shops. Though the women had ceased publicly begging when they took their vows, keeping them out of the public view, the attached church remained a spiritually suspect threshold with the outside world. The abbot, according to a later biographer, exclaimed to the other people on the bridge:

> 'As far as their souls are concerned, [they] are in Satan's jaws ... Women on a pier of a bridge, without a guide, without government, and with no advice at all? If the river flooded … who [would] free these women from impending ruin? Maybe you think it appears to be a decent thing, without scandal, that these women live in such a place, where a person cannot so much as pass by without them hearing? ... Is the noise and uproar of the people who

> continually pass there not certain to be a disturbance to their every devotion?'[10]

So, Gomez 'promised to help them, taking charge of removing them from there'. Sister Giustina tells us that Agata, the abbess at the time, 'very wisely' accepted the abbot's help because 'they should not wish to tempt God rashly', and they had so outgrown the small house on the bridge that it was 'unseemly'.[11] However, the abbot's biographer suggests that Abbess Agata was not so eager to move and contested his insinuation that their location was a cause for scandal:

> 'Say, venerable father, explain to us please the sentiment with which you talk in that way about us poor women, who maintain our quiet here in the service of Jesus, who is never absent from those who serve him faithfully? Fear of death doesn't disturb us in the least'.[12]

Sister Giustina, speaking with the benefit of hindsight, appreciated the relocation of the convent because she knew how much it would grow in the following decades. Abbess Agata, on the other hand, who may have been keenly aware of the issue of space, must have been equally aware of the dangers of not only horrendous young men, but of interfering, if well-meaning, religious men. Indeed, Sister Giustina tells us that the first years in the new house were a struggle despite the relative physical comfort. The new house had been granted to the women of Le Murate in exchange for the donor's daughter entering the convent. Sister Francesca, the last of the bridge-bound sisters, accompanied her new family in the procession from the Rubaconte Bridge to the house on Via Ghibellina, 'which seemed to be large enough for the entire earth'. The nuns' procession was accompanied by 'many devout persons with tears, psalms, hymns, and spiritual songs' as well as the prior and priests of Sant'Ambrogio, into whose parish they were moving.[13]

The nuns of Le Murate – now formally the nuns of Santa Maria Annunziata, a reference to the painting of the Annunciation kept over the altar of their church – chafed under the authority of the parish priest. According to Sister Giustina, the priest 'argued that they could not receive the holy sacraments or bury the dead without the ministers of that parish, or hang a bell … they could not even celebrate the feasts of the Annunciation and Saint Benedict, or accept offerings, along with many other severities and restrictions'. The nuns endured this 'harassment' for a decade though Sister Giustina tells us the restrictions 'irritated them not a little'.[14]

In the end, the convent was able to successfully argue their case – through the aid of Abbot Gomez – when Pope Eugenius IV (d. 1447) visited the city. In August 1434, he issued a bull in which he agreed that these restrictions were 'against good practice and unreasonable, and illegitimate, seriously damaging the monastery' of Le Murate.[15] The papal dispensation, which Sister Giustina describes as a 'liberation', placed the women of Le Murate directly under the supervision of their dear abbot who 'was very careful from the beginning not to submit them to religious authorities or any other superior except the pope' and the archbishop of Florence.[16] This first dispensation from the papacy was followed by several more as well as gifts over the course of the 1440s.[17] Eugenius was generous with the women of Le Murate for several reasons. For one, Abbot Gomez had been a loyal representative of the papal court for several years. Additionally, Le Murate had aligned itself with the ideals of the Observant reform movement. Eugenius was supportive of this fledgling movement which had been officially recognized by the church in 1415. It was their Observant style of monastic life which had made the nuns so beloved among the people of Florence as well.

Observance reform had grown out of the Franciscan Order and, like several earlier reform movements, centred on a rigorous return to an ascetic lifestyle. The women 'occupied themselves not only in the contemplative life and the mortification of the body but also in manual labour'. They slept in straw beds 'without any other mattress or pillows' and 'went about barefoot, only wearing sandals, as was more the habit of hermits than of nuns'. The women's devotion to this asceticism had been a source of friction with the more traditional Sant'Ambrogio:

> 'In effect they lived like hermits because they spent entire nights praying, sleeping little or not at all. They stayed in their beds so as not to disobey the prelate who ordered that

> they all retire at the same time to the dormitory until the abbess signalled for them to celebrate matins'.

This level of piety was greatly respected among the Florentine elite but was also appreciated by the Florentine poor. Le Murate gained a reputation early after its move to larger quarters of accepting girls, some as young as two or three, with discounted dowries. In some cases, infant girls were even dropped off anonymously on the convent's doorstep. For this reason, the convent's numbers swelled, becoming the 'fastest growing convent' in the city. When they had left the bridge in 1424, there were thirteen sisters. By 1439, there were thirty-six, and in 1458, this number had almost tripled to 124 nuns along with two to three dozen servants and several widows who lived in the convent as boarders. None of this growth would have been possible while living under the thumb of the parish priest, but it also could not have been so rapidly achieved or successfully sustained without the leadership of one particular abbess, Scholastica Rondinelli (d.1475).

Scholastica, along with her eight-year-old daughter, entered the convent at Le Murate in the spring of 1439. Her husband had recently passed away and Scholastica had been a devotee of the convent for several years. She had given another daughter over to the nuns three years earlier. Perhaps her own entrance sprung from a desire to live with her daughters again. It is also possible that she knew how quickly her status would increase after she became a nun. Shortly before Scholastica took her vows, the abbess of Le Murate had passed away rather suddenly. The tight knit community – no more than thirty-six women at this point – was 'disconsolate and afflicted', so 'miserable … [that they] did not know how to proceed, preventing them from electing a successor'.[18] Sister Giustina tells us that it was then nearly miraculous that Scholastica had come to them in this moment. 'Inspired by God they unanimously elected' their new sister 'because the nuns knew her to be a woman of great spirit'. This was sometime in the winter of 1439.

Less than seven months after she had been widowed, Scholastica had been elected abbess of Florence's most promising convent.[19] She brought with her all the benefits of having been raised in one family in the lower tier of patricians and married into another. She was well-educated, well-known, and well-connected. She used her knowledge of the local banking and political scenes to the advantage of Le Murate. She obtained several tax breaks from the local government, the Signoria, as well as 'an annual gift of 10 *staia* of salt (720 pounds)'.[20] The abbess also called on old friends from her secular life. She and her husband had owned a country estate outside Florence and one of their old neighbours, Giovanni Benci (d. 1455), who had worked for years in the Medici banks, immediately became one of the most prominent patrons of the convent. Abbess Scholastica was able to complete a major construction project left unfinished at her successor's death and to begin several long-term expansions of her own with his financial backing, which was rumoured to have exceeded 10,000 florins by the time of his death. His sons would give another estimated 30,000 florins to the convent.[21]

The first project, which the abbess had inherited, was the completion of the church adjoining the convent in which lay people attended masses and other ceremonies. At the same time that Giovanni Benci provided money for this, he and Scholastica commissioned three altars to furnish a chapel, also funded by Benci. In her chronicle, Sister Giustina juxtaposes a celebratory singing of the psalms at the completion of the church and altars with two visions received by 'one of their old mothers from the bridge', Sister Benedetta, from her guardian angel. She does this in such a way that highlights the lofty ambitions, not only of the new abbess, but of the sisters as a unified community.

In the first vision, which Sister Giustina tells us was revealed as the nuns were singing those celebratory psalms, Benedetta saw 'a large vine covered with beautiful leaves, flowers, and fruits' falling from the sky above the church, encircling it, and then reaching back into the clouds. An exhortation from God to continue their good works, Abbess Scholastica declared, after being told of the vision. In Benedetta's other vision, which Sister Giustina tells us had been revealed many years before, she

> '... saw a cart coming to this convent full of many girls, dressed in various habits and fashions. Such a vision was interpreted in this way ... The diversity of habits and fashions represented the different places of origin and

> variety of heritages … people from every part of the world have come to our religious community…'[22]

Indeed, Le Murate, particularly in its early days of expansion, prided itself on its far-flung reputation and its willingness to accept almost any girl or woman who came to their door. Sister Giustina tells us, and other notarial records of the convent confirm, that there were women living there who had come from nearly every corner of the Italian peninsula as well as from Spain, Hungary, 'and from many other parts of the world'. There were even two, maybe four, converted Jewish girls who came to the house at the end of the fifteenth century – Sisters Fiammetta and Lucrezia Hebrea, and perhaps Sisters Innocent and Maria Benedetta.[23] This is perhaps not surprising given that the convent was founded by a woman from Siena, bolstered through the involvement of an abbot from Portugal, and then sumptuously patronized by a banker who had made his career in the international branches of the Medici bank. Abbess Scholastica was able to harness this potential network to enrich her new convent and in the following century, Sister Giustina lauded her achievements.

The expansion of the convent was cyclical. The completion of a beautiful church attracted patrons. The patrons gave alms in exchange for the recitation of psalms and prayers for their souls. The accumulation of these liturgical requirements demanded more intense recruitment. The recruitment of more women in turn required more construction. By 1460, 'there were so many nuns that they could no longer gather together' in the original oratory – the chapel set aside for the recitation of prayers. Abbess Scholastica oversaw this enlargement and, for good measure, 'added a third bay to the church'. The church and its accoutrements remained Scholastica's top priority in the first two decades of her tenure as abbess. Not only the building itself, but its decorations and its ambiance. She gave permission to a nun, Sister Donna Zelante, to teach several girls how to sing plainsong chant. When masses and other services were held in the new church, the trained nuns would sing in a choir room above the sanctuary. Le Murate quickly gained a reputation for the singing of its nuns, so much so that the abbess could justify spending thirty florins on an organ sometime in the 1450s. The organ and reputation may have been what drew Sister Eugenia, the daughter of a nobleman raised in Viterbo, to the convent in 1461.[24]

The music was not without controversy. In the 1490s, during a moment of political crisis and fervent religious reform, the convent was publicly criticized for allowing 'satanic' polyphonic singing. A century later, the convent's confessor would be dismissed from his role when it was discovered he was teaching music. Despite this, the same archbishop who dismissed the confessor also allowed the abbess to waive a girl's dowry if she was deemed musically talented, particularly if she could sing in a bass voice.[25] The talent of the nuns' choir won out, likely because the people of the city enjoyed these singers reciting psalms for the souls of their loved ones.

Abbess Scholastica sought several other means to bolster the reputation of her convent and to bring in money to support it. Though the convent was among the largest and most popular, courting patrons from most of the important families in the city, the large sums were too sporadic to be the exclusive source of income. The recruitment of nuns, as well as the growing number of boarders, often outpaced the alms. Abbess Scholastica responded to this issue the way any well-raised Renaissance Florentine would. While the first walled-in women of Le Murate had supported themselves through begging, and their successors on Via Ghibellina relied on alms, Abbess Scholastica dedicated much of her abbacy to expanding the convent's real-estate portfolio and to training the nuns in several lucrative labours. The abbess persuaded 'the gentlemen lords of the republic to donate to the convent a street' between Via Ghibellina and 'three plots purchased by Abbess Simona, Scholastica's predecessor'. She also purchased a plot and enclosed it to make a garden and later three houses were added to expand the infirmary. Workrooms were equipped for the production of silk, gold thread, embroidery, and books. By the 1450s, the nuns of Le Murate were earning an average of 500 florins per year – enough to cover the annual living costs of thirty-five nuns.[26]

An opportunity for expanding the convent further, both physically and fiscally, came at the end of the following decade. In 1467, the Arno River flooded, devastating the entire city. The convent's infirmary, gardens, and scriptoria were ruined. The waters had risen so high that several lay people broke into the convent, heeding that distant call from Abbot Gomez, 'If the river flooded … who [would] free these women from impending ruin?'[27] Fortunately, none of the women or their rescuers perished, but Abbess Scholastica did have to send a representative to the papal court to plead their case; to enter a convent without the express permission of the vicar or archbishop was an excommunicable offence.[28] The rebuilding of the city moved along slowly, but in 1470 the city government granted 400 florins 'to complete the building of a new and much-needed infirmary'.[29]

In addition to the infirmary, Abbess Scholastica oversaw the expansion of the kitchen and the installation of a dispensary, 'where they could distill liquids and other necessary things, with the equipment and furnishings they used' to make medicines.[30] It is unclear when Le Murate began producing and selling medicines, but by 1500 they were one of six conventual pharmacies in Florence that provided services and treatments to the women of the city.[31] The practice grew out of the need for nuns to provide their own medical care to their ill and infirm and was bolstered by the Observant movement, particularly the preaching of Girolamo Savonarola, which encouraged selfless care for the poor and sick. In this spirit, the nuns often sold their medicines at a discounted rate. They could do this because they grew many of their own ingredients in their extensive gardens and orchards – Abbess Scholastica had overseen their expansion in the 1440s. This later earned them the ire of other non-monastic apothecaries but gained them the stalwart support of several leading physicians in the city who relied on their cheaper products.

Conventual gardens and apothecaries became increasingly essential over the course of the sixteenth century. During this time Florence experienced several sieges and consequent crises of famine and plague. With the citizens barricaded behind the city walls, the interior sources of food and medicine became vital to the city's survival. Consequently, the convents' pharmacies were of such importance that the nuns who directed them were afterwards often promoted as abbesses.[32] The role of head apothecary provided a nun with several years to interact with and broaden a vast network of suppliers, physicians, civic leaders, and other elite lay people like the Medici. A century after Scholastica's initiative to expand the infirmary and dispensary, the Le Murate apothecary, Sister

Umiliana Lenzi, had a long-term working relationship with the Grand Duke's apothecary and operated out of an expanded pharmacy that took up the first floor of several houses.[33]

In the year after Le Murate acquired the funding to expand the infirmary, the convent suffered a serious fire. Very early in the morning of 13 August 1471, 'fire attacked a room beside the oven where the laundry was boiled during the day. In an instant, it burned the kitchen and antekitchen'. Fortunately, the fire was extinguished before it could consume the rest of the convent. Lorenzo de' Medici, the young Lord of Florence, had been out for a walk in the neighbourhood. He was able to raise the alarm and summon a group of volunteers to fight the fire. Afterwards, he funded, and due to Abbess Scholastica's age and a recent illness that had left her weak, helped oversee the reconstruction of everything that had burned as well as the expansion of several other sections of the convent, including ten writing rooms, a laundry with new plumbing from a nearby well, two dormitories, a drainage system and several storage rooms 'with vaults to discourage the outbreak of fire'.[34] Sister Giustina tells us that the construction lasted three years and cost Lorenzo 5,000 florins. During this time, he 'respond[ed] to many other needs as well, providing grain, wine, and oil, always helping with favours, money, and support'. He also provided for several feasts, sent the women legumes for Lent and marzipan candies during the rest of the year.[35]

Lorenzo's relationship with Le Murate was 'always deeply affectionate', particularly during Abbess Scholastica's tenure. She had been abbess for a decade when Lorenzo was born. She had made connections with Lorenzo's grandfather, Cosimo, through Giovanni Benci. The abbess was present at the boy's baptism and was named one of his godparents. Throughout his life, he and Abbess Scholastica maintained a relationship through letters. Many of these survive and reveal a 'maternal intimacy' between the abbess and the young lord.[36] She acted as a moral and spiritual guide while also deftly directing his affections – and alms – to Le Murate. Though he 'did not wish to place his alms anywhere, choosing to hide [his] liberal, generous act of charity', the link between Lorenzo de' Medici and Le Murate was well-known and resulted in a stream of other patrons who wished to curry favour with the man in charge of the city.

When Abbess Scholastica died in 1475, she left behind a beloved, aspiringly self-sufficient, and generously funded convent with almost 200 inhabitants. Sister Giustina tells us that 'she left such an opinion of herself and of her convent that the nuns owed her a great debt and were left disconsolate and afflicted by her loss'.[37] Scholastica's son, Ugolino, himself a monk, paid for an inscribed marble plaque to be placed as a marker above her tomb. Sister Giustina writes that when the plaque arrived, 'they discovered that her body was intact and fragrant, surprising everyone as a marvellous sign'.[38] The nuns then felt reassured that she had been granted a place in heaven for all of the good she had accomplished for the convent.

The years that followed were markedly less expansive though not entirely stagnant. Abbess Caterina Ubaldini was elected and 'began very well'. She obtained a handful of large donations and purchased some land. Unfortunately, the real estate deals were bound up in some lawsuits for several years. A plague outbreak in 1478 that lasted until 1481 put a strain not only on the convent's finances but also exposed the convent to the outside world. Sister Giustina describes a near constant flow of 'beasts of burden, doctors and surgeons, priests, family members and other benefactors'.[39] Consequently, once the plague had subsided, Caterina had the convent door reconstructed and then sealed for five years 'for her convent's peace and quiet, for holy, just respect'. Sister Giustina simply comments that 'our mothers declare that the results satisfied her intention'. As the fifteenth century drew to a close, things took a turn for the worse in Italy. Plague and economic crisis had unsettled the tenuous peace held together by the far-reaching hand of Lorenzo de' Medici.

When Catherine de' Medici was removed from Le Murate in 1530, the city of Florence had been under siege for nearly a year and Italy had been engulfed in war for more than three decades. It was trapped between several shifting alliances between the papacy, the Holy Roman Empire, and the kingdom of France. In the preceding years, the papacy had allied itself with France, then the Empire, and then France again as both armies and their bands of mercenaries marched back and forth across the Italian peninsula. Florence, and several other Italian cities, states, and guilds, attempted to navigate a safe path through this era of turmoil caused by the ongoing series of Italian Wars (1494–1559).

The wars developed out of the long-standing rivalries between the several republics, duchies, and kingdoms of Italy. In the middle of the fifteenth century, these rivalries had been briefly settled under the guidance of such prominent men as Cosimo de' Medici of Florence and Francesco Sforza of Milan. The Treaty of Lodi, signed in 1454 by the five largest states on the peninsula (Florence, Milan, Naples, Venice, and the Papal States) put an end to three decades of warring in Lombardy, in central northern Italy. A fragile political equilibrium was then maintained for nearly forty years under the direction of first Cosimo and then his grandson, Lorenzo, sometimes called 'the Magnificent'. The death of Lorenzo in 1492 could not have come at a worse time for Italy. The Medici bank was faltering, a relatively new king of France, Charles VIII (r. 1483–1498), was eager to make claims on the kingdom of Naples, and a religious frenzy, with Girolamo Savonarola at its head, was sweeping through the region. Lorenzo's heir, Piero the Unfortunate (d. 1503), was no match for the unfurling political chaos. Within two years of Lorenzo's death, the peninsula was under siege.

The power vacuum left by the de' Medici was filled by Ludovico Sforza (d. 1508), heir to Francesco and the duke of Milan, who, in 1494, invited Charles VIII of France to invade Italy and stake his claim to the throne of Naples, a kingdom which comprised the entire southern half of the peninsula. The French army crossed the Alps in September and was in Rome by Christmas. In late October, Charles had reached the outskirts of Florence where he met with the hapless de' Medici heir. Piero arrived at the French camp with only a few loyal retainers and no bargaining chips. The peace talks were a devastating humiliation. Piero handed over control of the cities of Livorno and Pisa, the important seaport brought under Florentine control in his grandfather's lifetime and a pet project of his father who had drained the marshes and established a university there.[40] In exchange, Charles promised to recognize Piero as the ruling authority in Florence. News of the deal reached the city quickly and enraged the already disenchanted patrician class. When Piero and his men returned to the city they were pelted with mud. The agreement with the French was denounced by the city's government and messengers were sent to a cadet branch of the Medici family in the hope that they would send mercenary reinforcements while the city scrambled to organize the local able-bodied men into a defensive force. While the French army gathered outside the city walls, bounties were issued for Piero and his relatives on the inside. He and his immediate family were able to flee the city, but other de' Medici relatives were less fortunate as angry Florentines mobbed their homes and sacked the Palazzo de' Medici.

Florence was divided between those few but powerful families who had built their success around the Medici and those who had seen their fortunes diminished during the long reign of Lorenzo (r. 1469–1492). Beneath these patricians, there also lived a burgeoning class of craft guild members, lawyers, and ambitious merchant-bankers. In the midst of the crisis, many of the citizens tied their hopes and anti-Medici politics to the rising star of Girolamo Savonarola (d. 1498). The Dominican friar had gained a reputation as a passionate preacher, defender of the poor, and ardent critic of corruption in the church, particularly at the papal court, and among the Medici surrogates within the Florentine government.[41] He initially preached reconciliation with the Medici supporters and led the negotiations with the French king who marched into the city with 10,000 soldiers on 17 November. Even with Piero exiled from the city, Florence's position had hardly improved. They benefitted only from the fact that King Charles did not have Florence as his end goal in the peninsula but was instead in a hurry to reach Naples. He rescinded French claims on Pisa, though the city then declared itself independent, and dropped his demand that Piero be reinstated as lord of the city. Finally, in exchange for 120,000 florins (approximately 425 kilograms of gold), the French would neither sack Florence, nor station any French troops there. On 28 November, Charles took his army and marched south, leaving Florence to manage its own political fate.

Immediately, factions formed among the citizens – all property-owning, tax-paying male guildmembers or patricians. A divided patrician class was faced with perhaps the largest and most politically active middle class that Florence had ever held. It was these men who called a *parlamento* in the city's main square, the Piazza della Signoria. There, the majority voted to dissolve the Councils of One Hundred and of Seventy, the current legislative bodies, and called for a new constitution for the city. Again, Savonarola exerted his influence, preaching the supremacy of the Venetian style constitution.

> 'It was Brother Jerome alone who made it possible to avoid all this confusion and chaos. He introduced the Great Council … proposed the appeal to the Signoria … He brought universal peace… Without doubt these efforts saved the city … Because the results of his works were so good, and because several of his prophecies were fulfilled, many people continued to believe for a long time that he was truly sent by God …'[42]

At the end of 1494, as the French army was reaching Rome and Piero was selling the Medici family jewels in Venice, the Florentine public installed a new Great Council. Any citizen whose family had been eligible to hold a public office for at least three generations was now eligible to sit on the council – approximately 3,000 Florentine men were eligible by this standard. A new building to house this massive government body was begun right away and completed in 1496. As the walls of the new council went up, the political and social divisions of the city intensified.

The exile of the Medici had not been simply a rejection of one family, corrupted by power, but of their entire culture at court. While the Medici, and their supporters, had fully invested in the new humanist trends in literature and the arts, many others in Florence had continued to adhere to more traditional modes of knowledge and self-expression. In the dramatic shift of 1494, Savonarola found a place at the head of a social movement that resented the changes wrought by mercantile prosperity and the revival of 'pagan' motifs and philosophy. There was a hunger for prophecy, for austerity and piety, and for a religious revival, particularly among those Florentines who were not enfranchised by the series of government reforms during the fifteenth century. All of this was exacerbated by the humiliating failure of Piero de' Medici and the loss of Pisa, which would result in a drawn-out and expensive fight to retake the port city. The friar satisfied these appetites with his charismatic preaching against the 'modern' sins rife in the city and with prophecies about the sure and swift victory over Pisa that would result from the city's reconfirmation to Christ. Savonarola was leading his flock down a time-honoured path in medieval Italian culture, prophesying a way out of the second age – the Age of the Son, first proposed by the Italian monk and prophet, Joachim of Fiore (d. 1202) – and into the third age, the Age of the Spirit. To accomplish this transition first required that the church, the government, and the populace itself be purged of vanities, vices, and villains.

Savonarola and his most devout followers, the *Piagnoni*, or Snivellers, led the charge against gambling, prostitution, homosexuality, and usury (charging interest on loans to fellow Christians). Gambling was outlawed and the state-run brothels were shut down. Homosexuality, which was sometimes referred to specifically as the 'Florentine vice' by other Italians, had never been legalized in Florence, but had become tacitly accepted. Savonarola 'preached for the harshest penalties … such as death by stoning or burning'.[43] Young boys, sons of Piagnoni parents, were recruited into 'Bands of Hope' which patrolled the city looking for underground gambling dens and brothels, or harassing men suspected of homosexuality or women who were 'inappropriately dressed' by pelting them with rocks. Savonarola also preached against the presence of Jews in the city, particularly those who functioned as pawnbrokers and small-time bankers, providing loans to poorer guildsmen and businesses that were deemed insignificant by the larger Christian banks. In 1495, the Piagnoni faction in the Great Council was able to pass legislation ordering the expulsion of the Jewish population from the city, but it was not seriously enforced, and no major exodus occurred. The law was repealed the following year, signalling perhaps the declining religious fervour in the city, or at least Savonarola's increasingly precarious political position.

Savonarola's power reached its peak in February 1497, culminating in the 'Bonfire of the Vanities'. The friar preached that only by being 'reduced by these scourges to true and simple Christianity [could] Florence recover Pisa and whatever else it had lost'.[44] Coinciding with the time traditionally set aside for Carnival, he instead led a crowd through a religious procession that ended with the burning of anything deemed vain or sinful.

> 'At carnival, a day generally celebrated with a thousand iniquities, they first held a religious procession full of devotion; then they would go about collecting dice, cards, make-up, shameful books and pictures, and then would burn them all in the Piazza della Signoria … Every day the friar urged men to abandon pomp and vanity, to return to the simplicity of religion and the Christian life. To this end he proposed laws concerning the ornaments and clothing that women and children wore …'[45]

Savonarola even preached against the supposed vanity among the nuns at Le Murate who set aside time during Lent to make gold thread. In previous years, he had also condemned their use of music as 'satanic'. Shortly after pronouncing his criticism, however, he personally visited the convent to preach to the nuns. That sermon was much kinder, acknowledging the long-standing and well-respected piety of Le Murate. It was one of the few moments where Savonarola seems to have pulled back on his condemnations – a testament to the influence of the beloved convent despite its Medici ties.

Savonarola's message and methods were not only unpopular among the Medici loyalists, whom he would have described as lascivious and vain, but also among the church officials in the papal court, including Pope Alexander VI (d. 1503). The pope had first ordered Savonarola to stop publicly preaching in October of 1495. At that time, he had the full support and protection of the Florentine government. By the spring of 1497, the situation had changed. Piero had appeared in April at the city gates with a small armed guard, apparently encouraged by a conspiratorial group of patricians within the city. In June, Savonarola was excommunicated, and the threat of a papal interdict loomed over the city. The friar reluctantly retreated to his monastery of San Marco and refrained from preaching until Christmas. In February 1498, as the Lenten season began, he resumed preaching publicly but was quickly shut down by the Signoria.

Each piece of Savonarola's reform movement had inspired a countermovement. The 'Bands of Hope' found themselves coming up against anti-Savonarola gangs known as *compagnacci*. Their membership was made up of those young men put out of work by the crackdown on vices and their patrician clients who chafed under the moral restraints of the new government. On several occasions, these groups disrupted sermons by Savonarola and his loyal preachers. Within the Great Council, the Piagnoni-Snivellers were countered by a growing faction which they labelled the *Arrabbiati*, or 'The Rabid Ones'. At first, these 'rabid' anti-Savonarola groups were led mostly by patricians, either still loyal to the Medici family or nervous about the increasingly radical, perhaps even revolutionary, Florentine plebian classes, but as the fight for Pisa dragged on and conditions in Florence failed to improve, many began to abandon the Savonarola reforms.

The final blow to Savonarola's influence came in April 1498 when the Dominican friar was challenged to a trial by ordeal by members of the Franciscan Order, the rival branch of mendicant preachers. While Savonarola's star had risen, the Franciscans' had dimmed. The Dominican friar had adopted the Franciscan traditions of prophecy, particularly those prophecies pronounced by Joachim of Fiore which had declared that it would be the Franciscans who would usher in the next and final age of history. Savonarola had also made a name for himself through his preaching to the poor, to the marginalized, and to women. These groups had traditionally been audiences for Franciscan preachers. Now, the flow of alms and attention were redirected to the Dominican churches and houses in Florence. So, the Franciscans made a public summons, accusing Savonarola of preaching false prophecies.

On 7 April, a crowd gathered in the Piazza della Signoria to watch Savonarola's representative, Domenico da Pescia, and his Franciscan opponent walk through fire. Savonarola, holding a communion wafer aloft, arrived at the head of a train of Dominican friars 'dressed in their most formal robes', singing psalms. Around them a crowd of their supporters carried lighted torches. The stage was set, and the crowd was ready, but then the two factions of friars began to argue over the details of the ordeal.

> 'There arose some difficulty concerning the clothing Brother Domenico da Pescia [a Dominican] was to wear, for the Franciscans feared some sort of enchantment or spell. Since

> they could not agree, the Signoria sent two citizens for each side to iron out their differences … When they finally came close to a settlement … the Franciscans heard that Brother Domenico intended to enter the fire with the body of Christ in his hand. They objected very strongly, saying that if the Host burned, it would be a grave scandal … After long argument, with each side persisting in its position, no agreement could be reached, so they all went home without even lighting the wood'.[46]

In another account, the fire was lit but then extinguished by a sudden storm.[47] Regardless, the gathered Florentines were irate. Even as Savonarola took to the pulpit 'to argue that the fault lay with the Franciscans', the crowd was turning on him. It is easy to imagine the angry jeers and accusations flung against Savonarola and the Franciscans, perhaps even chasing them out of the public square. The squabbling and delaying had broken the spell of Savonarola's sacred charisma. The consequences were immediate and dire. The following day, a mob stormed the monastery of San Marco and the homes of several of Savonarola's political allies.

> 'Had [the mob] not been checked, it would have brought harm and destruction to the entire city, and ruined all the leaders of the friar's party. The mob then returned to San Marco, which was being stoutly defended … After a few hours they finally forced their way into San Marco, and took Brother [Girolamo], Brother Domenico, and Brother Silvestro da Firenze prisoners to the palace'.

The Great Council was summoned to a meeting and a new government was elected, ousting all of Savonarola's supporters. The three imprisoned friars were interrogated and tortured. Savonarola confessed to preaching false prophecies and agreed with his examiners that he, 'as a priest and a foreigner, had no right to engage in political activity in Florence'. These confessions were communicated to papal representatives who declared Savonarola a heretic. On 23 May, the three Dominicans were taken to the Piazza della Signoria, where they had so recently avoided fiery judgment, and were publicly hanged. Their bodies were burned and their ashes dumped in the Arno River.

Savonarola's arrest coincided with the death of Charles VIII. Only a few years later, Piero, Pope Alexander, and Ludovico would be dead. Still, war raged on with alliances between duchies, kingdoms, and states becoming increasingly convoluted. Florence continued to besiege Pisa which had the backing of several other Italian kingdoms as well as the Holy Roman Empire. Louis XII, king of France, continued to push French claims over the Kingdom of Naples, sometimes allying with Florence, sometimes with Venice, and other times with Spain, which also made claims on Naples. In 1508, after years of devastating sieges throughout the peninsula, resulting in thousands of deaths, Pope Julius II (r. 1503–1513) formed the League of Cambrai in the hopes of squashing the rising Venetian power, only to abandon this league in favour of the Holy League two years later, which aimed to oust France from Italy. Though this second league experienced some victory, it fell apart following Julius's death. In 1516, Louis XII died and his successor, Francis I, agreed to essentially splitting the Italian peninsula between himself and the King of Spain and for three brief years, there was a semblance of peace.

War broke out again following the death of the Holy Roman Emperor, Maximilien I, in 1519. His successor, Charles V, was not only Holy Roman Emperor, but also King of Spain, the Archduke of Austria, Lord of the Netherlands, and Duke of Burgundy. These territories created what is sometimes called the 'Hapsburg ring' around France. In a panic, France again allied itself with Venice and hoped for an alliance with the new pope, Leo X (r. 1513–1521), Catherine de' Medici's great uncle. Leo, however, sided with the Holy Roman Emperor in the hopes of securing aid in an attempt to suppress the early rumblings of the Protestant movement. The Italian peninsula was once again engulfed in war. It was not alone as fighting spread throughout Europe. The Holy Roman Empire seized nearly every French possession in Italy and successfully captured Francis I while he was leading forces into Spain. To gain his freedom, he renounced his claims to Milan and exchanged two of his sons as prisoners – the younger one, Henry, would later marry Catherine de' Medici.

Almost immediately after he was released, Francis entered an alliance with the papacy, which now feared the almost complete domination of the Holy Roman Empire on the continent. Unsurprisingly, the already decimated French forces were no match for the full weight of the empire. In 1527, imperial forces sacked the city of Rome. Sieges in Naples and Genoa resulted in several outbreaks of the plague, ripping through the already demoralized French army. Finally, in 1530, Florence fell to the imperial siege. Catherine de' Medici was removed to Rome and Alessandro de' Medici, believed to be her illegitimate half-brother, but more likely her cousin, son of Pope Leo X, triumphantly entered Florence. The Medici were back and would remain the unquestioned lords of Florence, and then of Tuscany as a whole, for two centuries.

During this chaos, Le Murate, like the rest of Italy, experienced increased factionalism and declining material conditions. Sister Giustina writes that at the end of the century, 'the city was afflicted with extreme misery so that the nuns received no donations'.[48] At one point during the final siege of the city, the convent became a refuge for 'a great number of gentlewomen, widows, married women, and girls of every age and condition retired in our community to flee the enemy's impetuous fury … They say there were more than a thousand of them'.[49] Looking back on this period of instability, Sister Giustina skims very lightly over the final three decades of the fifteenth century and the first few decades of the next. The exceptions to this omission highlight the fact that the convent was forced to look beyond the city walls for support. Over the turn of the century, the women of Le Murate would receive support from Milan, Jerusalem, Portugal, Rome, and France.

In 1450, many years before this chaos and during the time of Abbess Scholastica, Sister Eugenia Benedetta had come to the convent from Veneto, the region around Venice to the northeast of Florence, when she was thirty-three. She brought with her 'a fair bit of furniture and beautiful, fine linen'. The 'spirited young woman' ran into trouble with the convent's confessor who 'assigned what she [Eugenia] considered to be extraordinary acts of humiliation and penance to be performed by everyone'. She complained about this 'freely at every opportunity'. Irritated by this, the priest then forged a letter which he claimed was sent to him by the archbishop of the city. This letter ordered the abbess to expel Sister Eugenia from the convent because of her 'insolence, disobedience, and pomposity'. Sister Giustina tells us that the sisters of Le Murate did not want to send Sister Eugenia away, but out of their 'unfailing obedience', they provided her with a cloak and a singular florin to pay for food on her journey home.[50]

However, Eugenia did not go home. She asked the abbess for the archbishop's letter and 'went at once to the archbishop in Rome'. She presented the letter and told her story. The archbishop, 'full of just zeal', promised to support her case and to see that 'the person who had used episcopal authority with such arrogant presumptuousness' would be punished. Eugenia insisted that punishment was unnecessary and left Rome with the happy assurance that she could someday return to Le Murate. Sister Giustina writes that 'not long after her departure, the priest was called to Rome' and condemned to permanent exile.[51]

In the meantime, Eugenia 'dressed herself in men's clothes so that she could go anywhere' and entered a friary outside of Rome. She remained there, working alongside the brothers, until one day she accidentally exclaimed, 'I am exhausted!' using the feminine form of the adjective. When this caused a fuss, throwing suspicion on her, 'she left secretly, without delay', and entered another Franciscan friary in 'a new country'. There too, she was eventually suspected by one of the infirm brothers she cared for. So, 'with her usual shrewdness and wisdom' she departed. After this, she decided it would be best to go on pilgrimage to Jerusalem, rather than try another friary. On her way, she was allegedly imprisoned for a brief time but was able to break out of prison and continue to the holy city. She remained in Jerusalem, running a small hospital for pilgrims, 'until she was an old woman'. In her seventies, she resolved once again to go on a pilgrimage. First, she would go to Santiago de Compostela in Spain and then to Rome. It was on this pilgrimage that she was introduced to the Queen of Portugal, Leonora. Eugenia had fallen ill in Portugal on her way to northern Spain and was cared for by the queen and her household. During this time, while Queen Leonora cared for the old woman, Eugenia recounted her life story. She reminisced about Florence and her 'great familiarity and friendship with the venerable mothers of Le Murate … with a great flowing of tears and deep tenderness'.[52]

Afterwards, Eugenia did travel to Santiago de Compostela and then south through Spain, east along the Cote d'Azur of France, and finally back into northern Italy. Poor weather stalled her journey to Rome in Livorno on the west coast of Tuscany. There, she wrote to the sisters of Le Murate, requesting that she be allowed to return to her old convent to die. The nuns 'were delighted to have found [Eugenia] again, accepting her with singular piety and love'. She returned to Florence in 1492, just as the support of Lorenzo de' Medici was lost. The timing of Eugenia's return could not have been better. Shortly thereafter letters arrived from Jerusalem, Rome, and Portugal, inquiring after Eugenia's health.[53] Her return heralded an era of international patronage sent from the far corners of Christendom. The Queen of Portugal sent several gifts over the final years of the fifteenth century, but the first was the grandest. In 1497, the convent received '4 cases of fine sugar, weighing 1,000 net pounds, 300 pounds of *penniti* [sweet hard candies], a case of large *manuscristi* [pearl-shaped rose sugar candies], anises and candied almonds, 36 pots of apple marmalade, 6 jars of sugar and rose honey'.[54] The queen also sent 200 gold coins and a letter promising that she would send them sixty-five pounds of sugar every year and forty-eight pounds of fine sugar every three years. These donations from Portugal continued even under the next monarch with sugar, fruits, and candies arriving at the convent every year until 1559.

A year after the Portuguese treats began to arrive, Elena Orsini came to Le Murate. In her secular life, she had been the daughter of Lord Niccola Orsini, a count and 'general of the holy church and, eventually, of the Venetians'.[55] Fittingly, she was married off to a man of an equally important family, the Farnese. They lived together in Rome for a handful of years, attending 'the most important parties and splendid banquets', until her husband died. She then returned to her father and informed him that she wished to take the veil. Her entrance into Le Murate was accompanied by grand celebrations. She brought with her 500 florins and her father donated another 1,500 florins to the Florentine dowry fund. In her first years at the convent, she frequently received 'several lords and ladies from her family'.[56] In later years, she was able to call on her brother-in-law, Pope Paul III, who 'whenever she asked him, he sent at least 500' florins.[57] Several of her nieces followed in her footsteps bringing equally generous dowries and donations from family members. While she resided at the convent, she paid for the framing of the painting above the main altar, repairs to the organ and the furnace in the laundry, the drainage of the sewers outside the convent, and for the construction of a stone pergola in the garden.[58]

Sister Elena is indicative of a shift in Le Murate's recruitment. In the early days of the convent, the nuns had fulfilled the vision of girls of every fashion riding in a cart pulled by God's love. As the convent's reputation grew and as hard times strained the budget, it became both a given and a necessity that the newer sisters come from the upper echelons of society. While Elena Orsini was taking the veil, Caterina Sforza, daughter of the duke of Milan, turned her attention to the famous convent in Florence. Her first gift, thirty bushels of grain, arrived at a time when Sister Giustina tells us the nuns 'ate more dirt than bread'.[59] After this, 'she continually sent letters and other demonstrations of her love', including the money to construct a cell in which she intended to live, 'wishing to retire among them'.[60] It was in this cell that Catherine de' Medici, a relative of Caterina, lived for three years in the 1520s. Caterina did take the Benedictine habit in the final years of her life, dying at the convent in 1509. She was buried beside the altar in the church where, many years later, her grandson, Grand Duke Cosimo de' Medici built a sepulchre in her honour.

Catherine de' Medici was even more generous with the nuns of Le Murate as she 'confessed openly that they saved her life'. It is also easy to believe that Catherine's time at Le Murate may have been one of the brightest periods in her life. Both of her parents had died within a month of her birth. Her French mother, Madeleine de La Tour d'Auvergne, had died five days after she was born, likely from complications during labour, although there were rumours that she had died of the plague, or worse, syphilis contracted from her husband. Catherine's father died two weeks later 'from exhaustion' – he was only twenty-six. The infant Catherine was then removed to Rome where she was raised for a few years by a series of relatives, including her grandmother Alfonsina Orsini, under the protection of her great-uncle, Pope Leo X, and her other great-uncle, the future Pope Clement VII. As a child, she returned to Florence with her aunt, Clarice, but they were removed to the countryside almost immediately because of the danger of rebellion in Florence. The Medici men fled the city in 1527 and Catherine was placed under house arrest with her aunt, who died in the spring of 1528. It was after this that she was moved to her first convent and then to Le Murate, when an outbreak of the plague struck the first convent. During this time, she was a loathed asset of the Florentine Republic. The city was once again staunchly anti-Medici, putting them at odds with the invading imperial forces who backed Alessandro de' Medici. However, the city remained allied to France and the royals there took a keen interest in Catherine's security. When a French ambassador reported that the young girl was in good spirits, but 'little visited and esteemed' by the local government, the French king and queen insisted that her monthly allowance be increased. In the end, Catherine would be married to their second son, Henry, to settle peace between France and the imperially backed Alessandro de' Medici. Before Catherine left Florence to sail to Marseille for her wedding, she returned to Le Murate and granted them several gifts: twenty capes, 200 florins, the alms from a chapel outside the city and the rents from its attached farm, and the promise of 500 more florins the next year.

Catherine continued to send gifts for the rest of her life, thinking often and fondly of her time at Le Murate. Her life in France was only slightly less troubled than her life in Italy. Her husband was in love with another woman, Diane de Poitiers, on whom he showered gifts, chateaux, and public affection. The royal couple struggled to conceive a child, resulting in rumours about Catherine's fertility and suggestions that she should be put away and a new wife procured. These suggestions intensified when Henry's older brother died unexpectedly in 1536, and the couple became the dauphin and dauphine. After ten years, a child was finally born, with more in quick succession. Sister Giustina mentions that the sisters of Le Murate had offered up 'fervent and insistent prayers' for this conception and Catherine 'explicitly credited the sisters at least in part with her reproductive achievement'.[61] Indeed, throughout this period, Catherine had fostered an 'intensely intimate' relationship with the convent through the frequent exchange of letters and gifts, usually delivered by the ambassadors constantly moving between Paris and Florence.[62]

When Catherine became regent for her eldest son in 1559, she continued to lavish gifts on her favourite convent. The greatest of her gifts, however, came toward the end of her life. In 1584, only a few years before her death, she wrote to Le Murate 'to leave a memory of our singular love, benevolence, and grateful soul'. She still recalled her time there 'when Florence was besieged' and in hopes of returning the nuns' 'love, diligence, and liberality', she granted them extensive properties throughout Tuscany valued at 9,000 florins. Catherine also wrote to her relative, the Grand Duke Cosimo, requesting that he exempt these properties from any taxes for the sake of the convent, and sent an extra 500 florins to purchase more livestock for the farms attached to the properties.[63]

Sister Giustina dictated her chronicle in the decade after Catherine's death. Over the years, several copies were made. Most only survive in fragments, but the number indicates that the chronicle did have a decent number of readers. Or, perhaps, several copies were made to send to different patrons or potential patrons around the world. The convent's network was vast and cosmopolitan. Le Murate had come a long way from that small house dangling on the Rubaconte bridge. They had become an internationally recognized institution whose vast complex occupied several square blocks along the Via Ghibellina. Among their patrons had been duchesses, cardinals, popes, grand dukes, and queens. Many of these connections had been made by nuns and abbesses who had seen and seized every opportunity that was available in the rapidly changing scenery of Renaissance Italy. The business savvy of Scholastica Rondinelli, the self-confident ambition of Eugenia Benedetta, and the throng of increasingly wealthy Medici and Orsini women who flocked to Le Murate carved out a space in Florence where women could learn to read, sing, sew, mix medicines, grow herbs and orchards, or write songs and histories celebrating not only their God, but their city, their families, and their sisterhood.

Chapter Six

A Nun on the Run

As midnight approached, the nuns of San Sebastian gathered in their convent's choir to sing the psalms. Their 'mournful tone' filled the room as a young novice impatiently waited for the first lesson to begin.[1] As the music came to an end and the first lesson began, Catalina de Erauso approached her aunt Ursula, the abbess, asking to be excused from the late-night ritual because she felt ill. Ursula pressed her hand to her niece's forehead and sent her to bed. Catalina did not go to bed. Instead, she grabbed a lamp and hurried to her aunt's cell. She had been sent there earlier that day to fetch a book and had spotted the keys to the convent 'dangling from a nail on the wall'.[2] She had left the cell door unlocked. It was lucky her aunt had been busy that evening and had not returned to lock it. With the keys in hand, Catalina rummaged through her aunt's desk and cabinets for the other supplies she would need: a needle, thread, and scissors. She found all three as well as some money.

From her aunt's cell, Catalina proceeded through the convent, opening several doors and then locking them behind her. Finally, at the last one, standing on the threshold to the world outside, she 'shook off [her] veil and went out into a street [she] had never seen'.[3] The fifteen-year-old Catalina had lived in the convent since she was four. Her only knowledge of the world had come from convent chronicles and the occasional peek through a high window. 'Without any idea which way to turn', she began her journey. For three days, she hid in a chestnut grove on what she assumed was the 'outskirts of the convent grounds' while she made a plan. She turned her blue bodice and green petticoat into a doublet, breeches, and hose. She deemed her nun's habit 'useless' and threw it away. She did the same with her hair, taking the stolen scissors and lopping off what must have been several inches to create a boyish cut. Sufficiently disguised, Catalina set out, 'threading [her] way down roads and passing villages, until [she] came to the town of Vitoria'.

In Vitoria, a few days' walk south of San Sebastian, Catalina's luck held out. She met Francisco de Cerralta, a doctor of theology, who happened to be married to one of her aunts. For three months, Catalina, now going by the name Francisco Loyola, lived with the theologian and his wife, helping with Latin readings and chores. It was a pleasant enough situation; Cerralta provided new clothes and desperately wanted Loyola to stay on as his assistant.[4] He even went so far as 'to lay hands' on the young man, 'pleading and insisting' that he stay. This was too much for the young runaway who had perhaps fled the convent of San Sebastian, in part, to escape a nun who had beaten her.[5] So, Loyola/Erauso 'relieved' his hosts of a bit of money and hopped on the first wagon out of town.

Erauso was diving into a world he did not know, but he was not alone. Even the people living outside the convent walls sometimes struggled to recognize the world they inhabited. The sixteenth century had witnessed radical changes, not only on European maps but in nearly every aspect of life. New plants and foods, new animals, new languages and religions were all being documented, collected, and evaluated for either eradication or incorporation. The revelation that two continents existed on the other side of the Atlantic was perhaps the greatest shock in history. The rush to conquer, explore, colonize, and profit from these places resulted in a Europe that hardly recognized itself and forced every European to reevaluate their place in the world. This was especially true in kingdoms like Spain, which was intensely involved in the process of colonization and expansion in nearly every corner of the globe.

Yet, it is difficult to know how much of this information made its way into the convent in San Sebastian. Catalina was a member of a well-connected family full of military men, ship captains, and government officials. Though rules around enclosure and communication with the outside world had tightened in the last century, the abbess, Catalina's aunt, would still have kept informed of major political and social changes. It was necessary to know about these things to maintain the social networks and supply chains on which the convent depended. We might imagine Catalina receiving word from her family through her aunt. All her brothers, like their father, had joined the Spanish military. One of them, Miguel, would become a secretary to a high official in Peru. One of their uncles captained a ship that escorted silver shipments from Venezuela. Did Catalina hear stories about them and long for similar adventures? Over the course of her life, Catalina would find adventure as a royal page, a sailor, a merchant's assistant, a soldier, a sword-wielding gambler, and, finally, a mule driver. During this time, she mostly went by the name Alonso, though she eventually settled on Antonio de Erauso. Information about Erauso comes from several documents, notably the petition and testimonies sent to the king in the 1620s, as well as an autobiography detailing the runaway nun's life.

The autobiography was also intended as a supporting document for the petition to the king for a pension for Erauso's military service in Peru and Chile. It is an easy-to-read adventure tale of a listless youth who meandered his way to the New World and then stumbled from one opportunity to another. Erauso's life was one of work, violence, evading the law, and taking advantage of religion. Through a series of events, Erauso eventually ended up back in a convent, but only briefly and with the intention of saving his own skin. Besides this brief re-enclosure and the signature on the petition to the king, Erauso never returned to women's clothes or his birth name, Catalina. There has been a dizzying amount of debate about how to handle this. Was Erauso a trans man? Or was Erauso a woman who knew that to be a man was to have more freedom of choice and more security from particular types of violence in sixteenth-century Spain? Did Catalina cut her hair and wear breeches and a sword as a desperate disguise, or because she found being a woman uncomfortable and unwanted? We can never know definitively and, frankly, the obsession over Erauso's 'real' gender and 'true' sexuality has been a distraction from other more interesting details in the autobiography, like the strained dynamic between church and crown which Erauso manipulates so well. Throughout this chapter I will use the series of names that Erauso used. Often times I will pair the name Erauso with his current last name – Loyola, Guzman, etc. – to indicate the tension between Erauso and his chosen disguise. I will also, almost exclusively, use he, him, and his in reference to Erauso. In my opinion, this is a common courtesy. For most of his life, even after his secret was revealed, Erauso used a man's name, dressed as a man, and lived as a man, so to refer to him repeatedly as the woman, Catalina, would be to ignore everything Erauso had done and written in his long and storied life.

* * *

This life really began in Valladolid, a city in north central Spain that was briefly the royal capital. Erauso arrived in June 1600, but tells us that the royal court had already moved to the city. The official move did not happen until 1601. This is, perhaps, one of the chronological inconsistencies in Erauso's autobiography. Living as Loyola, the boy was able to secure a job as a page with one of the king's secretaries. Perhaps this man, Juan de Idiáquez, had arrived in Valladolid ahead of the royal court to prepare the city and royal properties. Regardless, Erauso's autobiography tells us that, as Francisco Loyola, he worked for Idiáquez for seven months, only departing after his father arrived. Captain Miguel de Erauso, a decorated soldier and prominent citizen of San Sebastian, had come to report that his daughter had escaped her convent and to ask for help finding her. The sound of the 'anguish in [her] father's voice', spurred Erauso to leave the city. The next day, 'with no better idea of where to go, or what to do, than let [himself] be carried off like a feather in the wind', Loyola/Erauso paid for a seat on a wagon headed to Bilbao.[6]

There, Loyola/Erauso's luck faltered. There was no available lodging, and the runaway was stuck wandering the city streets. Other youths spotted this new-to-town young man and followed him, trying to corner him in a dark street or alley. Fed up, Loyola/Erauso picked up some stones and 'let one of them have it'. After the brawl that likely broke out, the whole lot of them were arrested. One of Loyola/Erauso's attackers was badly injured. Loyola/Erauso was detained in a Bilbao jail for a month. It would not be the last time. After it was apparent that the injured boy would live, Loyola/Erauso was released, but with significantly lighter pockets having had to pay for the stay in jail. Leaving Bilbao, he found more work as a page in the town of Estella to the east in Navarre. For two years, the page was 'well-fed and well-clothed', but he was restless. So, 'with no more reason than that it suited [him]', he returned to San Sebastian. There, in his hometown, he 'remained completely unrecognized, a well-dressed young bachelor'. Even Erauso's mother did not recognize the young man when he visited his old convent to hear mass.

Going unrecognized by his mother was perhaps the last push Erauso needed to leave his homeland in the Basque Country of northeastern Spain. Shortly after the encounter, he travelled to the port town of Pasajes and boarded a ship to Seville. There, he met a Basque captain, 'a native of [his] own province', and secured work as a ship's boy on one of the galleons escorting a general's fleet to Venezuela. Coincidentally, the captain of that ship, Esteban Eguiño, was a first cousin to Erauso's mother – the Basque Country was apparently quite small. Without this Basque connection, Erauso would have had significantly more trouble getting on a ship to the colonies. At the turn of the century, the Spanish authorities had ramped up an effort to control the flow of Spanish men out of the kingdom. In 1607, only a few years after Erauso sailed the Atlantic, the punishment for crossing without the proper paperwork, or for aiding someone in the crossing, was elevated to the death penalty.[7] This would not be the last time that Erauso relied on the aid of fellow Basques. The strong, almost unconditional, loyalty between Basques would be one of his most precious currencies in the Spanish colonies.

Though Captain Eguiño took a liking to Erauso, making him his cabin boy, the work was difficult and dangerous. On the journey from Seville to Venezuela, the fleet encountered enemy ships – Erauso's first experience in battle – and many men died of disease at one of the ports on the way. In the first quarter of the seventeenth century, an estimated 36,000 sailors 'failed to return to Spain,' many died, but others, like Erauso, likely seized the opportunity to go ashore and find work in the markets and mines of the west.[8] When the ships were loaded with silver to return to Spain, Erauso 'dealt [the captain] a heavy blow, helping [himself] to five hundred pesos', before leaving the ship.[9] Having abandoned posts as a page and a sailor, Erauso managed to find work as a page for a treasury agent. Finding work would be an easy endeavour for Erauso in the first several years of living abroad. An able-bodied, literate Spanish man was a prized commodity, and few people asked any follow-up questions of the Basque lad. The treasury agent left Venezuela for Panama where, once again, Erauso, displeased with the low pay, changed jobs. Juan de Urquiza, a successful merchant, hired Erauso and took him from Panama to Ecuador and then to Peru.

It was in Peru that Erauso's life began to unfurl into the violent chaos that would thrust him into the limelight. Things started well enough with Erauso proving to be a skilled assistant, capable of organizing transport for large shipments of grain, silver, and pack animals, and surprisingly trustworthy for someone who had made a habit of 'relieving' others of money so he could skip town. Then Erauso's troubles began. An angry exchange with another man at a theatre resulted in a fight and overturned the comfortable life Erauso had started to build in Peru. Erauso murdered the man and had no choice but to flee the city. A vengeful friend of Erauso's first victim followed the trail only to end up on the wrong end of Erauso's blade as well. Erauso again had no choice but to flee, but not without the help of his boss, who provided 'two suits of clothing, two thousand six hundred pesos, [and] a letter of introduction'.

This was how Erauso arrived in Lima, the largest city in the Spanish colonies, and home to an archbishop, the royal courts, and one of the most important ports in the western hemisphere. Dubbed the 'Very Noble and Loyal City of Kings', Lima was a city in a constant state of expansion. The viceregal court and booming merchant class ensured that the city's buildings were large and opulent. It also housed a cathedral, 'much like the one in Seville', as well as twelve convents, eight hospitals, a hermitage, and a university.[10] Situated in a verdant valley at the confluence of two rivers, Lima was well-positioned to become the imperial centre of New Spain. The sea breeze kept the city cool and less prone to disease than many other cities in the west.

Though Erauso had come to Lima with a letter of introduction and found work with Diego de Solarte, a wealthy merchant friend of his previous boss, it would not last. After nine months, Erauso was told he 'should think about making [a] living elsewhere'. The young assistant had earned Solarte's ire after he was discovered flirting with one of

Solarte's sisters-in-law. So, 'in a sticky spot, with no work and no friends', Erauso joined the army.

In the same way that none of the bureaucrats or merchants who had hired Erauso asked many questions, neither did the military. The Spanish conquest of South America had stalled in central Chile, along the Bio-Bio River, almost a half century before Erauso enlisted. The Spanish had been at war with the Mapuche, a people they called the Araucanians, since 1546. By 1600, the year Erauso escaped the convent, the war was only beginning, and the Spanish crown had spent more than four million pesos on the war – a tenth of the total cost. In the decade leading up to Erauso's enlistment, every Spanish town south of the Bio-Bio River had been razed by Mapuche forces. The threat of resistance spreading north of the river was met by the Spanish authorities, who began an intense campaign to recruit soldiers for a standing army of unprecedented cost and size – besides supplying armour and weapons, each soldier was to be paid an annual salary of 280 pesos. Signing up to be a soldier in this army was seen as a desperate last resort. So desperate that Solarte's anger was erased, and he tried 'to speak to the company officers and get [Erauso's] enlistment annulled'. Erauso waved him off, however, insisting that he 'had a mind to travel and see a bit of the world'. So, he left Lima 'in a troop of one thousand six hundred men' and went to Concepción in Chile.

Erauso claimed in a later petition to the king that he served in the army in Chile for fifteen years. Other friends of Erauso, writing letters to support the petition, claimed Erauso had served for twelve or eighteen years.[11] In reality, Erauso signed on as a soldier in 1608 and served for no more than four years. Later, Erauso would re-enter the army and serve for another year or so. In the first stint of service, Erauso, now going by the name of Alonso Diaz Ramirez de Guzman, was originally meant to be stationed at Paicabí, 'a soldier's worst nightmare', but, once again, Erauso encountered a relative – his older brother, Miguel. As usual, Erauso went unrecognized, but benefited from the Basque connection. Miguel, who was working as a secretary to the governor, had been taking roll of the new soldiers, asking their names and origins. When he heard that Guzman/Erauso was from San Sebastian, 'he dropped his pen, threw his arms around [Guzman/Erauso], and asked for news of his father and mother, his brothers and sisters, and his beloved Catalina, the nun'. The two had supper together and Alonso/Catalina tried to give Miguel as much San Sebastian news as possible without revealing who he was. After this, Miguel pulled some strings with his boss and had his new friend from San Sebastian transferred to his own company.[12]

For three years, according to the autobiography, Alonso Diaz Ramirez de Guzman was his 'brother's soldier, and dined at his table … all the while never letting on to [his] secret'. Things might have continued peacefully, but the siblings fell out over a woman. Miguel had a mistress in town who Alonso also visited, sometimes with Miguel and other times alone. When Miguel discovered these solo visits, 'imagining the worst, he told [Alonso] that he'd better not catch [him] at it again'. Yet, Guzman/Erauso returned to the woman's house, unaware or unbothered that his brother was spying on him. When Guzman/Erauso left the house, Miguel 'lit into [him] with his belt'. The ensuing brawl brought the attention of an army captain who broke up the fight but advised Guzman/Erauso to 'take refuge in the church of San Francisco'. There, Guzman/Erauso waited until Miguel returned a few days later to inform him that he had been banished to his original post, Paicabí.[13]

Erauso describes the time in Paicabí as 'three years of misery'.[14] The outpost itself was named after a Mapuche chief who had been killed in 1553 in an early battle of the long-running Araucanian War (c. 1546–1880).[15] Though it was the headquarters for all military operations on the Chilean frontier, it was little more than a singular fortress on the edge of a wide plain. The army of 5,000 Spaniards was forced to set up camp in the surrounding open fields. Only a few years before Guzman/Erauso arrived, Mapuche forces had raided and sacked the entire area, burning most of the fortress to the ground. The army was there to rebuild and rebuff Mapuche successes. Erauso recounts that the Spanish and Mapuche battled 'three or four times', with the Spanish taking the upper hand until Mapuche reinforcements arrived for a final battle.

> '… it went badly for us, and they killed many of our men, captains, my own lieutenant, and rode off with the company flag. When I saw the flag being carried off I rodc after it, with two horsemen at my side, through the midst of a great

> multitude of Indians, trampling and slashing away and taking some wounds in return. Before long, one of the three of us fell dead… then my other companion went down, spitted on a lance. I had taken a bad blow to the leg, but I killed the chief who was carrying the flag, pulled it from his body and spurred my horse on… until at last I reached our own lines and fell from my horse'.[16]

Guzman/Erauso was carried to a medical tent where his wounds were treated. Several of Guzman's friends, including Miguel, his brother, came to his bedside when news reached the higher ranks. The wounds were serious enough that the two soldiers put aside their earlier quarrel and were friends again. A few months later, Guzman/Erauso received the flag he had rescued and a promotion to lieutenant. The autobiography tells us that Guzman/Erauso served as a lieutenant for five years and was almost promoted to the rank of captain – equal to his brother and father. During this time, the army 'rampage[d] … slashing and burning Indian croplands', and occasionally met Mapuche warriors in battle. The Spanish 'all but ate, drank, and slept in [their] armour'.[17] Despite these dangers, or perhaps because of them, Erauso seems to have remembered these days fondly, describing it as a 'quiet life'. The quiet did not last as 'chance toyed with [Guzman/Erauso], turning every scrap of luck into disaster'.[18]

Once again, an angry exchange, this time at a card game, resulted in Guzman/Erauso's blade hilt deep in a man's chest. When a judge attempted to arrest the lieutenant, he received the same treatment. Guzman/Erauso fled into a nearby church and hid, claiming sanctuary for several months. This would become one of Erauso's favourite strategies. Having been raised in a convent and not averse to befriending friars and priests, Erauso had learned how to manipulate the ongoing tensions between the church and the crown. The concept of sanctuary – a person's right to protection from civil authorities by calling on the church and remaining on sacred grounds – had been outlawed in 1570. This was part of a much longer trend of civil courts attempting to eliminate loopholes provided by canon law and ecclesiastical courts. In the eyes of a civil lawyer, it was bad enough that clergy could request that they be tried exclusively in their own courts. The abuse of sanctuary by the laity went too far. However, the Catholic Church resisted this change and continued to encourage clergy to protect the right of sanctuary into the nineteenth century.[19] On multiple occasions, Erauso not only sought sanctuary, but was offered it by friars, priests, and bishops alike who, rather than approving of Erauso's violent crimes, were making a clear political statement about the Church's rights.

The stalemate between the soldier and the law lasted long enough that 'the general air of alarm seemed to lift, and as [Guzman/Erauso] began to feel more at ease and even receive visits from friends', he agreed to act as a friend's second in a late-night duel. The lackadaisical atmosphere – Guzman/Erauso 'dined and chatted about one thing or another' before heading to the duel with his friend – was abruptly broken when the duel dragged on. The original fighters landed several blows and Guzman/Erauso and the other second stepped in. They fought in the darkness so thick that Guzman/Erauso had 'suggested [he and his friend] should tie [their] handkerchiefs around [their] arms so that, whatever might happen in the next couple hours, [they] would not mistake one another'.[20] Finally, Guzman/Erauso landed a fatal blow. His opponent fell the ground, shouting, 'Ah, traitor, you have killed me!' It was the familiar voice of Miguel de Erauso.

Stunned, Guzman/Erauso ran back to the church and brought two friars to perform Miguel's last rites. The church was surrounded by the governor's personal guard. Guzman/Erauso 'watched from the choir' as the friars buried his brother. Charged with rebellion, Guzman/Erauso remained in the church for several months before an opportunity arose to flee. Equipped with a horse and some weapons from a friend, Guzman/Erauso rode out of town and out of Chile. Guzman/Erauso was, as he later complained, running out of luck. The tragic turn of events in Concepción marked the beginning of a troubled decade for Guzman/Erauso.

The route out of Chile was difficult and deadly. Guzman/Erauso made two companions on the road up into the Andes. Neither survived the road down. Our fugitive barely made it, surviving only through a chance encounter with two ranchers who took him to their boss, a wealthy widow, 'the daughter of a Spaniard and an Indian woman'.[21]

Guzman/Erauso benefited from the woman's kindness and from her desire to marry off her daughter, 'a girl as black and ugly as the devil', according to Erauso.[22] The woman allowed Guzman/Erauso to recover from the arduous trek through the mountains and escorted him to the nearest town, Tucumán. There, Guzman/Erauso made a series of excuses to put off marrying the woman's daughter while he looked for work. He 'struck up a casual friendship with the bishop's secretary', and scored an invitation to a card game where he met yet another eager matchmaker who proposed that Guzman/Erauso marry his niece. Not wanting to offend the members of the bishop's social circle, '[Guzman/Erauso] pretended to be quite humbled by his flattering intentions'. He met with the girl, who he dubbed the 'little vicaress', and happily received the small chest of gifts she sent to him 'simply as a compliment, and having nothing to do with the dowry itself'. Having acquired an entirely new wardrobe, including a new velvet suit, Guzman/Erauso 'saddled up and vanished. And [he] never heard exactly what became of the black girl or the little vicaress'.[23]

It was a journey of three months from Tucumán in northern Argentina to Guzman/Erauso's next stop, the infamous mining town of Potosí. Along the way, Guzman/Erauso 'fell in with a soldier', a welcome partner to ward off the loneliness and the thieves. Despite the 'hard travel and several bad scrapes' the two survived, going their separate ways in the new town where neither of them knew a soul. Guzman/Erauso put his new suit to good use and was able to secure employment as a steward to an alderman visiting from La Plata. For 900 pesos a year, Guzman/Erauso, assisted by a team of eighty natives, was supposed to drive several thousand head of llama between towns. However, his new boss got 'mixed up in an unpleasant business … and the whole thing led to quarrels and hostages and the confiscation of property'.[24]

This was practically business as usual for the men who worked in and around Potosí. The mining city, like much of the Spanish colonies, was intensely hierarchical. The Spanish-born men ruled from appointed positions over nearly every aspect of society. Spanish men who had been born in the colonies, whether they had two Spanish parents or only one, were barred from holding these enviable positions because the Crown preferred to use them as gifts to loyal supporters. Given the restrictions on immigration from Spain and the persistent lack of Spanish women, many Spaniards in the colonies were considered *criollos* and were relegated to a permanently lesser position. Some discontent was dealt with by granting these men power over the African and native slaves who worked in the mines and on the *encomiendas.* However, in times of economic difficulty, discontent boiled over into rebellion. This was the case in the early seventeenth century as the price of silver began to tumble and the prosperity of the Spanish Empire, already restricted to an exclusive minority, began to dry up. So, when work with the alderman fell through, Guzman/Erauso, considered a Spanish-born veteran, was recruited by the mayor to put down a rebellion of embittered *criollos*.

Alonso Ibañez, a local with a reputation for rallying the 'poor and lost vagabonds' of the city, led a brief uprising. It was a violent affair, but one of surprisingly little note in the historical record.[25] It culminated in a street battle between the mayor's forces and the band of rebels. The rebels cheered for liberty, and the mayor led the charge, bellowing out, 'Long live the King!' When the dust settled, nine were dead 'with a pile of wounded on both sides', and thirty-six rebels were arrested. For his part in the fight, Guzman/Erauso was hired as an attaché to the sergeant major. For two years, Guzman/Erauso lived and worked in Potosí until the governor 'issued an order to raise soldiers for Chuncos and El Dorado, a region of hostile Indians ... and a land rich in gold and precious stones'. Erauso recounts how the soldiers found a riverbank covered in gold dust. Many of the men filled their helmets with the stuff before moving on. Yet, the expedition was short lived with most of the troops, including Guzman/Erauso, deserting after the governor ordered them to restrain themselves during an attack on a village.[26]

Again, Guzman/Erauso fell on hard times. Moving on to a smaller mining town, La Plata, to the northeast, he briefly worked for a Basque mine owner before being falsely accused of murder. Guzman/Erauso was arrested and accused of disguising himself as a native to attack Francisca Marmolejo, a woman who had been feuding with his hostess, Catalina de Chaves. Both women were of such high standing – the victim, Francisca, was related to a count – that a justice of the high court was called to town to investigate the case. Several town officials were arrested, and Guzman/Erauso was tortured in an attempt to extract a confession.

> 'Then the justice came for my confession. I told him I didn't know the first thing about it – he ordered me to be stripped and tied to the rack. A lawyer stuck his head in and pointed out that I was a Basquero, and therefore exempt from torture by the privilege of nobility. The justice didn't pay him any mind … They gave the screws a turn and I held fast, steady as an oak'.[27]

This was a rare moment when Erauso's Basque heritage did not help, even though it legally should have. All Basque men, by virtue of a long-standing custom, were born as *hidalgo* – literally, 'the son of someone' and a sort of technical nobility. Consequently, they were supposed to be exempt from torture. In the colonies, however, there was significantly less oversight. So, the torture continued until a note arrived from Catalina de Chaves, which prompted the justice to have Guzman/Erauso taken down from the rack and returned to his cell. It is unclear what the note said, Erauso does not tell us and perhaps never knew. The case dragged on and Guzman/Erauso was sentenced to a decade of indentured servitude in Chile. With the help of other Basqueros in town, he appealed the conviction and 'one day a ruling came down from the Royal court saying that [Guzman] was free to go'. Erauso quips in his autobiography, 'It just goes to show that persistence and hard work can perform miracles, and it happens regularly – especially in the Indies!'[28]

Guzman/Erauso left La Plata as soon as possible and headed to Charcas where he had delivered 12,000 llamas several months before while working for the alderman who was once again hiring. For a few months, Guzman/Erauso transported llama one direction and bushels of wheat or ground flour on the return, but he could not keep out of trouble. One day, again at a card game, a heated exchange turned into a brawl that ended with a stabbing. Guzman/Erauso 'retreated to the safety of the cathedral' and then slipped out of town a few evenings later, but things turned out just as poorly in the next town and in the exact same way.

In Piscobamba, a Peruvian town on the way to Lima, a Portuguese fellow argued with Guzman/Erauso over cards, and later that night, they crossed swords in a dark street. Again, our fugitive was arrested and 'they tried to torture [him] into talking, but [he] denied everything'.[29] Unfortunately for him, when the case went to trial, he 'found himself face to face with witnesses [he'd] never laid eyes on before'. They testified that Guzman was the murderer, and he was convicted. He appealed, but it was rejected. This was the closest Guzman/Erauso had come to facing consequences for his long series of violent crimes and 'now [he] was getting worried'.

> 'A priest arrived to confess me, and I refused – he insisted, and I held my ground. After this, it rained priests, I was drowning in them – me, a self-professed Lutheran! They dressed me up in a taffeta frock and put me on a horse. The priests cried and pleaded but the sheriff had a mind to hang me … They rode me out of the jail and down a series of unfamiliar back streets, all the while trying to keep clear of the priests – and I arrived at the gallows half out of my mind with the priests' shrieking and flailing … I had to stand on tiptoe while they gave me the *volatín*, which is the thin rope they hang you with, but the executioner was still having trouble getting it around my neck, so I said to him, 'You drunk! Put it on right, or don't put it on at all – I've got my hands full with these priests!'[30]

It was fortunate for Erauso that the executioner struggled. It bought the time necessary to stay the execution. A messenger from La Plata arrived, leaping from a horse and hurrying to the edge of the gallows. The witnesses that had testified against Guzman had been arrested themselves for some crime which Erauso could not recall. They had been sentenced to hang, and in the process of their confession, had admitted that they had been bribed to testify. Guzman/Erauso was free to go, having once again narrowly escaped punishment.[31]

For a few brief months, it seemed that Guzman/Erauso may have attempted to turn his life around. He left La Plata and headed to the next town, Cochabamba, only about a day's ride to the east, to take care of some business for his boss, the alderman. He needed to settle some accounts with Pedro de Chavarría. The business went well with the two reminiscing about the Basque Country – Pedro was from Navarre himself. Guzman/Erauso exchanged pleasantries with Pedro's wife, promising to carry some messages from her to her mother, a nun in La Plata, and then went to have a meal with friends. The quick and easy business trip took a foul turn as Guzman/Erauso headed out of town that evening. A crowd had gathered at the entryway to the Chavarría house. When Guzman/Erauso stopped to see what the fuss was about, the lady of the house, María, 'stuck her head out of the window and cried, Take me with you, Señor Capitán – my husband is trying to kill me!' And with this, she jumped out the window'.[32]

Two friars convinced Guzman/Erauso to save the lady by taking her back to La Plata to be with her mother. María had been caught with another man and her husband had killed him and locked her in the room from which she had jumped. The friars put her on the back of Guzman/Erauso's mule and they were off, not stopping until late in the evening. The next morning, they forded a river and took a short break at an inn along the road. Despite their pressing pace, Guzman/Erauso's mule was no match for María's husband, Pedro, who, riding alone on a horse, was able to catch up. Erauso recounts in his autobiography a thrilling chase into La Plata:

> 'We continued toward La Plata, somewhat cheered by the sight, but suddenly doña María tightened her arms around me and cried, 'Oh, señor – my husband! I turned, and there he was, coming up behind us on a horse that looked half-dead from the road … he took a shot at us with a rifle and missed, the bullet whizzing by so close to our ears that we could hear it sing. I spurred my mule on and plunged down a brambly hill. After four long leagues, going breakneck the whole way, I got to La Plata in a pitiful state, knocked at the door of the Augustine convent, and handed doña María Dávalos over to her mother'.

As the two women returned to the convent, Guzman/Erauso turned back to the road and 'collided with Pedro … who came at [him] sword in hand without bothering to wait for an explanation'. The two crossed swords, parrying back and forth, with Pedro pushing the 'bone tired' Guzman/ Erauso through the open doors of the convent church. Pedro landed two blows, but Guzman/Erauso lunged at him, pushing back against the altar 'and drove [his] blade a span's length between his ribs'. A crowd had gathered at this point and several officers of the law barged in to pull the duelling men apart. Pedro was arrested, but, in the chaos, some Franciscan friars from the monastery across the street sneaked Guzman/ Erauso away – likely with the aid of one of the constables who was the brother-in-law of Guzman/Erauso's boss.

As the dust settled, the alderman was called to town and spoke in defence of his employee who, he argued, 'had no choice but to help the woman in question, who had thrown herself at [Guzman], fleeing bloody murder'. After this, the whole ordeal was settled by the married couple taking vows to enter separate religious houses. María went to live with her mother where Guzman/Erauso 'went quite often to visit [his] little nun and her mother, and some of the other ladies there, all of whom were invariably pleased by [his] company and made [him] many gifts'.[33] María's mother also recommended him for a job investigating a murder in a small town nearby before he moved on to La Paz.

By the time Guzman/Erauso made it to La Paz, the terror of the noose seems to have faded away. Only a few days after arriving in the new city, 'without a care in the world', Guzman/Erauso decided to speak with one of the servants of the sheriff. Erauso does not record why or even what the conversation was about, except to say that 'the devil must have been stirring the coals, because it ended with the fellow calling [Guzman/ Erauso] a liar and slapping [him] across the face'. Unsurprisingly, Guzman/Erauso stabbed the man and was promptly arrested, tried, and sentenced to be hanged. Since there had been several witnesses, and not a single one required a bribe to testify, Guzman/Erauso had to devise a different means to escape the noose. He 'spent two full days confessing' to buy time and on the third day, when a mass was performed at the jail, he took the communion wafer, chewed it up, and 'spat the wafer out into [his] right hand and shouted madly', calling on the church. Erauso tells us in his autobiography that it was a priest who gave him this idea.

'Complete bedlam ensued'. The friars kept shouting that he was a heretic until the priest could calm them down and ordered everyone to stand clear of Guzman/Erauso. After the mass was completed, the priest and friars encircled the now heretical convict, 'they lighted candles, unfurled a canopy over [his] head and carried [him] in procession into the sacristy'. There, the friars scraped and washed Guzman/Erauso's hand several times before leaving him alone in the church. A month or so later, the priest gave him 'a mule and a little cash' and sent him on his way to Cuzco.[34]

After this, Guzman/Erauso meandered between Cuzco and Lima, falling into precarious situations in both cities. In Cuzco, he was accused again of a murder he had not committed. In Lima, his luck was even worse. The city was under siege. Eight Dutch warships had appeared in the port of Callao. Guzman/Erauso signed on to participate in the defence and sailed out with the five Spanish ships. The siege was ultimately unsuccessful, but Guzman/Erauso's ship was destroyed. There were only three survivors who were picked up by a Dutch ship. For a month, Guzman/Erauso, a friar, and another soldier were prisoners. Erauso recounts being certain that the Dutch meant to kill them or to take them back to Holland, but then dropped them off on a beach about thirty miles north of Lima. When he finally made it back to the city, he was almost immediately accused of stealing a horse and arrested. After proving his innocence, he went back to Cuzco.

There, in 'a city just as grand as Lima in both riches and people', Guzman/Erauso called on a friend of the La Plata alderman who had employed him. Lope de Alcedo was the local treasurer, and he supplied a room and, presumably, some work for Guzman/Erauso. Yet, trouble was around every corner – or at least in every gambling house. At a card game hosted by a friend, Guzman/Erauso met the 'menacing' and 'dark, hairy giant', who everyone called The Cid – a nickname which meant 'the master' and was a reference to a legendary eleventh-century Castilian knight. For some reason, which Erauso never discovered, The Cid wanted to fight. At one point in the game, The Cid 'stuck his paw in [Guzman/Erauso's] winnings, palmed some of [the] gold, and walked out'.[35] He came back and did the same thing a second time.

When he tried for a third time, Guzman/Erauso drove his dagger through the other man's hand.

A brawl immediately broke out, spilling onto the street, where Guzman/Erauso and The Cid drew their swords. This result was no surprise to The Cid, who had come to the card game with armour on under his clothes. Two passing Basque men jumped into the fray to help Guzman/Erauso, fending off The Cid's friends. The swordfight moved down the street, The Cid and his men gaining the upper hand. Guzman/Erauso took one blade through the shoulder and another in the side. As he fell, blood spilling into the street, everyone but The Cid fled. Guzman/Erauso pushed himself up, 'the taste of death in [his] mouth', staggering towards the door of the Church of San Francisco where The Cid lingered. Irritated that Guzman/Erauso was still alive, The Cid lunged at him with his blade. Guzman/Erauso 'forced the blow off to the side … and with a bit of luck managed to find the unprotected soft of his belly'. The Cid fell, 'begging for a priest'. Guzman/Erauso stumbled and fell beside him. Finally, the sheriff and his deputies arrived. The Cid was already dead, but by some miracle Guzman/Erauso held on as he was carried home.

Lying in bed, barely alive, Guzman/Erauso made his confession to a priest who had come. He and the others who had carried Guzman/Erauso insisted that a confession happen before surgery. Thinking that he might die, Guzman/Erauso confessed everything. The priest absolved him of his sins and gave him the last sacrament before he passed out and surgery began. For five days, he rested. When it was apparent he would live, the priest had Guzman/Erauso moved into a Franciscan monastery nearby to evade arrest. For five months, the friars and the sheriff argued over the fate of the man in the monastery. In the end, Guzman/Erauso again benefitted from having friends in high places and with deep pockets. They gave him a thousand pesos, three mules, three slaves, some weapons, and two Basque escorts for good measure.

At the edge of town, the sheriff was waiting with several friends of The Cid. With swords and pistols drawn, Guzman/Erauso's crew fought tooth and nail. Several men fell dead. Guzman/Erauso 'levelled the constable with a shot from [his] pistol'. He was officially on the run. Spurring his mule onward, he travelled through several small towns, dodging sheriffs, constables, and peering eyes who all seemed to recognize the fugitive. Finally, in the town of Guamanga, Guzman/Erauso was cornered in a gambling house. Though he shot his way out, the sheriff survived and saw to it that Guzman/Erauso's room at the inn was cleaned out. A local Basque man took the fugitive in, keeping him hidden for a few days in the hopes that things would settle, and the sheriff would assume Guzman/Erauso had fled.

> 'And all the while, there was no word of the case, no sign that the law was pursuing the matter, but still, it seemed like a good idea for me to move on – after all, why should the law be any different here than in some other town? And so, determined to slip away the first chance I got, I set off one afternoon just as night was falling, and I hadn't gone more than a few steps when, as my miserable luck would have it, I came face to face with two constables'.[36]

The ensuing sword fight summoned a crowd, including the sheriff and the bishop who had been dining together. Guzman/Erauso was completely surrounded, brandishing his sword this way and that in desperation. The sheriff shouted for someone to shoot the criminal, 'and shots [rang] out on both sides'. Then the bishop stepped out into the street 'and walked right into the middle of the whole thing'. Calmly, surrounded by four torch-bearing priests and his secretary, the bishop asked Guzman/Erauso to hand over his weapons. The bishop's secretary drew his own sword and escorted Guzman/Erauso away from the sheriff's men and into the church. This was how Guzman/Erauso met the man who would, perhaps unintentionally, thrust him into the limelight – sword drawn, on the run, moments away from death.

The next morning, sitting in the bishop's chambers, Guzman/Erauso recounted his life story. Then, 'a calm sweeping over [him, he] felt as if [he] were humbled before God, that things were simpler than they had seemed before', and Erauso let the truth spill out:

> 'Senor, all of this that I have told you… in truth, it is not so. The truth is this: that I am a woman…. I was placed

> in a certain convent with a certain aunt, that I was raised there and took the veil and became a novice, and that when I was about to profess my final vows, I left the convent… undressed myself and dressed myself up again, cut my hair, travelled here and there, embarked, disembarked, hustled, killed, maimed, wreaked havoc, and roamed about, until coming to a stop in this very instant, at the feet of Your Eminence'.[37]

Astounded and moved to tears, the bishop was speechless. He sent his new ward to bed and took the night to think over this unprecedented situation. Two days later, while the two were sharing lunch, the bishop voiced his doubts. The tale that Erauso had recounted was the most astonishing the bishop had ever heard. He asked more than once if it was true and how it could be true. Erauso assured the bishop that it was. If the bishop wanted, Erauso offered to allow other women to perform a physical examination to confirm it. That afternoon, two elderly women came and confirmed that Erauso was a woman and, more than that, a virgin. This elevated Erauso to a near holy status in the eyes of the bishop. Like Hildegund von Schonau or Eugenia Benedetta, the bishop declared that Erauso was 'one of the more remarkable people in this world', and promised to help 'in whatever you do, and to aid you in your new life in service to God'.[38]

This was the caveat of Erauso's confession. He was returned to a nunnery where '[he] once again donned the veil'. It was imperative that the bishop discover the status of Erauso's vows. If he had fled the convent after taking the final vows, then he would have to face charges from the Inquisition. While they waited for word from Spain, Erauso was allowed to make a tour of several convents in the region so that he could choose the best fit. Two years passed before it was confirmed that while Erauso had been raised in a convent in San Sebastian, he had never taken the final vows. Mail service between Spain and Peru only came once a year.[39] Tragically, Erauso's 'saintly bishop', died in 1620, only a few months after hearing Erauso's astounding confession. He was not the only one interested in the story, however. Even before Erauso had re-entered a convent, word had spread through Guamanga and along the roads to Cuzco and Lima. The day Erauso entered the convent of Santa Clara, the bishop escorted him 'through a crowd so huge, it was hard to believe there was anyone left at home'.[40] After the bishop's death, Erauso was summoned from the convent in Guamanga to meet with the archbishop of Lima. Again, as he entered the city, 'carried in a litter with a retinue of six priests, four friars, and six swordsmen … there were more people waiting than we knew what to do with, all come out of curiosity, hoping to catch a glimpse of the Lieutenant Nun'.[41]

Erauso had once again, and for a final time, successfully navigated the various ecclesiastical loopholes to avoid dire consequences. The murder of El Cid, and the various other individuals along the path from Paicabí to Guamanga, faded into the past. Those were crimes committed by the lieutenant and deserter Alonso Diaz Ramirez de Guzman, not the wandering nun, Catalina de Erauso; nor were they the crimes of Antonio de Erauso, the name by which he would be known for the rest of his life. When news arrived from Spain, freeing Erauso from the convent, he went first to Guamanga to say goodbye to the nuns of Santa Clara. Much like the nuns of La Plata, where Erauso had deposited the lady María Davalos after fighting off her husband, the nuns of Santa Clara doted on their fascinating new friend. Erauso stayed for a week, exchanging gifts and pleasantries, before setting off on the long journey home. Along the way, in New Granada, the archbishop of Cartagena de Indias, a city on the northern coast of modern-day Colombia, 'kept prodding [Erauso] to stay and take up residence in a convent of [his] order', but Erauso insisted that he 'had no order, and no religion, and that [he] was simply trying to get back to [his] country'.[42]

Erauso arrived in Spain, disembarking in Cadíz, in November 1624. It had taken another two years to travel from Lima with layovers in New Granada and the Canary Islands off the western coast of Morocco. In the second leg of the trip, Erauso had found a space on a general's ship where he was wined, dined, and provided with the opportunity to play cards and get in a small knife fight. Though this 'caused a great deal of disquiet', Erauso was simply transferred to another ship and, upon arriving in Cadíz, was still invited to stay with the general of the armada, Señor don Fadrique de Toledo.[43] It likely helped that two of

Erauso's brothers worked closely with the general. During his stay, Erauso became, perhaps for the first time, 'acquainted' with his brothers.

Erauso's autobiography provides no details about this acquaintance. This is the only mention of Erauso's family following his return to Spain. This may not be surprising given the shock that must have accompanied Erauso's reappearance after so many years, dressed and decorated as a soldier, saying nothing of his involvement in the death of their brother, Miguel. However, we know from other sources that Erauso did have contact with his family later and that the Erauso family had not forgotten their missing child. Erauso's father, who died before Erauso returned, had included Catalina in his will. Following Erauso's return to Spain, his mother included Antonio, listed among her sons, as an heir.[44] It seems his mother accepted, perhaps even forgave, Antonio. We might imagine his visit to San Sebastian, sitting with his mother in a house he had not seen since early childhood, recounting how, twenty-four years earlier, she had not recognized him after a mass at the convent; how might that have affected a mother's heart? In 1629, Antonio de Erauso signed over his inheritance – a portion of the family estate – to the one sister who had not become a nun in exchange for cash.[45] Perhaps the rest of the family in San Sebastian was not as welcoming to Antonio as his mother had been.

Antonio de Erauso was not in search of a home to settle in, however. He spent his time back in the 'Old World', meandering from place to place. From Cadiz to Seville and then on to Madrid, staying in each place only a week or two. At every stop, Erauso was bothered by 'swarms of people … trying to catch a glimpse'.[46] After Madrid, he moved on to Pamplona briefly, and then through southern France in a first attempt to visit Rome, but Erauso, accused of acting as a Spanish spy, was arrested by French authorities in Turin – the political situation in northern Italy had not improved much since the time of Catherine de' Medici. This imprisonment was fortunately brief, but Erauso was then forced to turn back toward Spain, 'penniless, barefoot, reduced to begging door to door' until he reached Toulouse, where he presented himself to a friendly count to whom he had previously delivered some important letters. The journey through France had been an unfortunate turn of events, but one that made Erauso's life story even more impressive as he recounted it to the king in Madrid a few weeks later. It was at this meeting that Erauso first made his request for a pension from the crown 'to reward [his] many services' and allegedly placed a self-authored memoir in the king's hands.[47] The pension – 800 crowns a year – was granted along with permission to continue living as Antonio rather than Catalina.

With that matter settled, Antonio de Erauso again set out for Rome. This time he travelled with a group of pilgrims, heading south to Barcelona to catch a ship. Along the way, the group was stopped by nine bandits, armed with shotguns, who stole everything, including Erauso's horse and clothes. Despite this setback, the pilgrims continued to Barcelona where Erauso once again claims to have been granted an audience with the king who, taking pity on the robbed pilgrim, granted an even larger pension. Erauso again writes that the king accepted a copy of his memoir. After this, things went smoothly – or as smoothly as Erauso could manage. In Genoa, he started a small brawl when an Italian man compared Spaniards to turds, but Erauso was able to sneak away before the city guards arrived. In Rome, Erauso's reputation and story preceded him.

> 'My fame had spread abroad, and it was remarkable to see the throng that followed me about – famous people, princes, bishops, cardinals. Indeed, wherever I went, people's doors were open, and in the six weeks I spent in Rome, scarcely a day went by when I did not dine with princes … and they made various gifts of this and that, and then, on special orders from the Roman Senate, wrote my name in a book as an honorary Roman citizen … All of them – or most of them – seemed remarkably pleased, even moved, to share my company'.[48]

Erauso even met with Pope Urban VIII, who, like the Spanish king, granted Antonio de Erauso a special dispensation to continue dressing as a man – surprising leniency from a pope who had banned smoking tobacco! One Spanish chronicle recounts that this decision was not universally accepted by the pope's cardinals. One of them allegedly reproached the pope in public, pointing out that cross-dressing was specifically prohibited. Perhaps this was one of the people Erauso alluded to when he recounted that only 'most' Romans were pleased to share his company. Urban VIII supposedly responded to the reproachful cardinal, 'Give me another Lieutenant Nun and I'll do the same for her!'[49]

When Antonio de Erauso returned from Rome, his rising star had yet to dim. While he had been visiting the Pope and touring the Roman Senate, authors, poets, and playwrights had been hard at work. The most famous of these was *La Comedia de la monja alferez,* typically attributed to the Madrid-based playwright, Juan Perez de Montalban (1601–1638), but possibly penned by the Sevillian, Luis de Belmonte Bermudez (c. 1587–1650). The plot of the play hardly resembles Erauso's life story. Instead, it mixes elements more like Shakespearean comedies: The disguised Catalina must deal with her incompetent and effeminate squire while trying to hold off the advances of a beautiful young woman; a close friend of the disguised soldier loves this same woman; a convoluted series of events involving mistaken identities, disguised lovers, and violence results in Guzman/Erauso returning permanently to the convent.[50]

Much like this play, a series of pamphlets purporting to tell the story of the Lieutenant Nun, published in the 1620s and 1630s, were more about the sensational and scandalous than the lived reality, complicating our modern understanding of Erauso and the position he held in early modern Spanish society. There are similar problems with the text purporting to be Erauso's autobiography. The only dated copy belonged to Juan Bautista Munoz who deposited the manuscript in the Bibliotéca de la Réal Academia de la Historia in Madrid in 1784 – 134 years after Erauso's death. This copy was itself a copy of a suspect manuscript made by the poet, Candido Maria Trigueros (1736–1798). Trigueros had claimed to base his copy on the original manuscript, deposited in a Madrid printing house in 1625, but this original has never been found. Two other copies were discovered in Seville in the 1990s, but they have not alleviated the debate around the autobiography's authenticity.[51] For some, the autobiography is as true as the genre of autobiography allows, a sort of subjective hybrid between diary, history, and public petition.[52] For others, the autobiography was a means of self-promotion, full of exaggerated violence and excuses.[53] Beyond this, a few argue that the autobiography is almost completely fictional, an expert manipulation of the popular picaresque novel, like *Don Quixote,* in which Catalina crafts and then 'remains in character for almost two decades'.[54] Were it not for the mass of administrative and epistolary evidence we have for Antonio de Erauso, this line of debate might completely erase the historical figure in favour of a literary read.

Fortunately, Antonio de Erauso, sometimes still called Catalina, was well-documented through the petition process. The more detailed autobiography, which falls under intense scrutiny as a potential fabrication, generally lines up with the narrative presented to the Council of the Indies. Several letters written by former bosses and fellow soldiers, and pilgrims prove that Erauso was a real individual. Though everyone who had known Erauso as Alonso Diaz Ramirez Guzman was astounded to find out that he had once been the female novice, Catalina, they praised Guzman's bravery and valour in service to the Crown. By all accounts, Guzman/Erauso was the ideal Spaniard, particularly in a colonial context. He had been intelligent, ambitious, trustworthy if well-paid, honour-bound, and talented at violence against rude gamblers, Mapuche warriors, and rebellious *criollos*. The young Basque had lived up to every expectation of a young man in the Spanish Empire and was rewarded in kind.

Against this backdrop, contorted in a moment of physical expansion *and* financial collapse, an individual could be lost – lost at sea, lost to disease, lost in the flood of thousands of petitions to a king – or suddenly crushed between the various forces trying to control this vast empire that stretched from Austria to Peru – the bureaucracies of the court or the Council of the Indies, the interrogations of the sheriffs or the Inquisition, the imperial navies competing to control the coasts of South America or the native populations rising up to push those empires out. Besides these forces, historians have often presented a picture of an Imperial Spain filled with individuals who had internalized the ideals of the Inquisition. These individuals repressed their own identities and policed the identities of others in an attempt to assure conformity to a Catholic and Spanish ideal of either a devout virgin or a valorous conquistador. There is plenty of evidence to corroborate this picture of the empire in the seventeenth century. Etiquette literature promoted nostalgic ideals of masculinity and femininity, emphasizing a potential 'crisis of masculinity'.[55] Laws outlawing bestiality, sodomy, and cross-dressing were repeatedly issued.[56] In the first decade of the century, an unprecedented number of people were convicted of witchcraft and burned at the stake by inquisitors; an anonymous accusation could suffice to send a person to the flames.[57] Yet, there was Antonio de Erauso.

Antonio, who had been raised in a convent, had become a page, a sailor, a merchant's assistant, a soldier, and a violent gambler. These were just his occupations. Erauso was also a Catholic novice who dodged vows, courted heresy charges to avoid the noose, and claimed, at one point, to be a Lutheran. The autobiography that Erauso allegedly presented to King Philip IV contained detailed descriptions of several crimes including cross-dressing, theft, and murder. Moving from convent to ship to battlefield to prison cell and back to a convent, Erauso evaded both civil and canon law. Instead of facing charges and execution, Erauso was briefly a celebrity. Granted a royal pension and permission to continue dressing as a man, Antonio even met the pope and toured the richest dining rooms and salons in Rome. While Erauso was in Italy, a play about the life of the Lieutenant Nun was written and produced in the Spanish capital. The play captured the excitement around the roguish celebrity but took many liberties with the story.[58] After returning to Madrid, Erauso was painted by Juan van der Hamen y Léon, one of the king's many court painters.[59] Copies of the painting were made to be included in touring cabinets of curiosities. This intense public interest in Erauso's story explains, in part, the freedom granted to the rogue nun; the spectacle of the Lieutenant Nun was too big to be contained by social norms.[60]

Antonio de Erauso was also likely allowed to live as he pleased because – excluding those first few months of touring rich dining rooms in Spain and Italy – he rejected the fame that came with his story. After his mother's death, selling his inheritance to a sister, Erauso returned to the Spanish colonies. Taking the cash payment and perhaps some savings from a few years of royal pensions, Erauso set up shop as a mule driver near Veracruz, Mexico. The route between Veracruz and Mexico City was notoriously dangerous – a perfect job for a retired soldier and gambler who wanted to be left alone. The historical record around Erauso, which had been so abundant in the 1620s, decreased to a trickle by the time he died in 1650. A few sensationalist reports claimed either that Erauso had retired on the royal pension to live a life of luxury in Mexico or that he had died, poor and lonely, begging a young woman to leave her fiancé. A truer account came in 1645 from the monk, Nicolas de la Rentería. He had encountered Erauso while travelling through Mexico and reported that the man, 'large and olive-skinned, with a thin moustache'[61] was respected by the locals for his courage and skill. He dressed plainly, armed with a silver-embossed dagger and sword, and sported a small, wispy moustache. The exact date or cause of Erauso's death is unknown. In the church where he was allegedly buried, the relevant page of a book recording burials was torn out sometime between 1650 and 1920. One source, written by a Spanish friar in 1653, claimed that Erauso had been venerated as a local saint after spending the last years of his life devoted to prayer and dressed as a nun – an obvious attempt to reclaim the young would-be nun who had lived as a man for fifty years.[62]

Notes

Introduction

1. There is a 1927 edition that translates the story in its entirety, but it was not digitized until after I had already done my own translation. Gregory of Tours, *The History of the Franks*, Volume II, trans. O. M. Dalton (Oxford: Clarendon Press, 1927).

Chapter One – War in the Convent

1. JoAnn McNamara, *Sainted Women of the Dark Ages* (Durham: Duke University Press, 1992), 75, fn. 53: 'The choice of deaconess rather than nun or sanctimonial seems to be deliberately indicated. Suzanne Wemple, *Women in Frankish Society: Marriage and the Cloister, 500-900* (Pennsylvania: University of Pennsylvania Press, 1985), 142, gives a cautious overview of the questionable legal status of a deaconess in this period. There is no reason to suppose that a deaconess was bound to celibacy. Conceivably, Médard had found an ingenious solution to his particular dilemma in consecrating a woman who was still married to the king. On this point, Delaruelle, "Sainte Radegonde", 67, remarks that the promotion of women as saints and their role in the sanctification of public life was an innovation of Merovingian spirituality. He sees Radegund as exempt from the restrictions of claustration in Caesarius's rule because of her diaconal status, which explains her charity and social life. Our text, however, suggests that once she entered her nunnery at Poitiers

she did live as a cloistered nun, but that was after Clothar's death'. Emphasis my own. On this final point about enclosure, I disagree with McNamara. Fortunatus and Baudonivia describe Radegund as experimenting with enclosure, initially only locking herself in a cell over Lent.

2. Venantius Fortunatus, *The Life of the Holy Radegund*; Baudonivia, *Vita Radegundis*, trans. JoAnn McNamara in *Sainted Women of the Dark Ages* (Durham: Duke University Press, 1992): 70-105, 75.
3. *Epistolae,* 'A letter from Radegund of Thuringia (561-67?)', https://epistolae.ctl.columbia.edu/letter/914.html. Baudonivia, *Vita Radegundis*, trans. JoAnn McNamara in *Sainted Women of the Dark Ages* (Durham: Duke University Press, 1992): 70-105; Gregory of Tours, *Glory of the Martyrs*, trans. Raymond Van Dam (Liverpool: Liverpool University Press, 1988); Gregory of Tours, *Historia Francorum*, trans. Ernest Brehaut (New York: Norton, 1969): IX: 39-43, X:15. Baudonivia was a young nun who was raised at Radegund's convent. In the biography, she recalls a few childhood memories of the queen. Gregory of Tours was a famous historian of this era, bishop of the nearby city of Tours, as well as the uncle of a prioress in Radegund's abbey.
4. Baudonivia, *Vita*, 93. Emphasis my own. For a more thorough consideration of the role of women's intercession in politics and war, see Alison Creber, 'Women at Canossa: The role of royal and aristocratic women in the reconciliation between Pope Gregory VII and Henry IV of Germany', *Storicamente* 13, no. 1 (2018).
5. Enclosure is the act of sealing oneself in a cell or room for devotion to prayer. It was incredibly popular among the monks and nuns of late antiquity and the early Middle Ages.
6. *Epistolae*, 'A letter from Radegund'.
7. Gregory of Tours, *History of the Franks*, IX.39, trans. Lewis Thorpe (London: Penguin Classics), 1974.
8. Gregory of Tours, *Historiae francorum*, IX. 40: 'Ad hoc enim opus beatus Eufronius, urbis Turonicae episcopus, injungitur. Qui, cum clericis suis Pictavum accedens… Post haec, cum pontifices sui saepius gratiam quareret, nec posset adipisci'.
9. Baudonivia, *Sainted Women*, 98.

10. *Historiae*, Dailey, 69.
11. *Epistolae*, 'A letter from Radegund'. The letter likely does not imply Maroveus as the ultimate agent of harm because it predates his investiture by 1-7 years. However, the tone of the letter might indicate that it is a bit later than suggested, making Maroveus a likely suspect or it demonstrates the insecurity of the abbey regardless of who the local bishop was. Note that Agnes was consecrated by the bishop of Paris, another example of the bishop of Poitiers either refusing or being refused the lead role in administering the abbey. Though the choice of Germanus, bishop of Paris, was also likely an astute political move by Radegund to secure Agnes's authority as abbess.
12. Ibid.,: 'et a nullo neque saepe dictam abbatissam nostram, neque aliquid ad nostrum monasterium pertinens molestari, aut inquietari, vel exinde imminui, aut aliquid mutari permittant…'
13. Ibid.,: 'Te quoque, beate pontifex, successors que vestros, quos patronos in causa Dei diligenter ascisco, si, quod absit, exstiterit qui contra haec aliquid moliri tentaverit, pro repellendo et confutando Dei hoste, non pigeat ad regem, quem eo tempore locus iste respexerit, vel ad Pictavam civitatem, pro re vobis ante Dominum commendata percurrere, et contra aliorum injustitiam exsecutores et defensores justitiae laborare: ut tale nefas nullo modo suis admitti temporibus rex patiatur catholicus, nec convelli permittat quod Dei, et mea, et regum ipsorum voluntate firmatum est'.
14. Gregory of Tours, *History*, IX.40.
15. Ibid., IX:40: 'Reginae sumus, nec prius in monastyrio nostro ingrediemur, nisi abbatissa eiciatur foris'.
16. Ibid., IX:41: 'Tam immensus enim eos, et, ut credo, diabolo cooperante, pavor obsederat, ut, egredientes a loco sancto nec sibi valedicentes, unusquisque per viam quam arripere potuit, repedaret. Adfuit huic calamitati et Desiderius, diaconus Syagrii, Augustdunensis episcopi, qui non inquisitor Clenni fluminis vado, quo primum littus adtigit est ingressus; ac, natante equo, ripae ulterioris campo evectus est'.
17. Ibid., IX.43.
18. Ibid., IX.42.

19. McNamara, *Sainted Women*, 63; Gregory of Tours, *HF* IX, 45-46. The countryside between Poitiers and Toulouse was said to be plundered by this same band of former guards; V: 15: Prior to Chilperic's assassination, his 'army came as far as Tours and plundered this region and burned it and laid it waste, and did not spare St. Martin's property, but whatever he got his hands on he took without regard for God or any fear'.
20. Gregory of Tours, *History*, IX.33.
21. Ibid., IX.43.
22. Ibid., X.15.
23. Ibid., X.16.
24. Ibid., X.15.
25. Ibid., X.15.
26. In an interesting aside to the trial, Clothild points out a man in the trial's audience. Indeed, he is a man who dresses as a woman, but he claimed never to have visited the nunnery and explained that he felt it was necessary for him to dress as a woman because he was impotent. Clothild also accused the abbess of cavorting with eunuchs, at which point another member of the audience, a doctor Reovalis, stepped forward and described a testicular surgery he had performed on a boy who had visited the convent in the time of St. Radegund.
27. Gregory of Tours, *History*, X.16.
28. Ibid.
29. Ibid.
30. Ibid., IX.40. This nun, who goes unnamed, had also levelled several accusations against the abbess at the time, Agnes. A similar escape occurred from a convent established next to Gregory's own cathedral in Tours. There, when its founder, Ingitrude had gone to the king's court to file a complaint about her daughter, one of the nuns, Berthefled, who was a daughter of King Charibert, fled to Le Mans. Gregory tells us that 'she was a woman who ate and slept a lot, and she had no interest at all in the holy offices'. IX.33.
31. *Epistolae*, 'A letter from Caesaria, abbess of Arles (c. 550)', https://epistolae.ctl.columbia.edu/letter/915.html

32. Baudonivia, *Sainted Women*, 88, 91-92.
33. Ibid., 89-91.
34. In Fortunatus' *Vita Radegundi*, Chapters XVII to XXII, Radegund visits the sick, personally bathes and feeds the poor, and then *experiments with enclosure*: '*The first time she enclosed herself* in her cell throughout *Quadragesima…*' In Baudonivia's continuation of the *Vita*, XX: 'Before the year of her transition, she saw the place prepared for her in a vision'.
35. Ibid.
36. Fortunatus, XXI.
37. Gregory of Tours, *Glory of the Confessors*, trans. Raymond Van Dam in *Gregory of Tours: Glory of the Confessors* (Liverpool: Liverpool University Press, 1988): 79-81.
38. Brian Brennan, 'St. Radegund and the Early Development of Her Cult at Poitiers', *Journal of Religious History* VR II, 27 (1985): 340-354.
39. *Epistolae*, 'A letter from Fortunatus (after 567)', https://epistolae.ctl.columbia.edu/letter/960.html
40. Ibid., https://epistolae.ctl.columbia.edu/letter/977.html and https://epistolae.ctl.columbia.edu/letter/971.html and https://epistolae.ctl.columbia.edu/letter/938.html
41. Mother Maria Caritas McCarthy, *The Rule for Nuns of St. Caesarius of Arles: A Translation with a Critical Introduction* (Washington, D.C.: Catholic University of America Press, 1960), 179: 'She should also be subjected to like severity if she should presume with impious boldness to send letters or gifts to anyone'; and 183: 'You shall never provide meals either in the monastery or out of it for these persons: bishops, abbots, monks, clerics, laymen, women in lay attire, nor the relatives of the abbess or of any of the nuns…'
42. Gregory of Tours, *History*, X.16.
43. Ibid., X.17-18.
44. Ibid., X.17.
45. Ibid., X.20.
46. Ibid., X.20.

Chapter Two – 'Mothers of the Fatherland'

1. C. H. Talbot, *The Anglo-Saxon Missionaries in Germany, Being the Lives of SS. Willibrord, Boniface, Leoba and Lebuin together with the* Hodoepericon *of St. Willibald and a selection from the correspondence of St. Boniface*, (London and New York: Sheed and Ward, 1954); Mary Ellen Rowe, 'Leoba's Purple Thread: The Women of the Boniface Mission', *Magistra* 17, no. 2 (Winter 2011): 3-20.
2. Thomas Pickles, 'The Historiography of the Anglo-Saxon Conversion', in *The Introduction of Christianity into the Early Medieval Insular World*, Roy Flechner and Máire Ní Mhaonaigh, eds. (Belgium: Brepols, 2016), 61. Bede's *Ecclesiastical History* was published around AD 731.
3. Grzeorgz Kazimierz Walkowski, trans., *Annales Sacri Romani Imperii*. (Bydgoszcz, Poland: Remedia, 2014), 501. The tribute demanded by Charles is unspecified, but the tribute demanded by Pepin took the form of 'annual payment in the amount of 300 horses'.
4. Ingrid Rembold, *Conquest and Christianization: Saxony and the Carolingian World, 772-888*. (Cambridge: Cambridge University Press, 2017), 3. Mass baptisms are recorded in the years 744, 747, 748, and 753.
5. Walkowski, *Annales Sacri*, 502.
6. Ibid., 504.
7. Ibid., 505.
8. Thomas F. X. Noble, 'Carolingian Religion', *Church History* 84, no. 2 (2015), 289.
9. Talbot, *The Anglo-Saxon Missionaries*, 205-206.
10. Ibid., 207.
11. Ibid., 211.
12. Ibid., 223.
13. Ibid.
14. Other letters from the Bonifacian correspondence provide ample evidence of women longing to go on pilgrimage or missing fellow

nuns who had gone on pilgrimage or taken up the conversion mission. Diane Watt, *Women, Writing, and Religion in England and Beyond, 650-1100*, (London: Bloomsbury Academic, 2020). In one letter, Boniface advises a nun, Bugga, that it would be better for her to go on pilgrimage to Rome than to remain in the cloister and risk losing her 'quiet mind'. Bugga had written to Boniface expressing her loneliness after her sister, Wethburg, another nun, had already gone on pilgrimage to Rome and decided to stay there. In a letter between the Abbesses of Whitby and Pfalzel, the former in England requests that the latter in Germany provide hospitality and travel advice to a nun on her way to Rome. Even Leoba's contemporaries, who appear not to have travelled beyond their cloisters – such as the nun Hucburg (fl. c. 760–780) – chose to include detailed pilgrimage itineraries in their hagiographical writings.

15. Felice Lifshitz, Mary C. Erler, and Franklin T. Harkins, *Religious Women in Early Carolingian Francia: A Study of Manuscript Transmission and Monastic Culture*, (New York: Fordham University Press, 2014).
16. *Epistolae*, 'A letter from Boniface (742-46)', https://epistolae.ctl.columbia.edu/letter/375.html Given the topics of the letter ('heretics and schismatics and hypocrites') and the complaints from Boniface about the difficulty of being a shepherd to a people who do not know the Gospel, we might assume that this letter was written slightly later than 742. A mass conversion had been prompted by Carolingian military campaigns in the region in 744. Two more would occur in 747 and 748. It would make sense that this letter from Boniface was composed sometime between the first mass conversion and before the second and third; perhaps 745 or 746.
17. Talbot, *The Anglo-Saxon Missionaries*, 219-220.
18. Ibid., 216-218. Rudolf specifically writes that this miracle 'was done in public, it came to the ears of everyone'.
19. *Epistolae*, 'A letter from Boniface (735?-755)', https://epistolae.ctl.columbia.edu/letter/376.html

20. *Epipstolae*, 'A letter from Lul (732-755)', https://epistolae.ctl.columbia.edu/letter/377.html. The dating for this letter is too broad. It must have been written after Leoba's arrival in Saxony c. AD 738 as it references 'our master Boniface'. It also seems likely, though not a certainty, that the letter was written before Boniface's murder in AD 754, given that Boniface is not described as 'of blessed memory' or some other typical descriptor to indicate that he was no longer living. It could be argued that the letter was written in AD 754 after Boniface had departed for Frisia, but before news of his death had reached Saxony.
21. Talbot, *The Anglo-Saxon Missionaries*, 221-222.
22. *Epistolae*, 'A letter from Lul (755-86)', https://epistolae.ctl.columbia.edu/letter/382.html
23. *Epistolae,* 'A letter from Hrotsvit, nun', https://epistolae.ctl.columbia.edu/letter/21.html. This 'letter' is the preface to Hrotsvit's *Gesta Ottonis.*
24. Walkowski, *Annales sacrii*, 546.
25. Ibid., 528, 529, 546, 547.
26. Ibid., 526.
27. Ibid., 522.
28. Bergman, 'Liber tertius', 63-65.
29. Ibid., 67.
30. Ibid., 113.
31. Ibid., 69-77.
32. Walkowski, *Annales sacrii*, 518.
33. Felice Lifshitz, *The Anglo-Saxon Cultural Province in Francia: A Study of Manuscript Transmission and Monastic Culture*, (New York: Fordham University Press, 2014), 17-18; Janneje Raajmakers, 'Missions on the Northern and Eastern Frontiers, c. 700-110', in *The Cambridge History of Medieval Monasticism in the Latin West,* (Cambridge, United Kingdom: Cambridge University Press, 2020), 493.
34. Elisabeth van Houts, 'Sanctimoniales Litteratae. Schriftlichkeit Und Bildung in Den Ottonischen Frauenkomunitäten Gandersheim, Essen Und Quedlinburg by Katrinette Bodarwé. (Quellen Und Studien. Veröffentlichungen Des Instituts Für Kirchengeschichtliche

Forschung Des Bistums Essen, 10.), *The Journal of Ecclesiastical History* 57 (2), 2006: 329-330.

35. Frederick S. Paxton, *Anchoress and Abbess in Ninth-Century Saxony: the Lives of Liutberga of Wendhausen and Hathumoda of Gandersheim*, Washington D. C.: Catholic University of America Press, 2009; Mary Bernadine Bergman, *Hrotsvithae Liber tertius, a text*, (United States: The Sisters of Saint Benedict, 1943).
36. Justine Audebrand, review of *Commemorating Power in Early Medieval Saxony. Writing and Rewriting the Past at Gandersheim and Quedlinburg* by Sarah Greer, *Revue d'Histoire Ecclesiastique* 117 nos. 1-2 (July 2022): 331-333.
37. Katherine M. Wilson, ed. *Hrotsvit of Gandersheim: A Florilegium of her Works. Translated with Introduction, Interpretive Essay and Notes.* (United Kingdom: D. S. Brewer), 1998; Stephen L. Wailes, *Spirituality and Politics in the Works of Hrotsvit of Gandersheim* (United States: Rosemont Publishing), 2006.
38. Ibid., 53-55, 77.
39. Justine Audebrand, 'Impératrices et abbesses : les *dominae imperiales* ottoniennes (X^e -XIe siècle)' *Clio* 53 (2021), 250. Sophie appears as an intercessor or beneficiary in approximately ten per cent of her brother's charters.
40. Helene Scheck, 'Queen Mathilda of Saxony and the Founding of Quedlinburg: Women, Memory, and Power', *Historical Reflections/ Réfexions Historiques* 35, no. 3 (Winter, 2009), 23.
41. John W. Bernhardt, *Itinerant Kingship and Royal Monasteries in Early Medieval Germany, c. 936-1075* (Cambridge, UK: Cambridge University Press, 2009).
42. Justine Audebrand, 'Impératrices et abbesses, 241.
43. Ibid., 242.
44. *Epistolae*, 'A letter from Widukind', https://epistolae.ctl.columbia.edu/letter/23743.html.
45. Walkowski, *Annales sacrii*, 520.
46. Manfred Mehl, *Die Münzen des Stiftes Quedlinburg* (Hamburg: Manfred Mehl, 2006), 42-49.
47. Audebrand, 'Impératrices et abbesses', 244.
48. Walkowski, *Annales sacrii*, 512-513.

49. David A. Warner, trans. *Ottonian Germany: The Chronicon of Thietmar of Merseburg* (Manchester, United Kingdom: Manchester University Press, 2001), 154.
50. Walkowski, *Annales sacrii*, 513.
51. Ibid., 514.
52. Eckhard Müller-Mertens, 'The Ottonians as kings and emperors', in *The New Cambridge Medieval History III* edited by Timothy Reuter (Cambridge, United Kingdom: Cambridge University Press, 2008), 256-257.
53. Audebrand, 'Impératrices et abbesses', 240-241.
54. Ibid., 248.
55. Walkowski, *Annales sacrii*, 520-525.
56. Audebrand, 'Impératrices et abbesses', 254.
57. Scheck, 'Women, Memory, and Power', 27; Elisabeth van Houts, 'Women and the writing of history in the early Middle Ages: the case of Abbess Matilda of Essen and Aethelweard', *Early medieval Europe* 1, no. 1 (1992), 61.
58. Sophie was replaced by her sister, Adelaide. After Adelaide, at least three other abbesses ruled concurrently over both Gandersheim and Quedlinburg in the course of the tenth and eleventh centuries.
59. Van Houts, 'Women and the writing of history', 68.

Chapter Three – Nuns and the Crusades

1. Robert the Monk, *Gesta francorum et aliorum Hierosolymitanorum: The Deeds of the Franks* trans. Rosalind M. Hill (London, 1962).
2. Fulcher of Chartres, *History of the Expedition to Jerusalem*, trans. in Oliver J. Thatcher, and Edgar Holmes McNeal, eds., *A Source Book for Medieval History*, (New York: Scribners, 1905), 513-17.
3. Connor Kostick, *The Social Structure of the First Crusade* (Boston: Brill, 2008), 272-273.
4. Ibid., 274-275.
5. Yvonne Friedman, 'Captivity and Ransom', in *Gendering the Crusades* by Susan B. Edgington and Sarah Lambert, eds. (New York: Columbia University Press, 2002) 135.

6. Albert of Aachen, *Albert of Aachen's History of the Journey to Jerusalem, Volume 1, Books 1-6: The First Crusade, 1095-1099.* Translated by Susan B. Edgington, Abingdon: Taylor and Francis, 2016, 72-73.
7. J. F. Michaud, *Bibliothèque des croisades* (Paris: A. J. Ducollet, 1829), 369-377.
8. Julia Bolton Holloway, trans., 'Margaret of Jerusalem/Beverley and Thomas of Beverley/Froidmont, Her Brother, Her Biographer', UMilta, British Library, 2017, https://www.umilta.net/jerusalem.html.
9. Ibid.
10. 'Your guide to Turkey's wild edible greens', *Daily Sabah* (5 September 2014). https://www.dailysabah.com/food/2014/09/05/your-guide-to-turkeys-wild-edible-greens.
11. Michaud, *Bibliothèque,* 573.
12. Holloway, 'Margaret of Jerusalem'.
13. Ibid.
14. Valerie R. Hotchkiss, *Clothes Make the Man: Female Cross Dressing in Medieval Europe* (New York: Garland Publishing, 1996), 43.
15. Ibid., 39. Also see the Hagiographical Appendix, 131-141.
16. Martha G. Newman, 'Real Men and Imaginary Women: Engelhard of Langheim Considers a Woman in Disguise', *Speculum* 78, no. 4 (October 2003): 1184-1213.
17. Hotchkiss, *Clothe Make the Man,* 34.
18. *Acta Sanctorum quotquot toto orbe coluntur, vel a catholicis scriptoribus celebrantur,* Joannes Bollandus et al. eds. (Paris: Palmé, April 2, 1865), 780-788.
19. Caesarius of Heisterbach, *The Dialogue on Miracles Volume 1,* translated by Henry von Essen Scott and C. C. Swinton Bland (New York: Harcourt, Brace, and Company, 1929), 52.
20. Ibid.
21. Ibid., 53.
22. Ibid., 54
23. Ibid., 55.
24. Ibid.

25. Natasha Hodgson, 'Nobility, women and historical narratives of the crusades and the Latin east', *Al-Masaq: Journal of the Medieval Mediterranean* 17, no. 1 (2005): 61-85.
26. James A. Brundage, *Medieval Canon Law and the Crusader* (Madison, WI: University of Wisconsin Press, 1969), 77.
27. Constance M. Rousseau, 'Home Front and Battlefield: The Gendering of Papal Crusading Policy (1095-1221)', in *Gendering the Crusade*, 36-38.
28. Ibid., 39.
29. Michael R. Evans, 'Unfit to Bear Arms: The Gendering of Arms and Armour in Accounts of Women on Crusade', 45-59; Susan B. Edgington, 'Sont çou ore les fems que jo voi la venir? Women in the *Chanson d'Antioche*', 154-164 in *Gendering the Crusade*. For an exception, see Keren Caspi-Reisfeld, 'Women Warriors during the Crusades, 1095-1254', 94-108 in the same volume.
30. Edington, '*Chanson d'Antioche'*.
31. Baha' al-Din, The Life of Saladin, trans. C.W. Wilson (London: Palestine Pilgrims' Text Society, 1897), 261.
32. Ibid., 195.
33. Orderic Vitalis, *The Ecclesiastical History of Orderic Vitalis*, translated by Marjorie Chibnall (Oxford: Oxford University Press, 1972-80).
34. Evans, 'Unfit to Bear Arms', 53.
35. Orderic Vitalis, 4:213.
36. Ibid., 4:215.
37. Ibid., 4:213.
38. Ibid., 4:213-215.
39. Frank Barlow, *William Rufus* (New Haven: Yale University Press, 2000) 283.
40. Alan V. Murray, *The Crusader Kingdom of Jerusalem: A Dynastic History, 1099–1125* (Oxford: Prosopographica et Genealogica, 2000), 203.
41. Anna Comnena, *The Alexiad*, trans. E. R. A. Sewter (London: Penguin Classics, 1969), IV.6.
42. Ibid.

43. Patricia Skinner, ''Halt! Be Men!': Sikelgaita of Salerno, Gender and the Norman Conquest of Southern Italy', *Gender & History* 12 (3): 622-641.
44. Anna Comnena, *The Alexiad,* IV:6.
45. Skinner, 'Sikelgaita', 623.
46. Ibid., 629-631.
47. Albert of Aachen, *Historia Ierosolimitana: History of the Journey to Jerusalem* (Oxford: Clarendon Press, 2007), 627.
48. Ibid.
49. Ibid., 631.
50. Kristoffer Ramsoy Fredriksen, 'Elite Medieval Women during the Crusades: A Comparative Study of Melisende of Jerusalem, Urraca of Leon, Matilda of Tuscany and Eleanor of Aquitaine', M.A. Thesis, Norwegian University of Science and Technology, 2023, 47.
51. Ibid., 47.
52. Hodgson, 70.
53. Helen J. Nicholson, *Women and the Crusades* (Oxford: Oxford University Press, 2023), 63.
54. Helen J. Nicholson and Anthony Luttrell, eds., *Hospitaller Women in the Middle Ages* (Burlignton, VT: Ashgate, 2006), 5.
55. Ibid., 12.
56. Alan Forey, 'Women and the Military Orders in the Twelfth and Thirteenth Centuries', in *Hospitaller Women in the Middle Ages*, Helen J. Nicholson and Anthony Luttrell, eds., 52.
57. Ibid., 13.
58. Ibid., 62-63.
59. Francesco Tommasi, 'Men and Women of the Hospitaller, Templar and Teutonic Orders: Twelfth to Fourteenth Centuries', in *Hospitaller Women*, Nicholson and Luttrell, 87-88.
60. Nicholson and Luttrell, 'Introduction', 15.
61. Ibid.
62. Tommasi, 'Men and Women', 87.
63. Forey, 'Women and the Military Orders', 46.
64. Nicholson and Luttrell, 'Introduction', 16.

Chapter Four – The Burned Beguine

1. Kathryn Kerby-Fulton, *Books under Suspicion: Censorship and Tolerance of Revelatory Writing in Late Medieval England* (Indiana: University of Notre Dame Press, 2006), 272
2. Guillaume of Nangis, *Chronique latine de Guillaume de Nangis*, trans. Elizabeth A. R. Brown in 'Marguerite Porete, John Baconthorpe, and the Chroniclers of Saint-Denis,' *Medieval Studies* 75 (2013), 319-320.
3. Sean L. Field, Robert E. Lerner, and Sylvain Piron, 'A return to the evidence for Marguerite Porete's authorship of the *Mirror of Simple Souls,' Journal of Medieval History* 43, no. 2 (2017): 153-173.
4. Maria Lichtmann, 'Marguerite Porete and Meister Eckhart: *The Mirror of Simple Souls* Mirrored,' in *Meister Eckhart and the Beguine Mystics: Hadewijch of Brabant, Mechthild of Magdeburg, and Marguerite Porete*, ed. Bernard McGinn (New York: Continuum, 1994), 71; David Kangas, 'Dangerous Joy: Marguerite Porete's Good-bye to the Virtues,' *The Journal of Religion* 91, no. 3 (July 2011), 310.
5. Ellen L. Babinsky, trans. *Marguerite Porete: The Mirror of Simple Souls* (New York: Paulist Press, 1993), 198.
6. Babinsky, *The Mirror,* 85, 87, 89, 90, 92, 99, etc.
7. Babinsky, 99.
8. Ibid., 104.
9. Kangas, 'Dangerous Joy,' 305-306.
10. Babinsky, *The Mirror*, 103-104.
11. Babinsky, 104.
12. Babinsky, 194.
13. Babinsky, 200.
14. Ibid., 222. Godfrey of Fontaines did not live to see Marguerite and her book burned. He died in either 1306 or 1309 after serving on the faculty of the University of Paris for twenty years. The other two supporters of Marguerite's work have made no other mark on the historical record despite Brother John's allegedly 'great fame'.

15. Justine L. Trombley, 'New Frontiers in the Late Medieval Reception of a Heretical Text: The Implications of Two New Latin Copies of Marguerite Porete's *Mirror of Simple Souls*,' in *Late Medieval Heresy: New Perspectives, Studies in the Honor of Robert E. Lerner*, eds. Michael Bailey and Sean L. Field (United Kingdom: Boydell & Brewer, 2018), 167.
16. Ibid.
17. Zan Kocher, 'The Apothercary's Mirror of Simple Souls: Circulation and Reception of Marguerite Porete's Book in Fifteenth Century France,' *Modern Philology* 111, no. 1 (August 2013): 23-47.
18. Lichtmann, 'Marguerite Porete and Meister Eckhart,' 66; Michael Frassetto, *The Great Medieval Heretics* (New York: Bluebridge, 2007), 147.
19. Huanan Lu, 'Marguerite Porete et l'enquête de 1323 sur le beguinage Sainte-Elisabeth de Valenciennes,' *Revue du Nord* 440, no. 3 (2021): 451-485.
20. Ibid., 468. My own translations from the French.
21. Ibid., 469-471.
22. Juan Marin, 'Annihilation and Deification in Beguine Theology and Marguerite Porete's *Mirror of Simple Souls*,' *The Harvard Theological Review* 103, no. 1 (January, 2010), 92.
23. Tanya Stabler Miller, 'More Useful in the Salvation of Others: Beguines, Religio, and the Cura Mulierum at the Early Sorbonne,' in *Between Orders and Heresy: Rethinking Medieval Religious Movements,* eds. Jennifer Kolpacoff Deane and Anne E. Lester (Toronto: University of Toronto Press, 2022).
24. Janice Marie Archer, 'Working Women in Thirteenth Century Paris,' (PhD diss., University of Arizona, 1995),110.
25. Tanya Stabler Miller, *The Beguines of Medieval Paris: Gender, Patronage, and Spiritual Authority* (Pennsylvania: University of Pennsylvania Press, 2014), 68-69.
26. Stabler Miller, *Beguines of Medieval Paris,* 65.
27. Ibid., 70.
28. Stabler Miller, *Beguines of Medieval Paris*, 21.
29. Sita Steckel, 'Hypocrites! Critiques of Religious Movements and Criticism of the Church, 1050-1300,' in *Between Orders and Heresy:*

Rethinking Medieval Religious Movements, eds. Jennifer Kolpacoff Deane and Anne E. Lester (Toronto: University of Toronto Press, 2022), 102.

30. William of Saint-Amour, *A Brief Tract on the Dangers of the Last Days* trans. Jonathan Robinson (Toronto: Self-published, 2014), 66-88.
31. Stabler Miller, *Beguines of Medieval Paris*, 17-18.
32. Ibid., 1.
33. Stabler Miller, *Beguines of Medieval Paris*, 40, 96-97.
34. Ibid., 38, 42.
35. Babinsky, *The Mirror*, 79.
36. Babinsky, 202-204.
37. Stabler Miller, *Beguines of Medieval Paris*, 88.
38. BnF lat. 16482, fol. 3vb.
39. Babinsky, *The Mirror,* 80.
40. Marin, 'Beguine Theology,' 93-97.
41. Beatrice of Nazareth, 'Seven Manners of Holy Love,' in *The Life of Beatrice of Nazareth,* ed. Roger de Ganck (Kalamazoo, Michigan: Cistercian Publications, 1991), 325.
42. Ibid., 331.
43. Hadewijch of Brabant, *The Complete Works*, trans. Mother Columba Hart (New York: Paulist Press, 1980), 145.
44. Stabler Miller, *Beguines of Medieval Paris*, 122-123.
45. Stabler Miller, 124.
46. Babinsky, *The Mirror,* 17-20; Frassetto, *Heretics,* 149; Lichtmann, 'Marguerite Porete and Meister Eckhart,' 68; Sean L. Field, 'The Heresy of the Templars and the Dream of a French Inquisition,' in *Late Medieval Heresy: New Perspectives, Studies in the Honor of Robert E. Lerner*, eds. Michael D. Bailey and Sean L. Field (United Kingdom: Boydell & Brewer, 2018), 32.
47. Paul Verdeyen, 'Le Procès d'Inquisition contre Marguerite Porete et Guiard de Cressonessart (1309-1310),' *Revue d'Histoire* 81, no. 1 (January 1986): 47-94.
48. Babinsky, *The Mirror,* 94.
49. Babinsky, 80-81.
50. A beghard was, roughly, an equivalent to a beguine, a layman who had taken no official vows with any recognized order, but had taken

personal vows of chastity and poverty. Like beguines unaffiliated with a beguinage, beghards also wandered from town to town, sometimes preaching, and living off alms.

51. Babinsky, 24; Verdeyen, 'Le procès,' 60.
52. Field, 'The Heresy of the Templars,' 25-31.
53. Verdeyen, 53. Nine of the twenty-one had sat on the council.
54. Ibid., 50.
55. Henry Ansgar Kelly, 'Inquisitorial Deviations and Cover-Ups: The Prosecutions of Margaret Porete and Guiard of Cressonessart, 1308-1310,' *Speculum* 89, no. 4 (October 2014), 936-973.
56. Norman P. Tanner, *Decrees of the Ecumenical Council, Vol. 1 (Nicaea I – Lateran V)* (Washington D.C. : Georgetown University Press, 1990), 383-384.
57. Babinsky, *The Mirror,* 11.
58. Stabler Miller, *Beguines of Medieval Paris,* 155-158.
59. Stabler Miller, 170.

Chapter Five – The Walled-In Women of Florence

1. Sister Giustina Niccolini, *The Chronicle of Le Murate*, trans. Saundra Weddle. (Toronto: Iter Inc. and Centre for Reformation and Renaissance Studies, 2011), 182.
2. Niccolini, *Chronicle*, 183.
3. Jacopo Nardi, *Le storie della città di Firenze*, vol. 9 (Florence : Bartolommeo Sermartelli, 1584), 371.
4. Niccolini, *Chronicle*, 48.
5. Ibid., 52.
6. Ibid., 52-53.
7. Ibid., 54.
8. Ibid., 54-55.
9. K. J. P. Lowe, *Nuns' Chronicles and Convent Culture in Renaissance and Counter-Reformation Italy* (Cambridge: Cambridge University Press, 2003), 136.
10. Placido Puccinelli, *Historia dell'eroiche attioni de' BB. Gomezio portoghese abate di Badia e di Teazzone romito con la serie delle*

badesse dell'insigne monastero delle Murate di Firenze (Milan: G. Pietro Ramellati, 1645), 34-35.

11. Niccolini, *Chronicle,* 56-57.
12. Puccinelli, *Historia* 35.
13. Niccolini, *Chronicle*, 58.
14. Ibid., 61.
15. Bull of August 23, 1434. Archivio di Stati di Firenze, CRSGF 81n104, insert 4.
16. Niccolini, *Chronicle,* 69.
17. Sharon T. Strocchia, *Nuns and Nunneries in Renaissance Florence* (Baltimore: John Hopkins University Press, 2009), 70.
18. Niccolini, *Chronicle,* 72-73.
19. Ibid., 73. '... so that in a span of seven months, she found herself change states three times: widow, nun, and then prelate, in which state she was confirmed and blessed by Monsignor Amerigo Corsini, archbishop of Florence'.
20. Strocchia, *Nuns and Nunneries*, 103.
21. Niccolini, *Chronicle,* 90.
22. Ibid., 77-78.
23. Ibid., 77: 'For example, one can clearly find that there were even four Jews who, after God washed them with baptism's sacred water, were kept by him in the knot of holy religion in this convent'.; Lowe, *Nuns' Chronicles,* 157.
24. Lowe, *Nuns' Chronicles*, 272; 277-278.
25. Ibid., 275.
26. Strocchia, *Nuns and Nunneries*, 114, 77: 'Convents used a baseline similar to the one set by the Florentine tax officials, who estimated the annual cost of living at 14 florins. Nuns spent a roughly comparable sum, despite certain economies of scale achieved in running any sizeable institution'.
27. Puccinelli, *Historia,* 34-35.
28. Lowe, *Nuns' Chronicles*, 144; Niccolini, *Chronicle*, 107.
29. Lowe, *Nuns' Chronicles*, 138.
30. Niccolini, *Chronicle,* 88.
31. Sharon T. Strocchia, 'The nun apothecaries of Renaissance Florence: marketing medicines in the convent,' *Renaissance Studies* 25, no. 5 (November 2011): 629.

32. Ibid., 642.
33. Ibid., 639.
34. Niccolini, *Chronicle*, 109.
35. Ibid., 108.
36. Strocchia, *Nuns and Nunneries*, 103-104.
37. Niccolini, *Chronicle,* 115.
38. Ibid., 116.
39. Ibid., 126.
40. Kenneth Bartlett, *Florence in the Age of the Medici and Savonarola, 1464-1498* (Indianapolis: Hackett Publishing, 2018), 50.
41. Ibid., 45-48.
42. Francesco Guicciardini, *The History of Florence,* trans. Mario Damandi (New York: Harper & Row, 1970), 147-148.
43. Bartlett, *The Medici and Savonarola,* 61.
44. Giucciardini, *The History of Florence*, 115.
45. Ibid., 146-147.
46. Ibid.,140.
47. Bartlett, *The Medici and Savonarola,* 66.
48. Niccolini, *Chronicle*, 142.
49. Ibid., 186.
50. Ibid., 128-129.
51. Ibid., 130.
52. Ibid., 131.
53. Ibid., 133-134.
54. Ibid., 135-136.
55. Ibid., 145.
56. Ibid., 146.
57. Ibid., 148.
58. Ibid., 148-149.
59. Ibid., 142.
60. Ibid., 143.
61. Niccolini, *Chronicle*, 248; Susan Broomhall, *The Identities of Catherine de' Medici* (Leiden: Brill, 2021), 347.
62. Broomhall, *Catherine de' Medici*, 342.
63. Niccolini, *Chronicle*, 251-252.

Chapter Six – A Nun on the Run

1. Catalina de Erauso, *Lieutenant Nun: The True Story of a Cross-Dressing, Transatlantic Adventurer who Escaped from a Spanish Convent in 1599 and Lived as a Man*, trans. Michele Stepto and Gabriel Stepto (Boston: Beacon Press, 1997), 4.
2. *Lietuenant Nun,* Stepto, 4.
3. Stepto, 4.
4. The choice of Francisco Loyola as a first fake name is quite funny if we consider that Erauso's host was also named Francisco and the runaway had likely passed through the small town of Loyola on the way to Vitoria.
5. Stepto, 3.
6. Stepto, 5.
7. Zogbaum, 22.
8. Zogbaum, 28.
9. Stepto, 8.
10. Stepto, 16. Erauso tended to enumerate all the most important buildings in the cities listed in his autobiography.
11. Matthew Goldmark, 'Reading Habits: Catalina de Erauso and the Subjects of Early Modern Spanish Gender and Sexuality,' *Colonial Latin American Review* 24, no. 2 (2015) 219.
12. Stepto, 19.
13. Stepto, 19.
14. Stepto, 20.
15. Zogbaum, 50. Araucanian – or simply Indian – was used by the Spanish to label the Mapuche.
16. Stepto, 20.
17. Stepto, 21.
18. Stepto, 22.
19. Zogbaum, 36; Aresti, 403. Many churches continued to resist the abolition of sanctuary into the early nineteenth century. In the modern era, only three churches in Spanish territories still offer it.
20. Stepto, 23.
21. Stepto, 28.

22. Stepto, 28.
23. Stepto, 29.
24. Stepto, 31.
25. Zogbaum. A local chronicler did not mention it, but the editor of the volume added a short note in the margin. Erauso passes over it very quickly and would not have mentioned it at all if he had not been involved.
26. Stepto, 32.
27. Stepto, 36.
28. Stepto, 38.
29. Stepto, 42.
30. Stepto, 42-43.
31. Stepto, 43.
32. Stepto, 44.
33. Stepto, 47.
34. Stepto, 49-50.
35. Stepto, 55.
36. Stepto, 63.
37. Stepto, 66.
38. Stepto, 66.
39. Zogbaum, 117.
40. Stepto, 66.
41. Stepto, 68.
42. Stepto, 69.
43. Stepto, 71.
44. Nerea Aresti, 'The Gendered Identities of the "Lieutenant Nun": Rethinking the Story of a Female Warrior in Early Modern Spain,' trans. Rosemary Williams, *Gender & History* 19, no. 3 (November 2007): 404.
45. Zogbuam, 119.
46. Stepto, 73.
47. Stepto, 74.
48. Stepto, 81.
49. Zogbaum, 118.
50. Jules Whicker, 'The Representation of Manliness in the *Comedia de la monja alferez*,' *Bulletin of Spanish Studies* 90, no. 7 (2013): 1091-1104.

51. Sonia Pérez Villanueva, 'Crossing Boundaries: Authority, Knowledge, and Experience in the Autobiography *Vida y sucesos de la monja alferez,' a/b: Auto/Biography Studies* 28, no. 2 (Winter 2013): 298-300.
52. Villanueva, 'Crossing Boundaries,' 299, 307-309.
53. Stephanie Merrim, 'Catalina de Erauso: Prodigy of the Baroque Age,' Review essay in *Literature and Arts of the Americas* 24, no. 43 (1990), 40.
54. Christopher Kark, 'Latent Selfhood and the Problem of Genre in Catalina de Erauso's *Historia de la Monja Alférez,' Revista de Estudios Hispanicos* XLVI, no. 3 (October 2012), 532-538.
55. Edward Behrend-Martinez, 'Making Sense of the History of Sex and Gender in Early Modern Spain,' *History Compass* 7, no. 5 (2009), 1303.
56. Zogbaum, 6. Cross-dressing was outlawed in the Spanish Empire in 1600, 1608, 1625, and 1641.
57. Zogbaum, 15.
58. Whicker, 'Representations of Manliness,'1093.
59. Marta V. Vicente, 'Trans Visual Narratives: Representing Gender and Nature in Early Modern Europe,' *Journal of Women's History* 35, no. 4 (Winter 2023), 61.
60. Mary Elizabeth Perry, 'The Manly Woman: A Historical Case Study,' *American Behavioral Scientist* 31, no. 1 (September/October 1987), 93; Merrim, 'Prodigy of the Baroque Age,' 38; Vicente, 'Trans Visual Narratives,' 64.
61. Perry, 94.
62. Zogbaum, 7.

Bibliography

Primary Sources

Acta Sanctorum quotquot toto orbe coluntur, vel a catholicis scriptoribus celebrantur. Edited by Joannes Bollandus et al. Paris: Palmé, 2 April 1865.

Albert of Aachen. *Albert of Aachen's History of the Journey to Jerusalem, Volume 1, Books 1-6: The First Crusade, 1095-1099.* Translated by Susan B. Edgington. Abingdon, United Kingdom: Taylor and Francis, 2016.

Anna Comnena. *The Alexiad.* Translated by E. R. A. Sewter. London: Penguin Classics, 1969.

Annales Sacri Romani Imperii. Translated by Grzeorgz Kazimierz Walkowski. Bydgoszcz, Poland: Remedia, 2014.

Baha' al-Din. *The Life of Saladin.* Translated by C.W. Wilson. London: Palestine Pilgrims' Text Society, 1897.

Caesarius of Heisterbach. *The Dialogue on Miracles Volume 1.* Translated by Henry von Essen Scott and C. C. Swinton Bland. New York: Harcourt, Brace, and Company, 1929.

Catalina de Erauso. *Lieutenant Nun: The True Story of a Cross-Dressing, Transatlantic Adventurer who Escaped from a Spanish Convent in 1599 and Lived as a Man.* Translated by Michele Stepto and Gabriel Stepto. Boston: Beacon Press, 1997.

Francesco Guicciardini. *The History of Florence.* Translated by Mario Damandi. New York: Harper & Row, 1970.

Fulcher of Chartres. *History of the Expedition to Jerusalem*, trans. in Oliver J. Thatcher and Edgar Holmes McNeal, eds., *A Source Book for Medieval History*. New York: Scribners, 1905.

Gregory of Tours. *Glory of the Martyrs*. Translated by Raymond Van Dam. Liverpool: Liverpool University Press, 1988.

Gregory of Tours. *Historia Francorum*. Translated by Ernest Brehaut. New York: Norton, 1969.

Gregory of Tours. *History of the Franks*. Translated by Lewis Thorpe. London: Penguin Classics, 1974.

Hrotsvit of Gandersheim. *Hrotsvithae Liber tertius, a text*. Translated by Mary Bernadine Bergman. United States: The Sisters of Saint Benedict, 1943.

Jacopo Nardi. *Le storie della città di Firenze*, vol. 9. Florence: Bartolommeo Sermartelli, 1584.

Marguerite Porete. *Marguerite Porete: The Mirror of Simple Souls*. Translated by Ellen L. Babinsky. New York: Paulist Press, 1993.

Orderic Vitalis. *The Ecclesiastical History of Orderic Vitalis*. Translated by Marjorie Chibnall. Oxford: Oxford University Press, 1972-80.

Placido Puccinelli. *Historia dell'eroiche attioni de' BB. Gomezio portoghese abate di Badia e di Teazzone romito con la serie delle badesse dell'insigne monastero delle Murate di Firenze*. Milan: G. Pietro Ramellati, 1645.

Robert the Monk, *Gesta francorum et aliorum Hierosolymitanorum: The Deeds of the Franks* trans. Rosalind M. Hill. London, 1962.

Sister Giustina Niccolini. *The Chronicle of Le Murate*. Translated by Saundra Weddle. Toronto: Iter Inc. and Centre for Reformation and Renaissance Studies, 2011.

Secondary Sources

Archer, Janice Marie. 'Working Women in Thirteenth Century Paris'. PhD diss. University of Arizona, 1995.

Aresti, Nerea. 'The Gendered Identities of the "Lieutenant Nun": Rethinking the Story of a Female Warrior in Early Modern Spain'. Translated by Rosemary Williams. *Gender & History* 19, no. 3 (November 2007): 401-418.

Audebrand, Justine. 'Impératrices et abbesses: les *dominae imperiales* ottoniennes (Xᵉ -XIᵉ siècle)'. *Clio* 53 (2021): 237-260.

Audebrand, Justine. 'Review of *Commemorating Power in Early Medieval Saxony. Writing and Rewriting the Past at Gandersheim and Quedlinburg* by Sarah Greer.' *Revue d'Histoire Ecclesiastique* 117 nos. 1-2 (July 2022): 331-333.

Bailey, Michael and Sean L. Field, eds. *Late Medieval Heresy: New Perspectives, Studies in the Honor of Robert E. Lerner*. United Kingdom: Boydell & Brewer, 2018.

- Field, Sean L. 'The Heresy of the Templars and the Dream of a French Inquisition'.
- Trombley, Justine L. 'New Frontiers in the Late Medieval Reception of a Heretical Text: The Implications of Two New Latin Copies of Marguerite Porete's *Mirror of Simple Souls'*.

Barlow, Frank. *William Rufus*. New Haven: Yale University Press, 2000.

Bartlett, Kenneth. *Florence in the Age of the Medici and Savonarola, 1464-1498*. Indianapolis: Hackett Publishing, 2018.

Behrend-Martinez, Edward. 'Making Sense of the History of Sex and Gender in Early Modern Spain'. *History Compass* 7, no. 5 (2009): 1303-1316.

Bernhardt, John W. *Itinerant Kingship and Royal Monasteries in Early Medieval Germany, c. 936-1075*. Cambridge, UK: Cambridge University Press, 2009.

Brennan, Brian. 'St. Radegund and the Early Development of Her Cult at Poitiers'. *Journal of Religious History* VR II, 27 (1985): 340-354.

Brown, Elizabeth A. R. 'Marguerite Porete, John Baconthorpe, and the Chroniclers of Saint-Denis'. *Medieval Studies* 75 (2013): 307-344.

Brundage, James A. *Medieval Canon Law and the Crusader*. Madison, WI: University of Wisconsin Press, 1969.

Deane, Jennifer Kolpacoff and Anne E. Lester, eds. *Between Orders and Heresy: Rethinking Medieval Religious Movements*. Toronto: Toronto University Press, 2022.

- Miller, Tanya Stabler. 'More Useful in the Salvation of Others: Beguines, Religio, and the Cura Mulierum at the Early Sorbonne'.
- Steckel, Sita, 'Hypocrites! Critiques of Religious Movements and Criticism of the Church, 1050-1300'.

De Ganck, Roger. *Life of Beatrice of Nazareth.* Kalamazoo, Michigan: Cistercian Publications, 1991.

Edgington, Susan B. and Sarah Lambert, eds. *Gendering the Crusades.* New York: Columbia University Press, 2002.

- Caspi-Reisfeld, Keren. 'Women Warriors during the Crusades, 1095-1254'.
- Edgington, Susan B. 'Sont çou ore les fems que jo voi la venir? Women in the *Chanson d'Antioche*'.
- Evans, Michael R. 'Unfit to Bear Arms: The Gendering of Arms and Armour in Accounts of Women on Crusade'.
- Rousseau, Constance M. 'Home Front and Battlefield: The Gendering of Papa Crusading Policy (1095-1221)'.

Field, Sean L., Robert E. Lerner, and Sylvain Piron. 'A return to the evidence for Marguerite Porete's authorship of the *Mirror of Simple Souls'*. *Journal of Medieval History* 43, no. 2 (2017): 153-173.

Frassetto, Michael. *The Great Medieval Heretics.* New York: Bluebridge, 2007.

Fredriksen, Kristoffer Ramsoy. 'Elite Medieval Women during the Crusades: A Comparative Study of Melisende of Jerusalem, Urraca of Leon, Matilda of Tuscany and Eleanor of Aquitaine'. M.A. Thesis. Norwegian University of Science and Technology, 2023.

Friedman, Yvonne. 'Captivity and Ransom', in *Gendering the Crusades* edited by Susan B. Edgington and Sarah Lambert. New York: Columbia University Press, 2002.

Goldmark, Matthew. 'Reading Habits: Catalina de Erauso and the Subjects of Early Modern Spanish Gender and Sexuality'. *Colonial Latin American Review* 24, no. 2 (2015): 215-235.

Hadewijch of Brabant. *The Complete Works.* Translated by Mother Columba Hart. New York: Paulist Press, 1980.

Hodgson, Natasha. 'Nobility, women and historical narratives of the crusades and the Latin east'. *Al-Masaq: Journal of the Medieval Mediterranean* 17, no. 1 (2005): 61-85.

Holloway, Julia Bolton. 'Margaret of Jerusalem/Beverley and Thomas of Beverley/Froidmont, Her Brother, Her Biographer'. UMilta, British Library, 2017. https://www.umilta.net/jerusalem.html

Hotchkiss, Valerie R. *Clothes Make the Man: Female Cross Dressing in Medieval Europe*. New York: Garland Publishing, 1996.

Kangas, David. 'Dangerous Joy: Marguerite Porete's Good-bye to the Virtues'. *The Journal of Religion* 91, no. 3 (July 2011): 219-239.

Kark, Christopher. 'Latent Selfhood and the Problem of Genre in Catalina de Erauso's *Historia de la Monja Alférez*'. *Revista de Estudios Hispanicos* XLVI, no. 3 (October 2012): 527-546.

Kelly, Henry Ansgar. 'Inquisitorial Deviations and Cover-Ups: The Prosecutions of Margaret Porete and Guiard of Cressonessart, 1308-1310'. *Speculum* 89, no. 4 (October 2014): 936-973.

Kerby-Fulton, Kathryn. *Books under Suspicion: Censorship and Tolerance of Revelatory Writing in Late Medieval England*. Indiana: University of Notre Dame Press, 2006.

Kocher, Zan. 'The Apothercary's Mirror of Simple Souls: Circulation and Reception of Marguerite Porete's Book in Fifteenth Century France'. *Modern Philology* 111, no. 1 (August 2013): 23-47.

Kostick, Connor. *The Social Structure of the First Crusade*. Boston: Brill, 2008.

Lichtmann, Maria. 'Marguerite Porete and Meister Eckhart: *The Mirror of Simple Souls* Mirrored', in *Meister Eckhart and the Beguine Mystics: Hadewijch of Brabant, Mechthild of Magdeburg, and Marguerite Porete*. Edited by Bernard McGinn. New York: Continuum, 1994.

Lifshitz, Felice Mary C. Erler, and Franklin T. Harkins, eds. *Religious Women in Early Carolingian Francia: A Study of Manuscript Transmission and Monastic Culture*. New York: Fordham University Press, 2014.

Lifshitz, Felice. *The Anglo-Saxon Cultural Province in Francia: A Study of Manuscript Transmission and Monastic Culture*. New York: Fordham University Press, 2014.

Lowe, K. J. P. *Nuns' Chronicles and Convent Culture in Renaissance and Counter-Reformation Italy.* Cambridge: Cambridge University Press, 2003.

Lu, Huanan. 'Marguerite Porete et l'enquête de 1323 sur le beguinage Sainte-Elisabeth de Valenciennes'. *Revue du Nord* 440, no. 3 (2021): 451-485.

Marin, Juan. 'Annihilation and Deification in Beguine Theology and Marguerite Porete's *Mirror of Simple Souls'*. *The Harvard Theological Review* 103, no. 1 (January 2010): 89-109.

McCarthy, Mother Maria Caritas. *The Rule for Nuns of St. Caesarius of Arles: A Translation with a Critical Introduction*. Washington, D.C.: Catholic University of America Press, 1960.

McNamara, JoAnn. *Sainted Women of the Dark Ages*. Durham: Duke University Press, 1992.

Mehl, Manfred. *Die Münzen des Stiftes Quedlinburg*. Hamburg: Manfred Mehl, 2006.

Merrim, Stephanie. 'Catalina de Erauso: Prodigy of the Baroque Age'. *Literature and Arts of the Americas* 24, no. 43 (1990): 38-41.

Michaud, J.F. *Bibliothèque des croisades*. Paris: A. J. Ducollet, 1829.

Miller, Tanya Stabler. *The Beguines of Medieval Paris: Gender, Patronage, and Spiritual Authority*. Pennsylvania: University of Pennsylvania Press, 2014.

Müller-Mertens, Eckhard. 'The Ottonians as kings and emperors' in *The New Cambridge Medieval History III* edited by Timothy Reuter. Cambridge, United Kingdom: Cambridge University Press, 2008.

Murray, Alan V. *The Crusader Kingdom of Jerusalem: A Dynastic History, 1099–1125*. Oxford: Prosopographica et Genealogica, 2000.

Newman, Martha G. 'Real Men and Imaginary Women: Engelhard of Langheim Considers a Woman in Disguise'. *Speculum* 78, no. 4 (October 2003): 1184-1213.

Nicholson, Helen J. and Anthony Luttrell. *Hospitaller Women in the Middle Ages*. United Kingdom: Routledge, 2006.

- Forey, Alan. 'Women and the Military Orders in the Twelfth and Thirteenth Centuries'.
- Tommasi, Francesco. 'Men and Women of the Hospitaller, Templar, and Teutonic Orders: Twelfth to Fourteenth Centuries'.

Nicholson, Helen J. *Women and the Crusades*. Oxford: Oxford University Press, 2023.

Noble, Thomas F. X. 'Carolingian Religion'. *Church History* 84, no. 2 (2015): 287-307.

Paxton, Frederick S. *Anchoress and Abbess in Ninth-Century Saxony: the Lives of Liutberga of Wendhausen and Hathumoda of Gandersheim.* Washington D. C.: Catholic University of America Press, 2009.

Perry, Mary Elizabeth. 'The Manly Woman: A Historical Case Study'. *American Behavioral Scientist* 31, no. 1 (September/October 1987): 86-100.

Pickles, Thomas. 'The Historiography of the Anglo-Saxon Conversion', in *The Introduction of Christianity into the Early Medieval Insular World*, edited by Roy Flechner and Máire Ní Mhaonaigh. Belgium: Brepols, 2016.

Raajmakers, Janneje. 'Missions on the Northern and Eastern Frontiers, c. 700-110', in *The Cambridge History of Medieval Monasticism in the Latin West.* Edited by Alison I. Beach and Isabelle Cochelin. Cambridge, United Kingdom: Cambridge University Press, 2020.

Rembold, Ingrid. *Conquest and Christianization: Saxony and the Carolingian World, 772-888.* Cambridge: Cambridge University Press, 2017.

Rowe, Mary Ellen. 'Leoba's Purple Thread: The Women of the Boniface Mission'. *Magistra* 17, no. 2 (Winter 2011): 3-20.

Scheck, Helene. 'Queen Mathilda of Saxony and the Founding of Quedlinburg: Women, Memory, and Power'. *Historical Reflections/ Réfexions Historiques* 35, no. 3 (Winter, 2009): 21-36.

Skinner, Patricia. 'Halt! Be Men!': Sikelgaita of Salerno, Gender and the Norman Conquest of Southern Italy'. *Gender & History* 12 (3): 622-641.

Strocchia, Sharon T. 'The nun apothecaries of Renaissance Florence: marketing medicines in the convent'. *Renaissance Studies* 25, no. 5 (November 2011): 627-647.

Strocchia, Sharon T. *Nuns and Nunneries in Renaissance Florence.* Baltimore: John Hopkins University Press, 2009.

Talbot, C.H. *The Anglo-Saxon Missionaries in Germany, Being the Lives of SS. Willibrord, Boniface, Leoba and Lebuin together with the* Hodoepericon *of St. Willibald and a selection from the correspondence of St. Boniface*. London and New York: Sheed and Ward, 1954.

Tanner, Norman P. *Decrees of the Ecumenical Council, Vol. 1 (Nicaea I – Lateran V)*. Washington D.C. Georgetown University Press, 1990.

Van Houts, Elisabeth. 'Sanctimoniales Litteratae. Schriftlichkeit Und Bildung in Den Ottonischen Frauenkomunitäten Gandersheim', Essen Und Quedlinburg by Katrinette Bodarwé. (Quellen Und Studien. Veröffentlichungen Des Instituts Für Kirchengeschichtliche Forschung Des Bistums Essen, 10.) *The Journal of Ecclesiastical History* 57, no. 2 (2006): 329-330.

van Houts, Elisabeth. 'Women and the writing of history in the early Middle Ages: the case of Abbess Matilda of Essen and Aethelweard'. *Early medieval Europe* 1, no. 1 (1992): 53-68.

Verdeyen, Paul. 'Le Procès d'Inquisition contre Marguerite Porete et Guiard de Cressonessart (1309-1310)'. *Revue d'Histoire* 81, no. 1 (January 1986): 47-94.

Vicente, Marta V. 'Trans Visual Narratives: Representing Gender and Nature in Early Modern Europe'. *Journal of Women's History* 35, no. 4 (Winter 2023): 57-75.

Villanueva, Sonia Pérez. 'Crossing Boundaries: Authority, Knowledge, and Experience in the Autobiography *Vida y sucesos de la monja alferez'*. *a/b: Auto/Biography Studies* 28, no. 2 (Winter 2013): 296-316.

Wailes, Stephen L. *Spirituality and Politics in the Works of Hrotsvit of Gandersheim*. United States: Rosemont Publishing, 2006.

Warner, David A. *Ottonian Germany: The Chronicon of Thietmar of Merseburg*. Manchester, United Kingdom: Manchester University Press, 2001.

Watt, Diane. *Women, Writing, and Religion in England and Beyond, 650-1100*. London: Bloomsbury Academic, 2020.

Wemple, Suzanne. *Women in Frankish Society: Marriage and the Cloister, 500-900*. Pennsylvania: University of Pennsylvania Press, 1985.

Whicker, Jules. 'The Representation of Manliness in the *Comedia de la monja alferez'*. *Bulletin of Spanish Studies* 90, no. 7 (2013): 1091-1104.

William of Saint-Amour. *A Brief Tract on the Dangers of the Last Days*. Translated by Jonathan Robinson. Toronto: Self-published, 2014.

Wilson, Katherine M. ed. *Hrotsvit of Gandersheim: A Florilegium of her Works. Translated with Introduction, Interpretive Essay and Notes*. United Kingdom: D. S. Brewer, 1998.

Index